Robinson Public Library Dist
606 North Jefferson Street
Robinson, IL 62454-2699

D1047380

Family Focused

A STEP-BY-STEP GUIDE
TO WRITING YOUR AUTOBIOGRAPHY
AND FAMILY HISTORY

Janice T. Dixon, Ph.D.

Robinson Public Library District
606 North Jefferson Street
Robinson, IL 62454-2699

MOUNT OLYMPUS PUBLISHING
WENDOVER, NEVADA

Family Focused

A STEP-BY-STEP GUIDE TO WRITING YOUR
AUTOBIOGRAPHY AND FAMILY HISTORY

by Janice T. Dixon, Ph. D.

Published by:

      Mount Olympus Publishing
      P.O. 3700
      Wendover, Nevada 89883

All rights reserved. No part of this book may be reproduced or transmitted in any form or by any means, electronic or mechanical, including photocopying, recording or by any information storage and retrieval system without written permission from the author, except for the inclusion of brief quotations in a review.

Copyright © 1997
by Janice T. Dixon
Printed in the United States

Library of Congress Cataloging-in-Publication Data
Dixon, Janice T. — 1st ed.
    Family focused: a step-by-step guide to writing your autobiography and family history / by Janice T. Dixon.

    Includes bibliographical reference and index.
    ISBN 0-9656919-6-9 : $19.95

    1. Family Focused   I. Title
    2. Autobiography, Personal History
    3. Family History
    4. Photograph Albums, Scrapbooks
    5. Genealogy
    5. Diaries, Journals
    6. Personal Letters
    7. Family Newsletters

Library of Congress Catalog Card Number 97-72333

929.2
Dix

Dedicated to
my husband, Willard, my daughter, Lucy
and Don Norton

who always believed I'd finish this book
and nagged until I did

and to my family,
past, present and future

Preface

No sooner had we set up our tent, pounded in the stakes and lifted the canvas high enough so we could almost stand tall, than our new neighbors from a nearby campsite dropped over to visit.

"Where ya from?"

"Utah. What about you?"

"California. What's your business?"

"Chemistry," my husband said, "And my wife is a writer."

"No kidding!" our new neighbor said. "A writer! Ya know, I've had a story I've been wanting to write. Happened to me a couple a years ago. I'll tell it to you, and you can write it down."

This is not an isolated incident. It happens all the time at parties, classes, PTA meetings and other social functions. The only problem is that the stories told to me are not my stories. They belong to the teller. If I did eventually break down and write one of these stories, then it would become my story and no longer belong to the person who told it to me. No one can write your story except you. You have a story inside; everyone does. Sometimes you have many stories: stories that happened to you, to your family, to your parents or grandparents that are waiting to be told.

"I don't know how to write," and "How do I start?" are the two most commonly heard laments. This book attempts to solve these two problems.

The actual writing process stops many would-be writers, but that is because you can only see it as an unsurmountable project. The secret is to take it one step at a time. Outline one story, add background, details and feeling until finally you are recreating your story the same way you have told it a hundred times. The only difference is that now you've written it down and it will not be forgotten. The major portion of the book is concerned with the writing. With this guide to direct you, you'll find that this is the most enjoyable part of putting your own book together.

I've tried to make this the most complete book possible in covering every facet of family writing. Not only are you writing about yourself, you learn how to write your family's stories.

After going through my mother's photograph album and not knowing half the people included in it, I realized how important it was to save those photographs, and also to know the stories behind the photos. Try using photographs as a stepping stone to your writing.

Personal letters and family newsletters are also a part of your family records. This book tells how to write them to make them more interesting and how to preserve them.

Writing in your diary can help you to know yourself in a way no other writing can. Try writing about one important idea/event/discussion/decision every day. This important concept allows you to put your life in perspective a day at a time.

I have included other helps for you: researching, organizing, polishing and publishing. I have also included memory joggers, a survey questionnaire, and reference material. This book is up-to-date, with information on computers, scanners, internet and desktop publishing. That's what makes this book so complete—I've covered situations that many people encounter. I've also given alternate suggestions; after all, there are many ways to write a book. In other words, I have systematically guided you through the writing process from the research, organization, writing, editing, reproducing and preserving processes.

Next time you meet a writer you won't have to say, "I have a great story, will you write it for me?" Instead you can smile smugly and show them your own personal and family histories

Janice Dixon

May 1997

Acknowledgments

During the writing of this manuscript, encouragement and technical experiences have been offered by a number of individuals whose services and interest are deeply appreciated. Among them are Peg Nichols, Alida Young, Mary Jane Whisenent, Barbara Williams, Lucy Armstrong and the manuscripters for their editing help and suggestions. Jeimi Woffinden and James Holman from Inkleys Inc. have advised me on the photography and scanning section. Brent Budd and Al Schmuhl from Salt Lake Community College have suggested ways to improve the book design and publication area. Ronald Coleman and Robert Hansen have read and given suggestions on genealogy. I would like to thank Paige R. Hansen, Pajun Photography, for the use of her photograph of my mother, Lucile Thorne on the cover.

Contents

Section Three
Photographs, The Images for Our Words
Genealogy, The Organizer

Section Four
Writing Diaries, Personal Letters,
Family Newsletters

Section Five
Polishing and Publishing
Personal and Family History

Appendix

Section One

Writing Your Personal History

CHAPTER ONE

Why Write Your History?

I was preparing a talk to present to a large group in San Francisco when suddenly a cyst started to grow on my eye. Within a week it had covered the area, and it was difficult to see. I contacted my doctor; and even though he was terribly busy, he agreed to take care of it. The waiting room was crowded, and I waited for a couple of hours before I was admitted to his office. I explained I was giving a talk in a week and hoped everything would be in order for me to give it.

"What is your subject?" he asked.

"Writing your personal history."

He filled a long needle with medicine and came toward me. The needle seemed about three inches long, and, as he thrust it in, he said angrily: "Personal history. I don't believe in it."

I'm not one to argue with a doctor with a three-inch needle, so I didn't answer.

"Nobody is going to get me to write my story," he grumbled.

I think he was getting ready for a fight, and inasmuch as he was fingering a scalpel by this time, I was put in a rather defensive position. And yet, writing a personal history was a subject in which I believed.

"You're an important person," I said. "I'm sure that you have learned many things you could pass on to your family."

"I've told them already."

"Did they listen? Did they really get the message you wanted them to have?"

He stopped a minute, thinking about it. "I don't know," he finally said. He proceeded to operate and didn't say anything for a while. After he bandaged my eye, he brought up the subject again.

"You think I should write it?"

"Yes, I do."

"How?"

As I sat there in the doctor's office, knowing that the waiting room was filling up, I told my doctor some of the things I have included in this book. He had put down his three-inch needle and his scalpel and was listening now.

"Your children don't have to have the same problems to face that you did, but they can learn from your experiences. If you write your stories down, the message is there. Writing personal history is a continuing process, one that contains the truths that you have found and want to pass on to your children?"

My doctor looked at me and nodded thoughtfully. "Maybe you're right," he said softly.

Writing your history will help you to learn about yourself in a kindlier, more accepting way. It will help you learn from each experience. If you haven't learned, you haven't grown, and that is what it's all about...learning from ourselves and learning from the stories of others. This book is here to guide you through that very process.

Each memory added together creates one unique person unlike anyone else. There are billions of us, each with our own memories. Everything that we have learned, experienced, interpreted and pondered is relegated to memory. Ours alone. No one else has ever exactly thought the same thoughts, gone through the exact same experiences, suffered the same sadnesses or been lifted with the exact same joys. There are many who have had similar memories but no matter how close we are to a parent, sister, brother, child, spouse, they still don't have the same memories.

As I was writing my personal history, many of my experiences were the same as those of my sisters and brother, and yet I remembered them in a different way. My account of the happening is not more or less accurate than theirs, but it is different. Because we each have our own story, which is our memory of our life there can be no other like it. Like a fingerprint, we have an imprint unique to ourself. Sharing these memories brings us closer to those we love.

In March of 1991, I marked the 50th anniversary of the death of my father. I was eight years old when he was murdered, and I hardly knew him. My memories of him were fragmented and distorted. He was a man who had never changed in fifty years, a picture over the mantle, and I could only remember as an eight-year-old.

It was a strange anniversary. I took the letters which he had written to my mother over a ten-year span and in the morning of that day, I started to read them. "Gosh, dear, how I wish that you were here with me to watch those mammoth waves come in and splash against the shore line throwing spray 25 feet in the air. Would you want to cuddle near me and enjoy that type of sport?..."

The picture on the mantle uses words! "Gosh!" He has been silent for so many years, and now he speaks to me in his letters. I treasure the day I heard my father speak. He was a young man when he started to write those letters, twenty-one years old, and deeply in love with my mother. My youngest son, Bill, is twenty-five and it is difficult for me to think of my father as a tall gangly kid. But there they were, the letters introducing me to my father.

My daughter and four grandchildren have come to stay for awhile. I look at the little ones ranging in age from six months to five years. I read Ryan and Greg stories about dolphins and gorillas, and sing to Christina who is two years old and hold Eric in my arms for hours and know that they will forget me if I should disappear suddenly from their lives. I want to be part of their lives forever, and know (sadly, yet gratefully) that I won't live forever, except through the stories I have written down.

I go to the cemetery and see the graves of my mother and father. I look at the tombstones. I know them very well, and I have made sure that we will remember them because of the book I have written about them and the letters they have left behind. And then I see the graves of my Grandmother and Grandfather Thorne close by and know that only a small part is written about them. There is nothing written about my great grandparents and all that is left is a small stone marking their graves. I wonder who will come to my grave, and who will remember my stories when I am gone.

I am not famous or rich, but I still want to be remembered. From the beginning of time people have wanted the same. I suppose the carvings in the caves are there because someone wanted to tell his story and didn't want to be forgotten.

History records the story of nations. Each nation, however, is made up of people, all kinds of people—cowards, heroes, artists, craftsmen, statesmen, farmers, teachers, builders, bullies. What each of those people does makes up the history of the nation. Biographies and autobiographies record the stories of individuals. If you put the biographies and autobiographies together they make up the history of a nation. Take the history of a nation and it becomes the autobiographies and biographies of its people. The two cannot be separated.

History is made up of individual men and women who have written of their lives. That's all history is, the interwoven stories of many people. These people have recorded the happenings of the day and the significance it held for them. Each of us wants to leave something so that we can be remembered. Sometimes we leave art or music. More often, we leave letters, stories, or memories for others. As you write, your life joins others and becomes part of a bigger history. Your autobiography should include the significant events in your life and how you feel about them.

There are many reasons to write an autobiography and I'm sure that you have your own motives or you wouldn't have chosen this book. However, if you need further reasons, I'll list a few, in addition to the ones you already have.

First, you are a witness for future generations. What you say about life is every bit as important as anyone else. As long as you add your comments, observations, feelings, experiences, then you exist as a unique voice in the eternal scheme of life.

The entire story of mankind has come to us from individual voices from the past. Each person who has written has contributed a small portion of the history we have today. Without the written stories, ideas and feelings of individuals, we would have no history and a very barren future.

Second, you introduce yourself to your posterity in a very real and wonderful way. Your words give new images of yourself. You have lived a good life and you should let your children and grandchildren know what you have learned and seen. They don't know about your memories and they never will unless you tell them. Everyone has one story to tell, her own. And though your immediate reaction might be, "My life isn't interesting," if you would think about it, there are many events in your life that are uniquely yours.

Some time ago I read the autobiography of my paternal grandmother Luella Ellsworth Thorne. As I read the entries, tears came to my eyes. My grandmother died of cancer when I was six years old and I never really knew her, and yet I shared her disappointments and her successes through her writing. She tells of the death of her third child, Aleen, her six-year-old daughter who died of diphtheria. In quiet terms she tells about her death:

"I never shall forget the night she was buried. The Relief Society sisters had made her such beautiful clothes and when we were ready to dress her I insisted on putting on every one of her clothes and combing her long golden hair. Then Father and I lifted her into the casket, I holding her head and Father her feet. Then we carried the casket into the yard and set it down and walked back to the house. Two men came and got the casket and placed it into a light wagon. The ground was rough and frozen. I could just shut my eyes and imagine I could hear that wagon for more than a year afterward."

Aleen Thorne, six years old. She was my father's older sister. Pleasant Grove, Utah, 1900.

The generations slipped away as I shared her grief for a moment. In reading her words I felt closer to my grandmother than I ever have. I'm sure she didn't know that I would read her personal history many years later. But if she had known, I think she would have been happy that she could be a part of my life. She allowed me for a few minutes the opportunity to be part of her thoughts and feelings.

I want to be part of the lives of my children and grandchildren and I know of no better way than to write my stories for them to read.

Third, you want your stories to represent you. If someone else writes your story, he may not tell it the way you want it told. Who knows you better than you? If you write it, there will be fewer mistakes.

Fourth, in writing your personal history, you put perspective and purpose in your life. You begin to understand yourself better than you ever have.

I spent a year writing my story which was also my mother's story and the story of our family. It was a most enlightening time for me, one I treasure, because it forced me to look at my life, re-shape it in many ways, and to laugh at things that I had taken so seriously before. I matured in many ways and became more tolerant and caring. It also freed me from some of my doubts and fears. In putting down my mistakes and fears I could examine them and realize that they were not as formidable as I had made them out to be.

There are many of us who don't know who we are. When you have finished writing your personal history, you will have a deeper sense of who you are and what is important to you.

A friend of mine is divorced. His wife allows him to see his children, but tells them terrible things about him. Nothing he says at this time is going to let his children understand his point of view. His health is bad and he won't live much longer. By the time his children are old enough to understand, he won't be there for them. This is why writing a personal history now is essential for him.

I know all the pitfalls in writing personal histories, because I hit all of them. You don't need to use these excuses as I did.

Watch out for those excuses like, "I need to clean out my closets (or cupboards or attic) first." I assure you when the closets are cleaned out, then you will have another excuse handy.

"I need inspiration." Inspiration seldom comes without effort.

"I have to have everything in my mind before I can put it down on paper. I don't want to make mistakes." There is nothing wrong with mistakes. Scribble on the paper. Make a happy face. Write down your thoughts and don't worry if it is spelled right. You can always come back and put it in better form.

"I don't know how to type. I don't have a computer. My pen just ran out of ink."   You can always write by hand with a pencil or ask a friend, daughter, or son to type it for you. If all else fails, you can tape your story into a tape recorder and hire someone type it up from there.

"I don't have time to write a whole book."   But you don't have to write a whole book. You only have to write a word at a time. Give yourself fifteen minutes a day, if that is all you have. If you have a notebook with you all the time, take time when someone puts you on hold and write a few words. Write while you are waiting for appointments. You will be surprised at how fast the notebook will fill up.

"I don't know how to write my personal history."   That's why you bought this book. Read it. It will take you step by step through the process.   If you follow instructions and let me help "brainstorm" with you, it will be an enjoyable experience. At the conclusion of each chapter is a challenge. If you meet each challenge as you go along, by the time you have finished reading this book you will also have created your own book.

Challenge

1. Let's get started.
    - Make a commitment to yourself to start your personal history.
    - Choose a specific time to write.
      Keep it a priority.

Getting Started

*L*et's start easy with short writings which can be done in one sitting. Don't worry about spelling, punctuation or grammar. Just write quickly, easily...whatever comes to mind.

CAPTION A SNAPSHOT

I can't think of anything easier than captioning a few photographs. Go to your photograph album and take out a snapshot of yourself. When was it taken? Write down the year on a paper. Think back for a few minutes. What prompted the photograph? See how much you can remember about that time. Write it down. Maybe it will be a few sentences, or maybe it will be a few paragraphs. If the writing goes beyond the photograph (like mine did) it still adds to your memories. If you can't remember the occasion, can you remember any story that happened about that time. This is the way my writing went.

1935.

I don't recognize the house, but it is probably in our home at 649 South West Temple. That area is now commercial in downtown Salt Lake about where a large motel now stands. At that time there were a lot of big old homes there. Grandfather Thorne owned an acreage that held three homes and we lived in one of them.

Mother told me a story about going to the twenty-fourth of July Parade which proceeded down Main street, a block east of our home. As we were walking toward the parade, a freak lightning bolt came down and hit so close we were knocked down. We were taken to the hospital, but we weren't hurt. I was carrying a Japanese parasol and it was ruined.

Myself (Janice) sitting on the front steps of my home in Salt Lake City, Utah, 1933.

Put the writing and the photo together on a paper. Don't they enhance each other?

This summer I took each of my grandchildren for an outing and, of course, took snapshots of the event. Afterward I wrote about what we did and the highlight of the day. I put the snapshots, the outing and the writing together with a copy for each child. This way we won't forget the fun time we had together.

Saturday, September 7, 1996.

Willard and I went to the Utah State Fair with Robert and Eric, both age 5. We started with the animal barns. Goats first. Robert loved to pet the animals, but Eric was hesitant. They had a stall where you could milk the goat. Both boys tried it, but didn't pull more than once. I don't think they believed that milk really came from an udder. In one barn there were baby pigs which Robert loved to touch. In another building an owner told the boys they could pet their steer. It was huge and Robert touched it carefully and quickly before he backed away. But Eric didn't want anything to do with it.

Grandson, Robert Dixon and unidentified cow at Utah State Fair, Salt Lake City, Utah, 1996.

When you write, you are investing time in yourself. How many vacation photos do you have with no idea of where they were taken, or what year you took that particular vacation? If you will jot down notes while you are taking your vacation and then add your notes to your photos, you will enjoy your vacation every time you look through your vacation album.

Start with a few of these short moments in your past as captured by a picture. Then try other moments.

WRITE ABOUT A MEMENTO

Do you have a memento from your childhood that you have saved? Maybe you have a first formal, an old uniform, a pretty vase or china dish. Take the memento (or the memory of it) and hold it. Think about the memories you have about it. I have an old doll given to me when I was twelve or thirteen. It was my last doll.

Christmas 1945

I knew Mother was going to give me another doll, and I didn't want it. I was thirteen, much too old to have another doll, even a bride doll. I wanted a bicycle, but the Second World War was going on and there were few bikes available. All the good stuff was going into the war effort. But there the doll lay, in a pink box hidden in the back of Grandma's closet, dressed in white satin with a frilly net veil. Mother had bought it for me late summer. Mother and Grandma thought they had it well hidden, but I was a snoop and knew practically the minute they smuggled it in. When I saw it, I hoped it was for one of my sisters. But one day Grandma called me to her and whispered in a stern tone that Mama had bought me a beautiful doll which was to be my last doll and "I was to be very happy with it." The whisper became a warning and a plan of action. I knew enough not to cross Grandma, and so I resigned myself to my ecstatic moment on Christmas morning. I don't know if I convinced anyone, but I still have that doll, never used. I think I love it more now than I did at age thirteen. And I don't think I love it because it is a pretty doll, but because Mother wanted me to have it.

FIND OLD MAGAZINES OR CALENDARS

Do you have any old calendars or magazines from a time past? Open them up and remember some of the events that you have experienced. If you don't have any in your possession, go to a library and ask for the Time-Life series, This Fabulous Century or the Album of American History. Go back in time and remember some of the things you did, or saw.

I looked back and saw a photo of a girl at a pajama party with her hair rolled in rags. The picture triggered this quick memory.

My hair was disgustingly straight in a time of curls. After all, Shirley Temple with her ringlets was the rage. Mother did everything to make my hair curly. I often went to bed with my hair rolled up in rags. That gave my hair some curl. Sometimes Mother would wrap my wet hair around her finger and put in bobby pins to make ringlets. She usually fixed my ringlets Saturday night so that I would look pretty for church.

Janice with ringlets.
Christmas 1940,
Provo, Utah

We also owned the predecessor to the electric curling iron. We would put the curling iron on our old coal stove until it heated. Before we dared curl our hair, we had to test it on a newspaper first. If the newspaper burned golden, then it was safe to curl my hair. Anything darker would scorch.

FOOD EVOKES MEMORIES

Sometimes a food will trigger memories. Do you have a favorite recipe or food that reminds you of a special time. This could be a treat (Grandma's Dolly Varden cake) or a disagreeable time (daily cod liver oil). In any event you are going to smile a bit as you remember. What was your mother's favorite recipe? You could even include it in your personal history.

Every September was canning time. Grandma was determined that our cellar was to be filled with canned peaches, pears, applesauce and grape juice. Grandma did the canning, but she recruited us to do the peeling. I remember the hot slippery peaches as she put them in our pans. We halved them and slipped off the skins. The fragrance in the house was wonderful, but I resented the long hours it took. Sometimes, during canning season I walked home from school slower than usual.

MUSIC EVOKES MEMORIES

Music is another memory jogger. Do you remember the music you used to dance to? What about songs you sang with the current popular vocalist of the time? What songs did Frank Sinatra sing? Did your Mother sing to you? Did your father have a favorite song he would sing when he was working? What songs did you sing to your children? Do you still have any phonograph records from earlier times? (I do, but I don't have a record player to play the old 78 records. I understand that phonograph needles are difficult to find also.)

Every time we got into our car, Mother would start telling stories or singing songs. *Jimmy Vallero* was one of her favorite songs, a ballad about an old cowboy. She sang it nearly every time, and we loved it. She sang every time we rode in the car.

At her death, we drove in the limousine behind the hearse and sang *Jimmy Vallero* all the way to the cemetery.

WRITE ABOUT YOUR NAME

Your name has been with you so long that you probably don't think much about it. For a moment though, consider it. Where did you get your name? What does it mean? Who gave you your name? Were you named after someone else? Who else in your family has the same name? Would you prefer another name?

I have written about my name in another section, so I'll go a different direction. What about family names? Are there any names that follow from generation to generation. In my husband's family, the name of Charles Dixon is given to the first born in each generation. The name goes back to the 1600's, and perhaps beyond that. Do you have any unusual names in your family?

There are many strange names in my family, but the name I enjoy the most goes back many generations with a grandmother called Thank Ye The Lord. Had I been brave enough I would have named one of my own children Thank Ye The Lord. I'm sure they are just as thankful that I didn't.

WRITE ABOUT A FIRST

We all remember firsts. Write about a first pet, a first car, a first date, a first job, a first home, a first baby, a first formal, a first time shaving, first day at school. The list is endless, but choose one and write about it.

I didn't want to go to kindergarten. I was happy at home with my sisters and mother. When Mother informed me that I was now old enough to go to school, I let out a howl. Not me! As the first day of school grew closer the more I resisted. On the appointed day Mother firmly took me out the door and we walked two blocks to the school. I started crying as we went out the door. The closer we got to the school building the louder I hollered. By the time I reached the school I was at a peak. Mother didn't know where the kindergarten class was, and so she entered the school at the opposite end of the building, where the big sixth graders went. Down the hall I yelled, with students and teachers peering out into the hall to see who was being hurt. Once in the schoolroom, I looked around and saw the blocks, and a big sandbox in the middle of the room. I stopped crying mid-wail and quietly went to play. Mother says that when she came to get me, I set up another wail at having to leave.

FAMOUS OR INFAMOUS ANCESTORS

Everyone has someone in the family who is famous or infamous? Do you have anyone who has done something unusual or heroic? How about a family member who does interesting things? Try writing about one of them.

Stephen Markham was my great grandfather, a man of great courage and devotion. He was a friend and bodyguard to the Prophet Joseph Smith. He was with Joseph in the Carthage Jail and was allowed to go in and out of the Jail to get supplies, deliver letters and run errands. It was a time of hatred and anti-Mormon violence. Men came in small groups and threatened to kill Joseph. Their catcalls and threats increased and more men gathered. Stephen watched helplessly as the mob grew. The men in the mob blackened their faces so they wouldn't be recognized. Joseph knew that he was going to be killed by the mob and asked Stephen to ride to Nauvoo, about twenty miles away, and get help. Stephen wanted to stay with Joseph, but was urged to go quickly. Stephen went outside the jail and the mob met him with jeers and threats. They lifted him onto his horse with their bayonets and spurred his horse on. By the time Stephen reached Nauvoo his boots were filled with blood, and Joseph and his brother Hyrum had been murdered by the mob.

MEMORY JOGGERS

In Appendix A I have included lists of ideas and questions that you can ask yourself. I suggest, however, that you continue in the book first, and then, later on, refer to the Appendix.

These are a few ideas to get you started. They don't take much time. You could probably write something in a spare moment.

GETTING ORGANIZED

Now that you have a few jottings written, you need to organize your writing so that you don't lose what you have. Buy or find a three-ring binder for your writing, acid-free, if possible. Try to use acid-free paper. The inexpensive papers contain acids which can cause your work to become yellow or brittle. If you are going to spend time writing, buy paper and binders that will last longer. Make a second copy of everything you write, in case it becomes lost. If you are using a typewriter or hand-writing your work, you can either use carbon paper or a copy machine. If you are going to video or audio tape, make a back-up copy.

The easiest way to write these days is with a computer. With a computer you can go back into the program and change it any way you desire. Be sure to save as you're typing, even if you haven't finished a section. I save my writing about every half hour. It is also prudent to make a hard copy at the end of a writing period. Another safeguard is to make a back-up copy on a second disc.

These are all precautions so that you don't lose your material. Put your working copy into your three-ring binder. File your second copy in a separate place. After each writing period, run a spell check. Some computers also have a grammar check. Let the machine work for you. Organize your writing on separate sheets in chronological order, i.e. 1945 will be placed before 1953. You may decide later on to use a different format, but for now, it is much easier to find what you have written if everything is placed chronologically in this notebook.

Challenge

1. Find a three-ring binder, preferably acid free, to put your notes and writing and any photos you will include in your story.

2. Caption a photograph. Give date, place, persons in photo and a memory. Include the photo and the writing in your notebook.

3. Write about a memento. Date it.

4. Look at some photos in an old magazine or book. Write a memory.

5. Let food or music stimulate a memory. Write it down.

6. Write something about your name, or about a famous or infamous family member.

7. Place all your writing in a notebook in chronological order.

CHAPTER THREE

Gathering Background Information

I don't know when I realized that Uncle Jim was the only person left who could tell me about my Grandfather Thorne. I've been hounding him to write about his father for about a year now and have finally come to the conclusion that, if I want the information, I'm going to have to interview him.

"I have to get dates and places," was his excuse.

Of course, he was right. Dates, places and names are the facts upon which hang all the stories, incidents and memories. They form the framework on which all else hangs.

This chapter deals with fact as a beginning to writing personal history. Collecting facts evokes little emotion, but as you gather those facts you remember times past and your memories may run the gamut from sadness, to anger to the greatest of happiness and all emotions in between.

There are certain occasions when dates and events are required from which no one can escape. We are constantly being asked for information about our family and ourselves. We include facts on questionnaires for schools, on job application forms, on the vita for a college degree, on marriage licenses and ultimately they become the information needed for our obituary.

Anyone trying to transfer a child from one school to another is required to supply many dates including birth certificates, school records, family data and health information. Many children have to retake vaccinations and immunizations because their health records have been lost.

Birth certificates may have been incorrectly filed and filled out and this information may not be discovered for many years, perhaps when the child starts into kindergarten. A friend of mine found out that she was recorded as the father of her child and her husband had been recorded as the mother. It took nearly a year before they could correct their records. Many adults apply for a passport only to realize that they are still "baby Prudden." Often the date of birth, place of birth, or parents are incorrect. Usually the birth certificate is filled out at the hospital while the excitement of a new baby is paramount. At other times, parents take the forms for birth certificate home with them because they haven't decided on the child's name and the hospital sends in the certificate without a name. Mistakes do happen and facts need to be checked and corrected. This is not only true of birth certificates, but of all legal documents, including marriage and death certificates. If you don't have all this information at hand, start gathering as much as you can. It won't be much of an autobiography without dates, places, and people.

Appendix C gives addresses and information in each state so that you can write to obtain the necessary information.

Some people think that other family members automatically keep all the records.

"Mama has all my records," said Andrea. (Andrea is 35 years old, married with three children).

Except that one day Mama missed Junior's birthday, and when Andrea called to find out why, Mama said, "I never can remember when Junior was born. Was it in 1988 or 1987 or maybe...and the last part of June or first of July?"

Maybe Mama doesn't have all the records.

You need to gather everything together yourself and organize your records.

There is always someone who is so organized that if you ask her the time her fourth child took his first step, she can open a little book and tell you the exact day, hour and minute. You don't ask her questions unless you really want to know the answer.

It might be handy to have some of these facts accessible, however. Like when you had your last tetanus shot, or the date of your mother and father's anniversary, or when you changed employment, and the manager's full name and address for reference. (Was that in 1967 or 1968? And his name was Norman Smith...or Wyman Brown, or was that the Vice President?) Mama may remember many things, but was it your brother who had the German measles when he was two years old, or was it you? She doesn't remember, but the doctor said it was the worst case he ever saw.

COLLECTING AND ORGANIZING THE FACTS

Don't rely on Mama, Dad, Aunt Gen, husband or wife to keep your records. That's your responsibility. It's your life.

What do you look for? Everything you can find. All legal documents, birth certificates, marriage licenses, wills, newspaper clippings, military records, baptism certificates, family histories, snapshots, passports, naturalization records, school diplomas, funeral programs, and obituaries, etc.

Appendix B is a survey for you to fill out. It lists where your documents have been stored. Properly filled out it becomes a resource for you and your family so that important documents can be easily found.

As you find your documents, you need to place them in acid-free folders or envelopes so that you can find them when you need them. You can now buy hanging files in legal and regular sizes along with an acid-free box. These hanging files make it easy to organize your documents. The legal size hanging files are preferable because they hold odd-size documents easier. Metal files are even better, but you may not want to go to that expense.

Make a photo copy of your certificates for everyday use and store your original copies. Make sure the original certificates are not folded, as they will become brittle in time and tear along the creases.

You may decide to place all your documents in carefully labeled envelopes, size 10" x 13", or larger. These envelopes must be placed in a safe place. For legal documents you should make a copy for your working files and place the original in a safety deposit box or metal filing cabinet for their protection.

It is easier to handle if you have separated your papers and memories into segments. Time-period organization is convenient for most people.

- Childhood
- Elementary school
- Middle school
- High School
- Post high school (college, employment, military, mission, Peace Corps)
- Marriage and/or beginning of career
- Raising a family, building a business or career
- Settling in (the balding, bifocal period)
- Grandparent or retirement years
- Family background

Other sections may include: friends, hobbies or simply miscellaneous.

This is only a suggested outline. Something else might work better for you. If you have traveled extensively, you may want to organize it by locations you have lived rather than the time periods suggested above.

As you gather each item, place it in the organizational slot that you have selected so that you can find it easily.

Challenge

1. Look for your certificates and documents.

2. Organize them in a meaningful manner. Protect them so that they won't become lost or destroyed.

3. Photocopy the most important documents.

4. File your documents and label the folders so that you can find them easily.

$\mathscr{F}amily\ and\ \mathscr{B}irth$

One of the problems of going on memory trips is that it is sometimes difficult to pull yourself away from them and start putting some of those memories on paper.

The easiest way to start is with three words..."I was born..." and go on from there.

Writing about my birth did not take too long, but I kept finding new material that I could add. The first extra material was a newspaper article about the Cranes Maternity home where I was born which will be fun to add to my history.

I was born May 9, 1932 at the Cranes Maternity on second south and University Avenue in Provo, Utah, which has been long torn down. My mother, Lucile Markham Thorne, tells me that when a woman was having a baby in those days, they were required to stay in bed for two weeks afterward at which time they were so weak that they could hardly walk. My father, Harold Arthur Thorne, was a proud daddy and took me from the nurse to hold. When the nurse objected, Dad managed to stay several steps away from her. Because I was born on May ninth, Dad wanted to name me Nina May, which my mother fought. As it was, they finally picked the name Janice.

*Baby picture of Janice
Salt Lake City, Utah, 1933*

After Mother's death I found her diary and she writes about being pregnant with me. Naturally I want to include this in my personal history.

January, 1931

Dear Diary,

Five months married, and still enjoying it. It is more fun every day. I love Harold more, and we understand each other to a greater degree. I meant to write a long time ago, but I just didn't. There have been so many things happening that I'm unconscious half of the time.

The big news I have for you is that we are expecting a baby on May 15th. We hope it will be a girl, and Harold wants brown eyes. However we shall be equally thrilled with a blue-eyed boy. We have even named it, whichever it is—Jean for a girl.

Jerold for a boy. And both for twins. Now we are prepared for any emergency. No more now. I must fix Daddy's supper.

Later on, I found a card with the following information on it:

Dated: 5:30 a.m. Monday Morning
Born May 9,1932, at Crane's Maternity Home in Provo, Utah. It was located at about 270 S. University Avenue (west side of the street.)

Sunday May 8 was Mother's Day, so Harold and I drove down from Salt Lake to visit our mothers. Both of them remarked that I had better stay down in Provo where my doctor was. Dr. Cullimore was the doctor, but he was away at a convention and his associate had taken over for him.

Well, we went back home. About one in the morning I had a couple of pains, the water broke, and we decided to start to Provo. On the way we stopped to tell Lou and Joe Page. By then the pains were five minutes apart, and Lou, a nurse, told us to hurry. On the way down, a car veered to our side of the road as it came toward us. Harold honked and slowed. It must have awakened the driver and he returned to his side of the road. We got to the hospital about 4:30 a.m. Harold called Mother, and the doctor took me to the delivery room. They were short one nurse, so Harold gave me the anesthetic. Janice was born at 5:30 a.m. George brought Mother down but they couldn't get in.

As you write this part include as much information as you know. You could include:

- Parents' names
- Place of birth including hospital, city and state
- Date of birth
- Name of doctor or midwife
- Circumstances
- Reason you were given your name
- Christening date

You may not have all of these details. Write what you are able and find out more, if possible. And if you find additional material after you have written about your birth, such as I did with Mother's diary and the newspaper article, you can always add to it.

Events at Your Birth

You could go to your local library and ask for a newspaper on the day of your birth. Note the happenings of the times. This will give you a wonderful feeling for the life into which you were born.

- Who was the President of the country?
- Was there a war going on?
- What was the economic situation (depression, inflation)
- How much did a loaf of bread cost?
- What did automobiles look like?
- Who was a popular singer, actor, sports figure?
- What was a current editorial topic?

When I add this background information to my history it reads like this:

> In 1932, the year of my birth, the world was a difficult place to live. In Germany, Hitler challenged President Hindenburg in the presidential elections and lost by a small margin, but by the next year he would become Chancellor and in 1934 would seize all power in Germany.

> In the United States the depression was at its worst. Nearly 1/4 of the working force was unemployed. For the first few months after their marriage Dad and Mother lived in a small house in an apple orchard which had no water or electricity. They earned what they could by picking apples and delivering them to market. They laughed about it later by telling of hauling their baskets of apples on an old horse drawn wagon. Each time the horses took a step they farted. As a kid we loved to hear this story.

FAMILY BACKGROUND

Nearly all the autobiographies I have read have also included family background. This might include:

- Name and background of each parent
- Nationality and social status of each parent
- Personality of each parent
- Occupation of parents and grandparents
- Something about grandparents and earlier ancestors
- Description of the home of family

Your Parents

Each autobiography is different, as yours will be. You may spend a long time on each parent, or only a paragraph or two. Concentrate on one parent at a time and tell as much as you feel comfortable with. You may include grandparents or even earlier ancestors if you are so inclined.

Important People in Your Life

Now that you are born and placed in surroundings, you need to bring in the significant people in your life. This would probably include brothers and sisters, parents and perhaps grandparents. But don't write about all of them at once. Choose one of them at a time and let us see them as you remember them.

> The first memories I have of my mother were of all five of us children lined up against a wall with mustard plasters on our chests (we were all coming down with whooping cough) and Mother telling us stories as she ironed.

This is only a fragmented memory, but it is a beginning. I suppose most memories include an action or happening. I always remember my mother doing something: checking out books at the library, teaching school, talking to me.

When I think back, what better way to describe my mother than to have her telling stories, because she was a master storyteller. She loved to read, and her home was always filled with books. She had her own personal collection in addition to the arms full regularly checked out from the library for herself and for us. A trip to the grocery story included a comic book along with the milk and butter. At one time she was criticized because she allowed us children to read comic books. "The important thing is that they are reading," she answered. "And they'll want something better." She made sure that better books were always available.

As I look back at this paragraph I realize that I know what she looks like, but a reader has no idea of mother's physical appearance. It is so easy to assume that because you know a person that everyone else will also. So, take the time to include a description of each person If you have a photo, include it.

My mother is a small woman, 5'4" and slim, barely weighing 100 pounds. She walks quickly and with purpose. She has brown hair and dark brown eyes, but more important, she is always interested in me and what I am doing. Whenever anything important happened in my life, I always told Mother first because I knew she cared.

My mother, Lucile Markham Thorne, Provo, Utah, about 1950

Along with the physical description should be the personality of that person. What is their attitude and demeanor?

If you say that your mother had a specific trait, try to include an example that would demonstrate.

My mother believed that a person shouldn't get something for nothing, and she was also compassionate. In those days of the depression many men came to the house begging for food.

"I will give you soup and a sandwich," she would tell them. "But first I would like you to move that pile of wood to the other side of the fence."

She always gave them something to eat, even though she didn't have much herself. When the next person came to the door asking for food she would tell them to move the wood back to this side of the fence. She never let anyone go hungry.

Think back on your parent's life. What stories demonstrate their characteristics.

Don't include all of these traits in each one of your family and friends, but you should include the most important ones. Do you know this much about your parents? You will notice that I didn't include all of these characteristics of my mother. I only gave you a list to help jog your memory. What do you know about your siblings? Your friends? As you write about one person remember them in relation to you. How does this person show love *to you*. What do you remember best about this person? How does this person show displeasure *to you*.

If this is difficult, try filling in some of the physical traits first and then add what you remember best. You can always go back and add to what you have written.

There are many important people in your life and you need to let others see them as you see them. Describe them, give examples of that description, let the reader know how you feel about them, tell stories about that person especially as they come into your life.

Be particular whom you choose or you will have a book filled with nothing but character sketches. Choose two or three people to write about and then as your story grows, add more as they fit into your story.

Tell about these people as they relate to you. Give your experiences with them and how you perceived what they did and what they said and what it meant in your life.

Even though there may be hurtful and hateful people in your life, try to see them in as an objective way as you can. Not all experiences are going to be happy and not everyone is good. Life isn't completely joyful and an autobiography without the good and the bad isn't being honest.

ADOPTED CHILDREN

I have just finished reading *The World Is My Home, A Memoir* by James Michener.[1] He writes of his background and the fact that he does not know his parentage, birthdate or birthplace. He is devastated when he is told at age nineteen that he is an adopted child. He tells about hiring a lawyer to find out about his birth mother, but is unable to find any information. He talks about the process he goes through in trying to locate his heritage.

Many people have asked me about how to write about adoption. I suggest that you read from Michener's book as this is one of the best models I have read. He writes about the facts, his feelings, and the subsequent decisions he makes. James Michener settled problems about his adoption in his own mind, as each adopted person must do.

In an article from the Reunion Research Report of Parent Finders, November 1, 1979,[2] the author talks about the trauma of children who have been adopted and feel the need to know about their roots. Joan E. Vanstone, National Director of Parent Finders, says that adoptees often need to find their birth parents, if only to establish their sense of kinship and identity.

Sometimes even though you have not been adopted, you may be missing a part of your heritage. My nephew married Dawn who had been raised by her mother in a single-parent home. Recently Dawn discovered that some of her father's family might live in a town in Texas. She looked in the phone book and placed a call. Moments later she discovered she was talking to a grandmother whom she had never met and the grandmother didn't even know that Dawn existed. Through the phone call Dawn discovered that she had aunts, uncles, and cousins. They are making plans to visit their new found family.

Where can you find information about your family? City
directories and telephone directories are found in public
libraries. Older city and telephone directories can be found in
libraries, museums and historical societies. If you know where
a family once lived, you can search cemetery records and vot-
ers' lists which are kept in courthouses in the county or
province.

You can also consult nonprofit adoptee support groups.
Some of these include:

- The International Soundex Registry, Carson City, Nevada
- ALMA (Adoptees Liberty Movement Association), New
  York City
- Yesterday's Children, Evanston, Illinois
- Orphan Voyage, Cedaredge, Colorado.

SETTING THE SCENE

Whenever you go to a movie or play you need to know what
is going on, a feeling of where you are, what is the year, and
who belongs on the scene. The same is true about a book. We
need to see you in your town/city/farm/home. Start with your
town or city first and your birth date. What kind of a place was
it? What were the people like? How big was it? Were you in
a depression or recession, war or peace, affluent or poor neighborhood? How did you fit into your environment? Were you
one of the ringleaders, or on the fringe? Set the stage for you
and your family. And then place yourself in the center.
Nowhere else are you going to get center stage like you are in
your autobiography. You are the star in every scene, so make
the most of it. Take the time now and write about the town or
city that you lived in as a child.

Your Home

Now that we know the location where you are living, let's
write about your home. Can you describe your home? Is it a
one family home, an apartment house, a condominium, a

duplex, mobile home? How is it built? Where was your bedroom? Did you share it with others? Where did you play?

I lived in several houses, as I have been told, but there is
only one house that I can refer to as the "family home." You
might want to list all of the houses you lived in, but a complete
description of each one would not only be tedious to yourself,
but also to the reader unless you have lived in only one or two
homes in your life. If you have a photo of your home or homes
you might want to include it in your personal history.

You need to be
selective of the
most important
places you lived
and write about
those that have
affected you the
most.

*Markham family
home, 365 North
1st East, Provo
Utah. This home
has been torn
down.*

My family home was located at 365 North First East in Provo,
Utah, one block south of the Brigham Young University lower
campus. It was a large old house with big rooms and high ceilings. Years before, my grandfather had remodeled the attic to
include upstairs bedrooms. He had done the work himself. This
meant that each room was distinctive. We had to duck our heads
on certain sides of the room because of low ceilings. Our front
room held a large gas stove with the word "Heatrola" printed on
the front. In the winters it was icy cold throughout the house,

and it took all the will power I had to throw off the bedcovers and rush to the front of the "Heatrola" to warm myself. One time I backed up too close and my flannel nightgown was branded with the Heatrola label.

SECOND-LANGUAGE DIFFICULTIES

There are some of you who have learned one language as a child and then adopted English as a second tongue. In this case, write in the language in which you are most comfortable. Few writers feel comfortable in their adopted language. One woman only two years in the United States, was trying to write her memoirs in English and was having a most difficult time. When she wrote in Dutch she started having problems with her spoken English, and when she wrote in English she couldn't express herself easily. Others might have the same problem, and there is no rigid rule to follow. You may need to try several ways before you find the method that is right for you. You could write in the language you learned as a child and have it translated or translate your thoughts down on paper. Another alternative would be to write in English substituting foreign phrases if you don't know the English word. You may find a compromise solution that will work best for you.

NOTES

[1]Michener, James, *The World Is My Home, A Memoir*, Random House, New York, 1992.

[2]Vanstone, Joan E., *Parent Finders*, National Director, 1408 West 45th Avenue, Vancouver, B.C., Canada V6M2H1.

Challenge

1. Write about your birth.

    *   Give the date and place.
    *   Tell about the circumstances surrounding your birth.
    *   Make a copy of your birth certificate.
    *   Make a photo copy of your baby picture. Place the original baby picture in a special file for protection.
    *   Place writings, copy of your certificate and pictures in a 3-ring binder.

2. At a library find a newspaper or magazine published the year of your birth and add anything of interest.

    *   What national events happened this day?
    *   Who was the leader of the country?
    *   What was the weather that day?
    *   Look at the fashions, cars, etc.

3. Write about each parent.

    *   How old were they at the time of your birth?
    *   Do you have any photos of them at this age? Make a photo copy of the pictures. Place originals in a special file.
    *   Show personality and representative traits of your parents.
    *   What do you know about their heritage?

4. Place everything in 3- ring binder.

CHAPTER FIVE

Turning Points in Your Life

If you have already started your writing, then you should have finished the story of your birth, the background of your family and something about your parents, so that others can see them as you see them.

Take a deep breath. Where do you go from here? There are many things you have done in your life and it is sometimes difficult to think about it all. It would be nice to write about everything, but it is probably impractical as well as impossible. For most people it is overwhelming. What then should you write about next?

I read the personal history of my grandmother, Luella Ellsworth Thorne. It is very short consisting of two stories. One is the story of the death of her six year old daughter, Aleen; the second is the story of my father and the time he was seriously hurt while climbing through a barbed wire fence with a loaded shotgun. This is an incomplete autobiography, but she wrote about two of the most important times in her life and she writes about them completely. They are very important to me.

In essence, if you don't have time to write a complete history, at least write about the most interesting and important times in your life. Start with them first. Write the turning points of your life.

TURNING POINTS

What are turning points? There is a pattern. Everything goes along smoothly and then, when you are lulled into complacency, something comes along and forces a change. A death in a family, moving from one house to another, financial reverses, school failures or successes, finding or losing a friend. These are all turning points.

One woman tells about her life. Her husband was there for her to help her in everything she did. He did the shopping for her. He drove her everywhere she went. He made all the financial decisions. And then he died. She was devastated. It took her several years before she took hold of her life and started making her own decisions. Her first turning point was when her husband died, and the second turning point was when she started to take hold of her life.

Another woman tells about being the only seventh grader in a one room school. The teacher had her go on to eighth grade and skip the seventh grade. The woman, although grown now, still feels a lack of knowledge because she missed that one grade in school.

How many people fall in love only to find that the love is not reciprocal. For a time they feel devastated, and then gradually they get used to the idea and can fall in love again. Marriage is always a turning point in a person's life. The decision not to marry a certain person is also a turning point.

The decision to have children is a turning point.

Choosing a career, deciding on an education, suffering from an accident or sickness and how you cope with these events, all these are definitely changes in your life.

One of the following may have been a turning point for you:

- I lived in one house all my life and suddenly the family moves. A sudden change! I don't walk the same way to the grocery store: I must seek out new friends; I have new teachers. Everything is different. It is a turning point!

- I am on the school ground on the teeter-totter. The school bell rings, and I jump off suddenly. My friend bumps to the ground and becomes angry. He takes after me and I run. A turning point. I must live the rest of my school days with the title "coward." And every bully has to prove my title.

- I run into the street and am hit by a car. My running days are stopped...at least for a time. In my cast and bandages I discover books and a land of my own imagination. My life has changed.

- I lose a quarter which I need to buy a birthday present. I decide to test God and see if He answers prayers.

- My mother objects to the crowd I'm going with. (Whichever way I choose is a turning point...away from my mother, or from my friends.)

- Death in a family.

- Financial reverses or successes.

- School failures or successes.

- Finding or losing a friend.

All these are turning points.

Not all turning points are positive. But they aren't all negative either. Because of the choices you have made or which have been made for you, this is where you are today.

There are many turning points in each person's life. Some are big and dramatic and others may not seem as big, but they still change your life. I started talking about turning points in the lives of my friends and family and discovered the excitement they felt as they remembered back.

"I remember when I was three," said one person. "We moved from a mining town to the city. It was a big change in my life."

"When I was in first grade, I hated my teacher," recalls another. "I was failing first grade because I refused to do anything for her. My father had to go to the superintendent of schools to get me transferred."

"When I entered junior high, all the popular girls banded together. They decided to exclude me from their group, and I was forced to find new friends. It was a traumatic moment to be told I wasn't good enough. I have spent my life trying to prove that I wasn't worthless."

By choosing the turning points in your life, you are giving direction to your autobiography and selecting the most important, decision-making times. You may want to add other events in your life, a few of the plateaus or quiet times, but each plateau is thrust forward by the changes and choices you make.

Usually there are not as many turning points in your early childhood years as there are later on. Most of the turning points during these years are forced upon you in the form of a move, an illness, or a death. However, it may be easier to look back on our childhood and have a better perspective of our turning points. The ones that are happening, even as we speak, may not be as obvious to us.

In my life the first turning point that I remember was the murder of my father, a traveling salesman, who was killed by a hitchhiker when I was eight years old. It meant not only the loss of one of my parents, but moving to a new home in a new city, new friends, my mother leaving the home to work, my grandmother stepping into my mother's role, and the hours and days that I spent at the murder trial. It was so traumatic that sometimes I chose to forget the pain associated with those memories.

How do you go about writing about your turning points? How much do you say? Of course, a lot depends on how much you remember and how old you were. If you were two years old (like my youngest sister, Sally) when your father was killed, you are not going to remember much. Ideally, your story would include:

- A background of what was going on in your life before this particular action occurred.
- Rising action. What were the immediate events that happened prior to the turning point in your life.
- The turning point that changes your life.
- Looking back on that event and showing or telling how it changes your life. An evaluation time.

The four basic areas are only a suggestion to help organize your story. The first turning point in my life, as I have mentioned, was the death of my father. To show you the various steps it takes, I'll outline my story for you.

Background

- My father was a traveling salesman in southern Utah.
- He had a wife and five children living in Salt Lake City. I was the oldest of the children.
- This was to be his last trip selling. He was going to start his own business.

Rising Action

- In March 1940, police tried to stop a car which ran a red light in Salt Lake, but the man panicked and a high-speed chase followed.

- Police discovered the car belonged to my father, but the man who was driving the car was Donald Condit.
- There was blood in the car.
- Donald Condit confessed to the murder of my father.

The Event

- The police informed my mother, and our lives were changed.

Analysis

- The change in my life was caused by the death of my father.
- How I feel about the turning point as seen now.

This outline was written in 1977. In 1989 my mother died and we found all of the letters, newspaper clippings and personal journals she had kept. With all this information, I went back and re-created this turning point in my life and it was different from the one I wrote in 1977. I had not written falsely before, but only from a different point in time for me. Now that I was able to look at the events that took place in my life, I found many things different from what I had remembered. I also realized that I did not have a small turning point, but a much longer one than I had written before.

If you have written one of your turning points, ask yourself the following questions:

- Do you have all the facts?
- Are they accurate?
- Do they follow in order?
- Why is this a turning point in your life?

There will be many turning points in your life. By writing the first one, you are learning the basic form, and you are time removed from the event, which makes it easier to be objective. Emotional events that have occurred within the last year or two, such as death or divorce, are more difficult to handle.

You will not want to write each story the same way, but as you write each one, you will discover that when you add details, the outline will flesh out and each story will be as different as people are different.

Sometimes the areas will overlap; other times you may not be able to include them all. You have to decide where the most emphasis should be. There are as many ways to write an auto-biography as there are people in the world. This chapter suggests ways of taking the most important times in your life and writing them. If you only finish one of your turning points, but finish it the best way that you can, then you can be proud of that accomplishment.

Challenge

1. Write a turning point in your life

   - Decide on the most important turning point in your life.
   - Write an outline to follow.
   - Following directions in the chapter, immerse yourself into this one story. Write it as complete-ly as you can.
   - Include any photos you might have.
   - Put your story and photos into your binder.

2 Write a second turning point.

CHAPTER SIX

Enhance with Details

$\mathcal{A}$dding details to your story makes it uniquely yours. Decide what you want to say and then choose those words that say it best. Don't try to embellish your story with unimportant words in an effort to impress. Give the details that will enhance your story, but don't go off the subject. Make sure your story is going somewhere.

If your story doesn't go anywhere, say anything or do anything, the reader will become distracted and put your book down.

You keep the reader's interest by making each word count. The word, "detail" is described in the dictionary as: "the small elements that collectively constitute a work of art."

You must use details in order to make your story clear, convincing and interesting. The correct use of details makes the difference between vivid writing and static writing.

Concrete Details

Concrete details are word pictures of things that can be seen and touched. The more specific you can get, the closer your reader can see as you do. Try to use general words in a limited way and be as specific as you can.

General words could be any of the following: dog, candy, teacher, mother. If you see any of these words written you have a general idea of what the writer is trying to say, but you probably will plug into one of your own memories and come up with something different from the one the writer wants to convey. Take these general words and create concrete images as follows: a dog becomes a yellow cocker mix with one eye missing, the result of chasing one too many cars: candy become a foot long black licorice rope given every time dad comes back from a trip; teacher becomes Miss Maeser, my fifth grade teacher at BYU Training school, an ageless woman with a hump on her back, a slight smile perpetually on her lips and a love big enough to encompass everyone. Your description of a dog, candy and teacher are completely different from mine.

If you say, "My mother was a good woman," people are going to be bored and not at all informed. It is up to you to fill out the details. You need to give specifics about your mother, stories that make her come alive. If your reader comes to know her in some ways as well as you know her, then she becomes a vibrant, exciting woman. Specifics make uninteresting writing come to life.

If I were to take one of these general words, "mother" and write about my own mother I would include the following:

My mother is Lucile Markham Thorne, born on Halloween day in 1906 to Joseph Markham and Mary Catherine Lewis.

Well, this isn't too exciting yet, but at least you know who she is specifically.

Description is the third section of detail. It could include any or all of the following: size, age, coloring, texture, weight, speed, thickness, sound, personality, education, temperature. Anything that helps a reader to see that object can be used.

Mother was small and lithe with energy to spare. Her short brown hair was bobbed and her dark eyes sparkled in the pictures we have of her as a girl.

After you have finished this part, then include a quality that is unique to this particular object.

By her own admission, she was a flirt. She had a way with words, and when a youth, wrote to half a dozen pen pals who repeatedly begged for pictures and wanted to visit her. She never lacked for boyfriends and had several proposals of marriage.

Lucile Markham Thorne, taken about 1931, just before her wedding.

Harold Thorne, taken about 1929, when he was leaving for a two-year mission in England.

The last part of giving details would be a story or example of that particular object or person.

When she started to date my father, Harold Thorne, he told her that he only dated a girl three times.

"Agreed," said Mama, and then she made sure that they had lots of fun. They always dated with a group, usually Dad's friends.

Mama was lively and fun, with a ready smile, a quick comeback and a willingness to get the most out of every minute.

At the end of the third date, she shook Dad's hand. "Thanks," she said. "I've had a lot of fun with you. I hope to see you around."

"What do you mean, 'thanks'" Dad asked.

"This is the third date and you never date a girl a fourth time."

Dad thought about it for a moment. "With you I'll make an exception."

Compare the statement, "My mother was a good woman" and contrast that to the paragraphs that I have written about her. You are beginning to see a person and not a generalized word, "mother." Unless you can make each person in your autobiography interesting and individual, then it won't be interesting to your reader. It isn't enough to know a person well. You have to present that person with a personality, with faults and virtues, with smiles and frowns, with words coming from her mouth and a flirty look in her eye.

Visual Images

Our modern lives are filled with visual images. We watch television, motion pictures, read magazines, books. We have seen just about everything that we want to see, and lots of things that we didn't want to see. Our memory holds these visual pictures in our minds and a word can readily recreate these visual pictures.

In our writing, we can use concrete details and know that visual images will flood into the minds of those who are reading.

We have been talking mostly about photographic memories. Are these memories frozen or are they moving? In your history you are always doing things, moving, thinking, reacting. Let your story be one of movement also. Instead of using lots of adverbs, make sure that you use verbs that create pictures. If you use the verb "to be" which includes "is, am, are, was, were, be, being, been" it may be possible to substitute a more vibrant word for it, such as fighting, screaming, flying, crawling, laughing, running. Show yourself doing things. Let the verbs work for you.

Adjectives and Adverbs

Most every beginning writer is afraid he is not going to be able to make his writing interesting, so he starts by adding description. He usually does this by piling on the adjectives.

Limit the amount of adjectives and adverbs you use. Most of them are superfluous and add nothing to the meaning. Keep your writing as clean and simple as you can.

USE YOUR SENSES

One time I attended the lecture of a noted poet. After the lecture, I watched him as he walked across the campus. He stopped by a tree and touched a leaf. He rubbed the leaf between his fingers and smelled it. He touched the bark, stood in the shade of the tree and looked up through the branches. It was the first time I was aware of someone enjoying and using the sense of touch and smell and sight. We take them for granted.

From the moment you are born you learn by using your senses: sight, sound, smell, touch, taste. A new-born baby, having tasted his mother's milk, will often reject bottled milk or refuse to suck water. As you grow older, you tend to depend on sight more, but the other senses are equally important.

Touch

My brother-in-law complains that my sister goes shopping with her fingers because she has to touch all the clothes on the rack. She loves the feel of the fabrics and knows by touching the clothes how it would feel on her body.

I have taken up the hobby of making porcelain dolls. I feel the greenware with my fingers, stroking away the blemishes. There is something calming about this and I suppose that I am developing my sense of touch.

I watch my talented niece play her violin and wonder how much of her music comes from her very developed sense of touch.

Smell

I spent a few minutes cooking a hamburger with onions and mushrooms. As I walked into another building, the odor clung to my clothes and immediately everyone wondered where the food smell was coming from. One person guessed it was garlic bread, another liver and onions, another guessed onion soup.

They were more sensitive to a food smell than to a perfume. At least they were more vocal about it. Some people are more sensitive to odors than others. My husband has had his sense of smell deadened somewhat because of his work with chemicals.

Taste

Closely akin to the sense of smell is the sense of taste. Imagine a hot day and you have been working in the garden at noon. You reach into the refrigerator for a cold glass of orange juice. You can imagine the cool liquid on your tongue.The sense of sweetness is there. Let your reader remember the taste with you. Other taste sensations include salty, sour, acrid, bitter, rancid, sharp, wet.

In your family are food traditions. What are your favorite foods? What do you serve on special occasions, such as birthdays, Christmas, New Year's. These play an important part of a family history because they evoke special memories. Can you recreate your mother's apple pie? What about her bread? Was she a lousy cook? So, no one's perfect.

Sound

The first thing in the morning you will probably experience the sense of sound before anything else. With your eyes still closed, you might hear birds singing or chirping, or the neighbor revving his motor, the toilet flushing somewhere in the house, a radio or television being played, a telephone ringing. Helen Keller said that of all her senses, hearing is the sense that she misses the most, even before sight.

Sight

I don't know why the game *Peek-A-Boo* is so much fun for a young child, but I can get my two year-old granddaughter to have a giggling good time by playing this simple game. Perhaps it is the momentary loss of sight enhanced by the visual image coming back into view. Most of our description is visual. Try to enlarge your description by including all the senses.

Use all five senses in your writing. It makes your writing vivid and real and helps your readers to feel the same way you did when you experienced it.

Let's go back to the story of the turning point in my life, my father's death, and start putting details in the story. By using details and as many of the senses as I can, I will try to show instead of tell the story. As it is written in Chapter Five, it is no more than an outline. By adding details, I am completing the picture, as I remember it. I must keep it from ending until I have included all the significant details. If I leave too many details out, or if I include too many, then my picture will be distorted.

First of all, I need to set the scene, let you know what the situation was, the peaceful condition of our life before the event happened. This section does not include anything but the background for my story:

This was to be my father's last trip! He was going to have his own business and never have to travel again. I knew that made

Mother happy, because she smiled all the time now. I looked up at him, past the long legs, and wondered if he would be able to play with me more if he were home longer.

Six-year-old Joyce and five-year-old Mary Lou played hide-and-go-seek around his legs, but I was too old for that. Daddy sold jams and jellies to stores in southern Utah. We had more strawberry jam than anyone in all of Salt Lake, I thought.

The year before Joyce and I went with Daddy on one of his trips. I remember that it was so hot my crayons had melted together in the back window. Daddy had been cross, because the crayons had made a drippy mess in his brand new car. I also remember the Indians sitting in the shade by the old stores. I had jumped the rope for one old Indian, and he had laughed. I think Daddy knew everyone we saw and they knew him.

Daddy sat down and picked up three-year-old Jimmy and two-year-old Sally and bounced them on his knee. I sat quietly by him and held onto Sally, so she wouldn't fall. I was eight years old and figured I knew more about baby-sitting than Daddy did. Through the blue serge suit pants, I felt his strong legs. I didn't know it then, but I would remember his legs longer than his face, or his smile, or his voice. My friend Dale, from next door, and I had arguments several times on the subject of "dads." I had conceded that maybe his father was probably stronger, but mine could run faster.

Dad stood up. All I could see were his legs. "I'll call you from Cedar City," he said and hugged us all. "It's the last time I'll be going away." And he was gone.

Check back and see if everything that was in the outline is included. Actually I had forgotten to mention that he was going into business for himself and had to go back and add it. Have I used all the senses?

- Sound: The Indian laughing, my father's voice
- Taste: Strawberry jam
- Touch: Feeling his legs, holding onto Sally
- Sight: Crayons, Mother smiling, hide-and-go-seek

- Smell: I goofed. I could have added that the sage-brush smell tickled my nose, or the dust of the desert made me scrunch down and wish I could smell rain or grass instead.

Time Controls

Write your story as you remember it happening. I use the flashback about going on a trip the year before.

Although flashback can be used, your story will be more effective if you continue in a forward sequence. If you use too many flashbacks or your flashback becomes too long, then it should be a cue to you that perhaps you should have started your story at an earlier point in time, or given more background.

SPECIFICS OR GENERALITIES

There are other questions you can ask yourself. Have you written in specifics or used generalities? As I go back over my writing, I see that I have used the word "car" in talking about "my father's car." Inasmuch as the car is important to the entire story, I should be more specific: "dark blue four-door Dodge with light gray upholstery," should have been used instead of simply "car." As I was describing my trip to southern Utah the year earlier, I could have also mentioned how lonely it was on the road and how few cars we saw on the desert. These are clues that I should give early in the story

It is easy for generalities to slip through, and sometimes it is better to use the general term. Try to be more aware of which you are using, and why.

You can add detail through concrete words or by using an example.

Be Concise

Professional writers use minimal words. You can have more impact by shortening your sentences.

Keep your descriptions short, but include the necessary.

Make sure that you do not go off on tangents. Decide what you want to say and keep to that decision. If a second story creeps in you may want to take it out and write that second story after you finish the first.

Polishing Ideas

Words that you should watch for are redundant words or wasted words.

- Redundant words include: yellow in color, 10:00 a.m in the morning, big elephant. Yellow is a color, 10:00 a.m can't be anything but in the morning, and elephants are always big, so nothing is added by including adjectives to modify.

- Wasted words: In regards to, according to, in this day and age, during the time that I lived in..."In regards to" and "according to" simply start out your sentence. You don't need them. "In this day and age" can be simplified to "today." "During the time that I lived in Texas..." can be simplified to "When I lived in Texas."

SUMMARY

Make sure that your examples, details or descriptions add to that main thought. Ask yourself, "What do I want to say first of all?" Then say it.

When you have finished, go back over what you have written and see if each detail is meaningful. Does it add or take away from your story? Do you need to add details? In your hurry to tell the story, have you only included general details. Does each detail serve a purpose?

In the final writing, no one can tell you which details to use any more than I can tell you which incidents and turning points are vital to your life. You have to ask yourself, "Does this detail add to my story?" and "Is there a reason for using it?" If you have a question as whether or not to use a detail, then leave it in. It is much easier to cut it out later than it is to add.

The easiest way to write your story is to write your story as you remember it happening and then go back and see what needs to be added or cut.

Don't be afraid if your writing is not perfect. There is no reason for it to be perfect. The important thing is to get it down the first time. Don't compare yourself to a published author who has written and rewritten his material many times and then had his words honed by an editor.

Challenge

1. Write about one of your homes

   - Describe it. Let us know how it smelled and felt.
   - What was the atmosphere in that home?
   - What kind of food was prepared.

2. Use as many senses as you can.

   - Tell us one story of an event in this home.
   - Give an example so that we can see that home.

CHAPTER SEVEN

Let Your Feelings Show

$\mathcal{A}$ man showed me his personal history, but it wasn't really his story, it was a list of his accomplishments, a resume. Every degree he had earned, every honor bestowed upon him, every organization to which he belonged was included. This man was a caring, accomplished man, but not once did his true personality show through in his personal history. I know that he cared for his mother-in-law in her old age. He took her into his home and never complained when she became burdensome. This was not included in his list of accomplishments, and yet by the greater standard, this was one of his greatest. In his resume we never saw his gentle humor, or the sad times in his life. We never even felt joy in his accomplishments. We have no record of anything he ever felt. No one can give that to us now because he died shortly after he compiled his resume.

Many people think that if we show our emotions, it makes us appear weak or foolish or vulnerable. They feel the ideal is to be strong and silent. But feeling is also the very essence of being human. In the Bible it says that "Jesus wept." He was not afraid to show his feelings. Attitudes, emotions, feelings—

these are the elements that make your autobiography uniquely yours.

By sharing your emotions with your reader, you become genuine in your writing. You have a favorite story, one you remember in great detail. Everyone has one. It is yours forever because you felt great emotion at the time that it happened and you remember it because of its emotional impact. You have forgotten many of the events in your life because your emotion did not burn it into you. But you do remember this event. This is a special story told from your heart.

When one of our loved ones die, one of the strongest emotions we feel is guilt. We remember every word spoken in anger, every action that distressed and we feel guilty that we didn't do more for them. We remember our neglect and thoughtlessness. And it is made even worse because we can no longer rectify our actions or say we are sorry. I remember watching mother's grief over dad's death and feeling that somehow I was partly responsible.

It is difficult to describe someone without displaying your personal feelings about that person.

You are going to remember people and places if you had strong emotions about them. Love, hate, pity, fear, embarrassment are all going to play strong points in your memory. If you knew a person but didn't care much about him, he was only incidental to your life. This is the person you will forget. The same is true of places and events. Emotion sorts out the memories you have and leaves you with the happy, sad or fearful at the same time as it dulls the tedious, repetitious, apathetic times.

When you write, how do you reveal your feelings?

The only way you can mean anything to another human being is to share *your* feelings. It is not enough to write facts and details. We need to know how you feel about them. A newspaper article includes facts and details but lacks personal feelings or emotion.

If you are a carpenter, let us know how you feel about the wood you touch, your tools, and what it means to you to build a bookcase. If you worked your way up to the top of your profession or business, what was your motivation? Tell how you met challenges. If you are a salesman talk about the people you meet and how you feel about them. If you are a housewife, tell how you feel about raising your family or how you feel as a woman. When you are telling incidents in your life, include your feelings. When you talk about your family and friends, a description isn't enough.

It is difficult to describe someone without displaying your personal feelings about that person.

The easiest method is to merely tell how you feel. "I was embarrassed," "I was afraid," "I hated," "I loved" are simple statements of feeling.

GIVE AN EXAMPLE

Illustrate your emotion by giving an example or a story you remember. A friend wrote about a trip she took:

Just now I can never see a fresh red rose without remembering the experience on the Queen Elizabeth on my first trip to Europe. A number of my former students who lived in New York had been to the pier with me. Now the great Queen ship was moving away from the shore. That evening when we were without skyline of New York, I went to my lower deck of the state room and began to open some of my gift packages. A knock came to my door. I opened the door and there in crisp cellophane see-through wrapping was a bouquet of tight red buds of more than a dozen roses. The messenger laid them on my arm.

"These aren't for me!"

"Yes, they are for you. Here is your name."

I opened the spray and real tears blinded my eyes. I cried for seconds, then lifted them in my arms and buried my face in the roses. I laughed and cried. Then I read the card. The flowers were from the other teachers at the school where I taught. I was not alone again on the entire trip to Europe.

I don't think there are any questions on how happy this woman was about a simple act from her friends.

General terms such as "lonely," "happy," "sad," "success-ful," are better understood when you *show* us in addition to telling us how you felt.

Go back over your material and find the places where you write such statements as:

"My mother didn't understand me."

"I had many happy times when I was growing up."

"My brother was lazy."

"My grandmother was an example in my life."

"I had good teachers and bad teachers."

These statements mean very little to us until they are filled out with examples and stories. Go back to the statements and ask "why?" Why didn't your mother understand you? Can you find an example in your life to illustrate it. What happy times did you have? Tell us some. In other words, show us how your brother was lazy or what your grandmother did to merit your admiration.

Use of the Senses in Our Feelings

One way to communicate our feelings is to be aware of everything around us and to use all of our senses in writing. When we feel emotion, it affects us physically. When we are happy, we see objects in colors and brightness, but when we are unhappy, blacks and whites are predominant. Our faces flush or are drained of color, depending on our emotion. We hear birds or thunder; our skin gets goose bumps; our hair stands on end; we sing; we walk on air; we vomit; our mouth is dry. Use the senses in writing and you will be showing us your feelings.

In your writing, be selective about your words and details. Try to create the same mood you felt when you were actually experiencing the situation.

Re-experience the Emotion

To re-experience an event is to recapture the emotion. As we record our memories we are also storing emotional memories. We can still remember the excitement we felt at winning a state basketball championship, the joy at seeing our first newborn child, the sadness at the death of a loved one, the despair at watching someone we love destroy himself. These emotions are still with us mingled with our memories of the event. However, those emotions are softened with time. We can only hold so much joy, sorrow, despair, excitement within us. We must let them soften in order to survive. At the time of the event you thought that you could never live through that experience, and yet, here you are, a survivor. You probably could not have written about it at the time, but now you can write about it.

One way of re-experiencing an event is to find a quiet place and meditate. Forget about your daily concerns for the moment and focus on the one story you want to tell. Hold onto it as long as you can. It will come back again each time stronger if you don't try to force it. When you feel you have reached the point of saturation and the impression is now fully developed in your thoughts, this is the time to start writing. Don't worry about punctuation or perfect sentences. Concentrate only on putting down your thoughts. After you have written what you can, let it rest for a day or more without looking at it so that when you do go back to it, you can see it more objectively. When you go back to it, you will find that some parts are better than others. The parts in which you actually were able to include the feelings will be more unified and vivid. Some parts are going to be easier for you to write than others, but do go back and try to rewrite those places that are unfinished. It will give you deep satisfaction when you find that you are able not only to put words onto paper, but also emotions and feelings.

Just as you are able to talk about an emotional time after the experience, so are you able to write about it.

"Wait a minute!" you might say. "I don't want to relive some of my life. I mean, it was bad enough the first time! I can't go through that again. I don't even want to remember it, let alone re-experience it!"

But these traumatic times stay in the background of your mind and slip out unexpectedly when something reminds you. If you are able to write this experience as clearly as you can, helping us experience how you felt, you will feel much better. If you can express your feelings rather than keep them bottled inside you, you will be able to see the situation in a new light. In time you might even be able to analyze it and perhaps understand a part of it, and finally accept it in your own way. Sometimes writing about a problem in your past acts as a therapy and is a healing process for you.

"All right," you might say, "maybe it is good for me to get it off my chest, but I sure don't want anyone else to know about it. I was embarrassed (or hurt or ashamed)."

Of course, what you write is entirely up to you, but isn't it possible that your experience might help someone else? Sharing your mistakes or embarrassment or hurt may prevent someone else from making the same mistake. Your assessment of it, or your acceptance, may open the door for someone who is at this very time going through a similar experience.

A friend of mine, a woman with a family of growing teenage daughters, was writing her story. She was a child of sexual abuse and harassment and didn't want her daughters to be subjected to the same problems that she went through. Her stepfather had continually tried to rape her. Her story tells about how she would come home from school and go into her bedroom. She would arrange the windows and furniture in such a way that she could escape through the window at a moment's notice. She writes about her abuse by saying, "He touched me and made me touch him." She did not need to go into the details. That was not necessary. She tells her story as a warning and help to her daughters.

However, there may be a time in your life that is of such a nature that you cannot write of it without pain. If this is your situation, wait until you can be more objective before writing about it. Finish your autobiography without it, and perhaps later—even years later—you may be able to complete your story. If you start having nightmares or reliving stress, then stop. Perhaps this is too much for you, and you need professional help in getting through it. "I don't mind being honest and frank about the things I have done," said a thoughtful woman, "but how do I write about a close family member who has saddened my life?"

I knew the woman and her circumstances. Her rebellious teenage daughter had experimented with drugs and alcohol and was now living at home with an illegitimate baby. She had given her mother several years of heartache, and yet the mother stood by her. Now the girl was trying to straighten out and the mother didn't want to write anything that would stop that progress.

In other words, "Are there some things that are better not said?"

Try to get perspective on the entire situation. Even though the actions of others have affected your life, it is still *their* story and not yours. Try to summarize in generalized terms what has happened to them. Rather than detail all their misdeeds or sins, put the emphasis on what you did and how you felt.

Use restraint, common sense, and the wisdom of hindsight in writing about the situation. If you can allow the bitterness and unhappiness to mellow into an honest appraisal of your successful and unsuccessful reactions, you could not only help others who are going through a similar problem, but will allow that family member to understand you better and realize that he/she isn't hated, outcast, or alone.

Sensitive matters such as suicides, insanity, drug dependency, divorce, criminality, illegitimate births are subjects difficult to accept in a person's life. When you write about them you need to use tact and diplomacy to explain. Do not be insensitive to the rights of others. If you feel that what you may write may be hurtful to others, then it is better to omit that story. Be sure that you tell the truth. Do not make up some story to cover up the problem. It is better to never mention a sensitive issue than to lie or distort the truth.

There are degrees of telling stories:

- You may go into detail.
- You may give only the most important details
- You may pass over the subject lightly.
- You can hint at it, but give no detail.
- You may make no mention of it

Everyone has problems. I know of no one who has completed his life without facing and solving problems. How you feel about it, and how you handle the problem is what is more important. Don't try to write your personal history by covering up your disappointments, failures and faults. However, these faults should not be dwelt upon. Talk about how you overcame these problems. This will ensure that your story will be an uplifting story, one that can be treasured.

By now you have probably realized that I am still working on the story of my father's death. It is easy for me to tell you to write about your difficult times. It is not as easy to tell about mine. It took me all morning to write the following account. The mailman and a neighbor interrupted my writing, and I'm sure they wondered if I always spent the day with tears streaming down my face. But at least now I can say to you that I understand how difficult it is to write about emotional times.

Strange, I can't even remember being told of my father's death, or of his funeral which I attended.

But I do remember my mother's tears. Mama put her arms around all of us and held us until Jim squirmed away and Sally squealed. Mama cried, a low moaning sound as though it hurt her inside, and I didn't know what to do.

"What have I done that's bad?" I thought. "It must be me." I tried to make it up to her,and so I picked one of the first daffodils of the spring from next door and placed it carefully in an empty strawberry jam jar. But it was dwarfed by the baskets of roses and lilies that began to fill the house. Some of the vases of flowers were bigger than Sally, and they smelled so sweet I wanted to open all the windows.

Everyone came to see Mama now...neighbors who lived down the block came to see us, even though they never had before...and Mama's friends...and those who said they knew my daddy. But he wasn't here any more and I didn't know why they came. They all made Mama cry more, and I wished they would all go away so we could be as before.

Something had changed. Something was different and I wasn't sure exactly what. We clustered close to Mama whenever we could, to give her strength or maybe to draw from her.

"Your daddy's dead," Dale said. "So my daddy can run faster."

"He was old anyway," I justified. (Dad was thirty-two years old.)

I didn't see Dale much after that. We moved to Provo and lived with Grandma. The moving was overshadowed by Condit's trial. It seemed to last such a long time. The trial took place in Parowan, Utah, the county seat where the murder had taken place. We stayed with a relative.

"Why is it taking so long?" I asked Mama

"Because they can't find enough people to make up a jury," Mama sighed.

It seemed to me there were plenty of people around. They all would pat our heads and murmur in low, sad voices, "And these are the children!"

Newspaper clipping of our family at the time of my father's death.
Left to right, Mary Lou, 5; Joyce,6; Jimmy, 3; mother; Janice,8; Sally, 2

The trial lasted into the summer, and it was hot and dry. The fine red dust covered my Sonja Heinie paper dolls and scattered into swirls as I jumped the rope. When Condit came into the court the first time, I knew him from the newspaper pictures. Jim's clear voice was heard throughout the court, "There's the man who killed my daddy." He had clear speech for a four-year-old. Condit had vacant blue eyes, so light the blue was almost white, and I stared at his eyes each time I saw him. He looked at us all during the trial, but I didn't know if he ever saw us because he never changed expression. I wondered if eyes without color could really see.

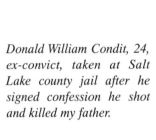

Donald William Condit, 24, ex-convict, taken at Salt Lake county jail after he signed confession he shot and killed my father.

I helped Mama with the younger children so she could hear the trial. She cried some then, but I watched her swallow hard and make the tears stop. She kept the tears inside until night, and then she'd bring them back in gulping sobs when she thought everyone was asleep.

Three weeks after jury selection, Condit was pronounced guilty and was given the death sentence, and one year later he was shot by a firing squad.

During the days after the trial, Mama seemed happy and she told us stories and taught us how to ride a bike and roller-skate and fold paper to make boats that sailed down the gutter. But for months after, in the night I heard her cry from behind closed doors, and I didn't know what I could do to make her stop.

Becoming older, I've known myself the grief she felt and I understand. As a child I felt inadequate in meeting grief. But instinctively we clustered close to her, and that was the only thing we could do. With all the wisdom I've gained now, the only thing that really helps is to open up my arms and say, "I love" and "I understand," and even now it seems inadequate.

Challenge

1. Tell a story that has influenced you strongly.

    - Give background
    - Rising action
    - The event
    - Analysis

2. Go back over the story.

    - Did you show how you felt at the time?
    - Do you feel strongly about it now?
    - Did you cry or smile while you were writing it?

3. Write a second story using your feeling.

CHAPTER EIGHT

Show Your Story Instead of Telling It

One of the basic tools of a writer is the ability to show an event happening. This is called dramatization, another word for dialogue and action. You too, can use this tool in your writing. It is the difference between *showing* the story of you and your family and *telling* about them. *Telling* is simply narrative and *showing* uses a variety of techniques such as using dialogue, describing the surroundings, and seeing people in action.

SETTING THE SCENE

When you go into a theater or movie you are uncomfortable until you know where you are in the plot, who the characters are and what is happening. The same is true about a story, even your story. You need to place your reader in the same spot as you were when the event occurred. In journalism you learn to report who is involved, when it happened, what happened, how it happened, where it happened and finally why it happened. This isn't journalism, but if you are sure to include these basics, it is a good start. As you start your story, include the following:

- People involved.
- Place and time of action.
- What is happening.

Example of Telling

Every married person has a time when he/she accepts another person into his/her life. It is a definite turning point and should be included in your personal history. But it should be given more space than merely the telling of the fact. Write the time when you made this decision. Give the facts and then go beyond that. Describe where you were, what you thought, who was there. Give the circumstances. The following statement is an example of *telling* of my engagement.

I was engaged to Willard Dixon on February 13, 1953.

This is completely factual, but not very interesting. Let me take you back to those few minutes when that particular event occurred.

Example of Showing

I was ready early for the Valentine Dance at the BYU and was waiting for Willard to arrive. But he was often late, and so I lay on my bed in my slip studying my book on Speech Correction. My formal hung in the closet ready for me to wear. I glanced into the closet and smiled. Willard loved me to wear red and this was a deep rich red color. It had yards of soft chiffon and lace with rhinestones and a beaded bodice. The doorbell rang and I could hear Mother go to the door.

"I'm early," I heard Willard say.

I glanced at my watch. An hour early! I couldn't believe it. He never came early! I peeked over the banister carefully. From my position at the top of the stairs I could see most of the front room. Mother, Grandma and Willard were gathered together looking at something. I couldn't see what.
"Oooo!" Mother said. "It's beautiful!" Mother's voice always carried, even when she was just whispering.

"Oh, my!" said Grandma. "Look at that!"

I couldn't see even though I kept watching. Maybe one of them would move so I could see. My peephole from the top of the stairs offered only their backs.

"A corsage?" I thought.

I put my books away, and took my formal out of the closet. I'd known Willard about a month and a half, and already he had started to give hints that he wanted to marry me. But he'd never actually asked me.

I heard my sister, Mary, give a little squeal.

Too much excitement for it to be a corsage.

A couple of my girlfriends had whispered to me, "I saw Willard in a jewelry store the other day."

"Are you sure it was Willard?" I had asked.

"It was Willard," they had said.

Oh my. Could it be tonight? Was he going to give me a diamond tonight? Was he going to show my entire family before he even ASKED ME?

Yes, I think he would. When he got something on his mind he was bulldogged about it. Friday the 13th, the day BEFORE Valentines. Yes, that wouldn't bother him.

I sat down on the bed. What was I going to say? "I don't know you well enough." But I did know him, even though we had dated such a short time. I seemed to know what he was going to say almost before he said it.

Would I say, "I don't love you?" But I did.

Yes. I did love him. So it was set. My decision was made. In my bedroom, standing in my bedroom alone, on Friday the 13th, 1953, the luckiest day of my life.

I slipped on my formal, checked my hair and make-up and went downstairs pretending I hadn't heard every giggle, squeal and exclamation.

Willard took my hand and placed a blue velvet box in my hand. I opened it to reveal a beautiful diamond ring, square cut with two smaller diamonds on either side.

I looked up into his eyes, and knew that I would love him forever. He placed it on my finger without even asking me if I would accept it. He knew I would without even asking. He knew me as I knew him.

In front of Mother, Grandma and sisters, I was asked, I accepted and words weren't needed.

Willard and Janice, engaged just three hours at the Valentine's Dance. Friday, February 13, 1953 at BYU Social Hall Ballroom.

USING DIALOGUE

When you go into a bookstore or a library, you may be attracted by the title. You pick the book up and glance through it. If the paragraphs are long, then you probably will put the book down and look for another one with "white" spaces. Using dialogue gives white spaces. A book becomes easier to read with many short paragraphs and few long paragraphs.

Conversation or use of direct quotes from a person offers many pluses. It breaks up long paragraphs; it pushes your story forward; it is useful for transitions; it shows characterization, and it shows more than one point of view. More than anything, however, it begins to *show* your story instead of merely telling your story.

Although you are not using exactly every word that was said, try to remember how it was said and what was probably said.

If you would like to give more than one point of view, dialogue is an useful tool. A conversation or argument can be effectively written, using nothing but dialogue.

Example of Telling

When we were married one of the most difficult things we did was to go shopping for groceries. Neither Willard nor I knew what to buy.

Example of Showing Using Dialogue

I was the first to leave home. I married Willard Dixon on June 8, 1953, but didn't realize how dumb I was until I went to the grocery store as a married woman the first time. I was not a cook. Grandma Mary had managed all the cooking and baking the past twelve years.

"No one's going to fool around in my kitchen!" she had announced many years before when I wanted to make cookies.

Willard and Janice Dixon, married June 8, 1953. Salt Lake City, Utah

That set the standard. We wouldn't invade her territory. It also left me unprepared. But I had eaten food all my life and I knew what should be in a kitchen.

So the first thing after our 12 hour honeymoon. (Willard was new on his job as a chemist at Geneva Steel and they would only give us a half-day off) we went to the grocery store.

"What do we need?" Willard asked.

"Flour," I told him, "sugar, eggs, milk." After that, I wasn't sure what we would need. But, of course, I wasn't going to admit my deficiencies so early in married life.

I sent Willard for the eggs and I went up and down the aisles trying to decide what a real cook would choose. I was all right in the vegetable and fruit section. I knew how to boil potatoes, although I didn't know how long it took to cook them.

When I came to the meats, I was completely stumped. Hamburger and hot dogs were the only two meats I knew how to fix. I chose a pound of hamburger. I looked at the pork chops, roasts, steaks and panicked. How would I tell my new husband that he had married such a dud! His mother was known for her gourmet cooking, and I had been to dinner at his home many times and knew she set a high standard.

Willard came toward me without the eggs. "Which size eggs should I get?" he asked.

"What do you mean, which size?" I thought an egg was an egg.

"They come in jumbo, extra large, large, medium and small," he informed me.

"Which is the best price?"

"The small eggs are the cheapest, but they have the least volume," he answered. "I've weighed each kind and divided by the price. The large eggs seem to be the best value, but to be accurate I would have to measure the shells separately."

I looked at him in amazement. It had taken him fifteen minutes to weigh the eggs. At this rate we would never finish shopping. "Just get the large eggs."

"Would you get the toothpaste?" I figured I could get all the rest of the shopping done while he did that.

I turned to heavier matters. Flour. There was bleached, unbleached and whole wheat in a variety of sizes. That wasn't difficult. I bought the kind Grandma always bought, only in the small size. I didn't envision myself baking cakes, pies or breads for some time.

"Toothpaste comes in large, medium and small," Willard said. He was carrying the large size.

"Did you weigh them?" I asked.

He grinned.

"It's hard to tell because of the weight of the toothpaste tubes, right?" I guessed.

"Right."

I looked at Willard with a whole new perspective. I had been married one day and I didn't realize we were going to go through life weighing things. Marriage finally hit me. I had volumes to learn about my new husband.

Our first trip to the grocery store cost ten dollars. It was the hardest ten dollars Willard ever spent.

DON'T GO INTO THE MINDS OF OTHERS

Be careful that you don't give the thoughts of other people. "He thought" is a phrase to beware of.

"I don't know which size eggs to get," Willard thought.

Willard can *say* these words, but he cannot *think* them, because we don't know that's what he is thinking. If he says the words out loud, then we can repeat them.

LET YOUR FAMILY SPEAK
THROUGH DIALOGUE

When you want to show the people in your story, the easiest way to do that is to let them speak. Think about some of the favorite sayings of your mother, father, grandfather, aunt, 3-year old child, etc. Start writing them down. How do they express anger, surprise, satisfaction. These can be used in your stories when you write about them. Some common expressions used in my family include:

"Let's get this show on the road!"

"I'm going to ride it on out."

"Do you want your dinner cold or burned?"

Sometimes these expressions are family codes. We all have them. They can be different for different relationships: husband/wife, parent/child, sister/sister, friend/friend. "Let's get this show on the road means, "Let's go," or "finish the project". "I'm going to ride it on out," is my 94 year old mother-in-law's way of saying, "I'll suffer the pain until I die, just forget about calling a doctor."

My neighbor, Gloria, phoned me late one night in desperation. "Henry is having a heart attack or a stroke. Can you drive me to the hospital!"

Gloria sat in the back seat of my car trying to console her husband while I drove quickly, but carefully to the nearest emergency room.

"What happened?" Henry asked.

"We were having a party," Gloria said, "And you got sick. We're taking you to the doctor."

The hospital was several miles away and I heard the same conversation over and over again. Henry didn't seem to comprehend what was going on.

At the hospital I stayed with Henry while Gloria signed the necessary papers.

"What happened?" Henry asked.

I tried to ignore his question, but when he repeated it, I answered, "We were having a party...and then you got sick."

Henry looked at me strangely. Hesitantly he asked, "...We were...having...a party?"

"Yes...yes," I answered.

It was only afterward that I learned that "having a party" was their code for "having sex."

GETTING STARTED

- First of all, you set the scene by giving background. Tell where and when the story took place.
- Then you tell us the people involved.
- Let the people in your story speak and move. However, keep the sentences short and to the point. They don't have to speak in paragraphs, in fact, few people actually do. Sometimes one or two words are enough.

You will find that your writing will become more vibrant and interesting if you *show* some of the times in your life instead of merely reporting them.

Challenge

1. Try showing one event in your life including dialogue.

   - How did you propose to your wife (or were proposed to).
   - How did you explain Santa to your young son or daughter. Give dialogue.
   - Write about the birth of your first child? the second?

2. Make a list of familiar family sayings.

CHAPTER NINE

Writing Humor

A woman called me last week and told me that she was writing a book about local women who had made a difference in the community. She wanted to include the story of Mother.

"Could you write something about your mother?" she asked. "Something funny..." she added. "My editor says that most of the sections read like resumes..."

What can I say about Mother that would let strangers know Mother better? I could say that Mother has a great sense of humor, but you're going to smile and nod, "Sure! Everyone says that."

I have to prove to you that Mother has a sense of humor. Simply telling you isn't enough.

I thought back. When she was in her seventies, Mother, my three sisters and I went on trip to Mammoth in California. We went hiking, shopping, and finally we talked Mother into going on a horse back ride. She had ridden a horse when she was younger, but it had been over 50 years since she had been on a horse. The ride was fun, into the mountains on a two hour trip. When we got back, however, Mother couldn't get off the horse. Her muscles had stiffened up and she couldn't throw her leg over the horse's back.

"Maybe I'd better just stay up here." Mama joked.

It took all four of us and two men to help her get off. She may have been embarrassed, but she was laughing too hard to let anyone know how she felt about it.

Mammoth California, 1981. Mother sitting on insepara-ble friend.

Perhaps you don't know my mother, but you know more about her than if I had said she has a sense of humor.

Until you can see a person's sense of humor, you do not really know that person well. Think about yourself. What makes you laugh? How do you respond to embarrassing situations?

There have been many funny incidents that have happened to you. Some are only smiling funny; others are chuckles; and a few may bring laughs. You need to show some of your enjoyable times. A person with a sense of humor can face life's problems much easier than someone who is stoic and lets his burdens weigh him down. We must be able to laugh at ourselves.

In the story about Mother, I showed that she was able to laugh at herself.

WHAT MAKES YOU LAUGH

Think back to things that make you laugh. Many times it is when you try something new and find the unexpected. Do funny things happen to you...

...when you are on a trip? (you sent your laundry out and everything came back pink) (you lost directions and found yourself in someone's back yard on top of a mountain)

...when you start a new job? (you were so nervous you spilled food down the front of yourself) (you parked your car in the boss' parking space. Well, it wasn't marked)

...get married? (find out that he snores so loud you can't sleep) (find out that she can't cook)

...have a new baby? (her water broke in the grocery store) (he was so nervous he forgot her packed suitcase for the hospital)

The world is new for you and you have to learn to face new challenges. Often you are surprised at the outcome. Surprise is always a part of humorous events.

When Mother was in her 60's she and a group of friends planned a trip to Taiwan. At that time, not many tourists had vacationed there and Americans were still a novelty. Everywhere Mother went, crowds of Chinese children gathered around her. Some of the little children came up to her and wanted to touch her hair. She nodded agreement and found that the whole crowd wanted to touch her. She touched their hair too.

"I felt like a 'petting zoo,'" she told us.

Often you can find humorous incidents such as this when you do something you are unaccustomed to doing.

The first time we attempt something we are often awkward, slow or accident prone. Sometimes it also shows how we can adapt or are inventive. It also exposes us when we are most vulnerable.

START WRITING IT DOWN

Don't try too hard. Write without trying to be funny. If you try to force humor, it will sound forced. Be yourself. I find that if you keep a notebook, you can often find humor in your life. Humorous things are happening all around you. All you have to do is look at the life you are living and enjoy what is happening to you.

Many of the techniques professional writers use to create humor do not work in personal and family histories. Exaggeration is one of the most used techniques. But you are aiming at accuracy and to compare your boss to a battleship discredits everything else you write. Yet comedy writers do it all the time to get a laugh. The purpose of writing a personal history should always be remembered. Do not distort for a cheap laugh.

An old friend came for a visit whom I hadn't seen for some time. It came as a shock to me when he confided, "I can't see much anymore. You are just a blur to me."

"Well, I haven't changed much," I told him in an attempt to lighten the conversation. "I still have a perfect figure, no gray in my hair, and I'm so brilliant you can almost see my brains." I was going to exaggerate even further when I heard his gallant reply,

"Yes," he said, considering it thoughtfully, "That's how I remember you."

I recently was asked to read and correct a personal history. The history was laced with spelling mistakes and poorly constructed sentences. But the humor was there. The woman had a way of putting words together that was very funny. I knew the woman, and she wrote exactly as she spoke. As I corrected the history I was careful to preserve her way of writing because it was unique in itself. You could almost hear her voice as you read her words.

SEE THINGS AS THEY ARE

In order to have a sense of humor you have to first of all see things as they are. Look at yourself. What are your weaknesses? Are you able to laugh about them? Are you getting older? What problems does that bring?

- Forgetfulness?
- Loss of strength?
- Releasing of authority?
- Physical complaints?

As I have grown older, I find that I cannot sleep through an entire night without getting up a couple of times to empty my bladder.

I can rationalize and say, "Well, I've always had this problem." But, did I? Am I only making excuses?

Funny? Not really. Except that this summer I'm planning a trip to French Guinea into the wilderness area. We are going to be floating down an alligator filled river in a long canoe with natives poling the water. We'll see the red eyes of the alligators in the water by night, fight poisonous snakes, keep our shoes on to prevent vampire bats sucking our toes, and at night sleep in hammocks covered with mosquito netting.

Now does a weak bladder begin to sound funny? I can see myself trying to push away the netting, adjusting the hammock, looking around for insects, snakes and alligators crawling under the hammock, all in order to relieve myself.

If I can't laugh at my problem, I am going to be faced with embarrassment or discomfort. I am laughing at myself before I can give anyone else a chance to do so.

The same can be true of any weakness. As a person gets older, he may lose some of his hair, or his hair goes gray...or both. Look at the paunch on the belly, the balding of the hair, the rooster neck. Definitely, these are not funny. But, short of surgery, intensive exercise and a wig, they are part of us, ready to stay until we die. So you might as well laugh. It makes it easier for us and for others.

ACCEPT THINGS AS THEY ARE

It is not enough to see yourself as you are. You must also recognize and then accept yourself. When you start to laugh at yourself, you are also accepting yourself as you are. Mother accepted the fact that she simply could not dismount from the horse, and that it took four daughters and two men to help her. If she had hurt herself, or cried, the story would not have been humorous.

Once you go through this process with each part of your life, then you can write about your problems and endure what is happening, and also allow others to see how you accept them. This is where humor begins. It is the accepting of a not-so-perfect person in a not-so-perfect world.

Find a good story from your past. Humor is found in the everyday, common times and not so much in the more important, dramatic times. Some subjects lend themselves to humor. Do you have any folk history in your family. How about pet sayings, or home remedies?

DON'T BE AFRAID TO LOOK RIDICULOUS

Two years ago, on a trip to Hawaii, my sister, Mary and I decided that we wanted to bicycle down one of the volcanos. Our husbands tried to talk us out of it, telling us that we were too old, too chicken and completely out of shape. The more they talked, the more stubborn we became. On the designated morning Mary and I slipped out of bed at 4:00 a.m. and drove to the tour area to receive our ride. We were issued yellow plastic suits and goggles which made us look like aliens, and driven to the rim of the volcano to see the sunrise. Our bicycles were transported to the top waiting for our descent. Of course, our husbands were there when we arrived, with cameras to document the occasion. Mary and I whispered together, wondering if they were right in questioning our sanity. However, we come from stubborn stock, and no matter how ridiculous we looked, we got on our bicycles, along with a dozen other stalwarts and started the 20 miles down. As the oldest members of the group, Mary and I were placed in front. It meant that we paced everyone else. I guess we gave them a good ride because not too many grumbled and neither one of us fell off.

I guess you never forget how to ride a bicycle. It has been a highlight of memories for me and probably the reason I'm willing to try the French Guinea trip.

GETTING ANGRY

Sometimes we over-react to situations, only to find that things aren't as they appeared.

> I was twenty years old and my sister, Joyce was eighteen when we went to Yellowstone to work for the summer. I felt responsible for my sister, especially because I felt she was flighty and impulsive. One time her friend, Paula, came to me. "Joyce and Tom have rented a cabin for the night," she warned.
>
> I was appalled! And angry! And worried! I thought about what Mother would say. I thought about Joyce's Eternal salvation and SIN and all the dark ugly things that happen to young innocent girls.
>
> "Which cabin?" I asked.
>
> Paula knew.
>
> I stormed out, Paula following and we ran over to the cabin area.
>
> Angrily I knocked at the door.

Joyce furtively peeked out, then slammed the door and locked it.

I hammered on the door. "You let me in right now!" I ordered.

Finally Joyce let me in. There sat Tom on the bed. His hair was put up in little pink curlers and the smell of permanent solution was strong in the room. He looked completely embarrassed.

"Tom has always wanted curly hair," Joyce explained. He didn't want anyone to know....

My anger, my worry, my frustration left...and so did my speech.

APPRECIATE OUR DIFFERENCES

We are all different, obviously. Instead of becoming annoyed when others are not like us, we should enjoy these differences.

My son, Bill spent a winter season at Alta Ski Resort in the dorms. His assigned companion, Brian, had strange habits. First Brian arranged all of Bill's belongings before Bill had a chance to put his things away. Bill objected, but didn't say anything. Then after work, Bill came back to his room and all of his belongings had been re-arranged. Some of his non-breakable items were hanging from strings from the ceiling. Each day was different. Bill started to get angry--but stopped short. After awhile it became funny to him to see the different ways his belongings were arranged.

We all have to get used to living with others and, although Brian did weird things, Bill was able to adjust. Can you remember adjusting to a roommate, a spouse, a mother-in-law, a new co-worker? Adjustment time can be upsetting, but if you adjust your thinking, it can be a lot of fun.

ATTITUDE

Look at your material with a smile. Enjoy the times when you have been embarrassed, awkward-looking or ridiculed. Your attitude will show in your writing.

Remember that you are human and, being human, you make mistakes. If you look ridiculous once in a while, it also makes you look human. One of my ancestors was held up as a paragon of virtue. He became human to me one day when I was told that one time his teen-age son exasperated him so much that he kicked the boy in the seat of the pants and broke his own toe. For me, this man had not existed until I was told this story. Now that he has become human for me, I can accept the other more praiseworthy stories about him.

SIMPLIFY YOUR WRITING

Keep your story simple. Don't go off on tangents. Sometimes it helps to outline your story first. Again, use the background, rising action and the event as suggested in writing your turning point. The difference will be your attitude toward the story. Plan the story so that the punch-line (or joke line) comes at the end.

DON'T BUILD EXPECTATIONS
OR EXPLAIN YOUR JOKE

Never tell your audience that you are going to tell a funny story, that it is the funniest thing that ever happened to you, or that they are going to laugh their heads off. By doing this, you are setting yourself up to fail, because then the reader is going to say to himself, "Prove it," or "I dare you to make me laugh." Never challenge your audience to laugh.

Don't try to explain your joke. Once the story is told, end it. If you have built your story with the proper background and let it proceed naturally to the punch line, you will have no need to add anything to it.

USE DIALOGUE

When you use dialogue it makes your story come to life. Keep the lines short and to the point.

> One time, Mother was tending the children while my husband and I went on a needed vacation. Steven, then about seven years old, wanted his way about something. He said to her, "Grandma, there's only one thing wrong with you."
>
> "What's that?" she asked.
>
> "You always have to be right."
>
> "That's correct," she retorted. "And that's the way it's going to be." She got her way, and Steven had to live with her decision.

Humor is the attitude with which you look at yourself. Become vulnerable and enjoy your awkward moments with others. When you show moments when you were not at your best, then you allow others to get to know you better. Your story will be better for the fun you have had in your life.

Challenge

1. Write something funny that has happened to you.
   - Try to include dialogue.
   - Save your best line for last.

CHAPTER TEN

Reinforce With Variety

We have stressed the importance of writing the turning points in your life. If you have chosen carefully, then you probably have written a good basic story of your life. You have learned how to write humor, to show your stories and to include dialogue. However, perhaps you sense that something is missing.

This is a matter of orchestrating or balancing your writing such as a composer does with his music. Think about the quiet times, the gentle stories, the people who are a part of you.

There are recollections of times in your life that you may want to include, such as memories of vacations, dating, early school experiences. There are also special events such as an accident or illness, learning to drive a car, a birthday. You may want to include places you have visited or lived, and people you have known. You should include your achievements, positions, honors, schooling, skills, and hobbies. Now is the time to look at Appendix A, Memory Joggers. Here are some other suggestions on how to write about some of these events.

NEED FOR MEMORIES

Why do you remember certain things in your life and forget others? There must be a reason. It might be that some events were significant in your life and you haven't taken the time to really think about them. Sometimes a memory will come back to you many times. This memory is important to you and should be written down. Perhaps later it will take on a significance to you and you can develop and explore it in more depth. For now, let the memory stand by itself. Other memories emerge unexpectedly and then slip back into the background of your mind with only a wistful remembrance.

These memories often become the transition between turning points and stories that you want to tell. Often they are generalized times in your life. Some memories might include:

- Daily chores you did as a young person
- Flowers you planted or loved
- Friends you grew up with and fun times with them
- Family trips, summer vacations
- Family traditions

The writing of a memory can be as long or as short as you want. Memories can be triggered at any time.

Next to our office in the middle of a busy business section of town is an old home with grass and flowers. The home is a relic from a quieter time. The roses bloom profusely and are a joy to everyone who passes.

But what I enjoy most is the patch of hollyhocks beside the fence. As a child I spent many hours making hollyhock dolls from our own patch of hollyhocks in our backyard. My favorite hollyhocks were the double petaled ones. These made beautiful skirts for my dolls. A barely opened bud supplied the head and fancy hat, and the single hollyhocks made bodices and long flowing sleeves. I put the dolls together with toothpicks. Some days I had a whole ballroom full of dolls for a most wonderful gala.

The list can go on. There is no beginning or ending to these memories; the recollections don't grow into a climax; they are there to ponder and enjoy.

PETS

Perhaps pets have been an important part of your life. Why not give some space to those animals that you have spent many hours of time loving.

The following is a story about a cat who grew up with us. She was a part of my life, but certainly not a great influence. Still, she was important to me, a fond memory.

Old Smokey was a prolific old cat, mottled, long haired, gentle. She offered us hours of great enjoyment and she allowed us to haul her around. It seems that we always had a litter of kittens to enjoy, courtesy of Old Smokey. When she was younger she hid her new-born kittens from us and we had to search the bushes, the garage, the old coal shed or under the house until we found them. It was better than finding Easter eggs, because she was creative in her hiding places.

When she grew older, Grandma prepared a place for her in a small closet in the kitchen. Then we didn't have to hunt for the kittens, only enjoy. Grandma always seemed to know when the kittens would be coming.

Smokey's kittens would come into the world, damp, skinny and hungry. Usually she would present us with golden yellow kittens, blue-gray ones, pure black ones and tiger-marked ones in the same batch.

We would admire the little ones, name them, love them, and as they grew older, dress them in doll clothes and take them for rides in our doll buggies. In times of stress the kittens would hear all of our problems. As we stroked their soft fur, our problems would lessen in our minds and we could cope with our daily lives. The kittens provided a needed release.

MEMORY OF PLACES

In addition to the home in which you grew up, there are other places that are important to you. These might include vacation times, places you go for seclusion or rest, a second home, your garden.

Madeleine l'Engle in *A Circle of Quiet*, tells about a retreat by a brook, quiet and away from everyone. Sitting in this quiet place she is able to restore her sense of calm. She says, "If I sit for a while, then my impatience, crossness, frustration, are indeed annihilated, and my sense of humor returns."

I received a ten page single-space typed letter from a friend. It told the day by day activities of a month long trip to Europe. If I could have felt the newness through my friend's eyes, or her feelings as she saw the wonderful adventure she was having, then I would have enjoyed it more. As it was, it could have been written by anyone. I suspect that some of the paragraphs had been copied from a travel brochure.

If you are going to write about a vacation, make sure it does not become a travelogue. If you went many places, choose the most significant part of the trip and be specific about that and generalize the rest. The following is a vacation we took as a family when my children were younger:

> Somewhere in Oregon we searched for an overnight camping spot to spend the night. It was getting dark and we were tired. Steven had been sick the entire trip with a throat infection and he was grumpy, and he set all the other off.
>
> At 8:00 we saw a sign which read: "Garbage dump and camping site...three miles."
>
> "I'm not sleeping at any garbage dump," Steven grumped. But it was getting late, and we turned off the main road and followed a one-lane road, winding off into the mountains. By the time we had set up the tent and fixed a hot meal, it was too dark to explore the area. But the next morning as we looked around, we discovered we had camped in a most beautiful camping site. A short hike led us to a natural swimming hole with a diving rock.

We spent the day relaxing and swimming. Shade trees and grass lined the river area.

"Let's stay here the whole vacation," Steven begged.

Douglass found a tree just right for climbing, and Dan and Charles explored some trails close by. We never did find the garbage dump.

We hadn't planned on spending the time in this quiet place. We had Disneyland to see and the California beaches. We were going to Fisherman's Wharf and the Golden Gate Bridge and then to Los Angeles and Universal City. We would stop by Grand Canyon and Bryce and Zion's on the way home. It was to be a cram-packed vacation. Our days were planned. How could we explain to waiting relatives that we had found a water-hole in Oregon!

After two days, the children were sunburned and scratched up and still begging to stay longer, but we moved on. We promised ourselves that some day we would go back. I doubt now if we could even find the place again, especially if they have taken down the sign: "Garbage dump and camping site...three miles."

NEED FOR PEOPLE

There are many people in your life and probably all of them have influenced your life and changed it in one way or another. You need to present some of them in your story. You have lived with members of your family and know all about them. Yet, how much have you said about them? You know their achievements, their sense of humor, or lack of it, their good qualities and their bad qualities. You have had many experiences together. So, how do you present this person to a reader who may never have met him.

You are not going to write about a person unless you feel strongly about him/her. You are going to love or hate him. Because you choose to write about him means that he has touched your life. Let those emotions show.

You need to show how that person is unique. Other people may know this person in a completely different way. Both of your impressions are correct, only different.

Be sure to make this person believable. This will include bad things as well as good things, sad times as well as happy times. A recent book was self-published about my great grandfather and was written by a distant cousin. It was so completely one-sided that it became almost laughable. Because it was so laudatory it lacked credibility. The book depicts my great grandfather as being almost perfect. He never did anything wrong and every conversation was a work of art. We know from old diaries that the marriage was less than perfect, with many arguments loudly voiced. Yet, the book describes the marriage as in complete harmony. In real life we know that his first wife left him and took their children with her to California. We never heard from her again.

It is also possible to focus only on the negative side of person. This is as objectionable as giving only the good qualities. Try to be as objective about a person as you can.

Show the human qualities of this person. Do this by presenting him/her as honestly as you can. Be specific. Describe and tell stories of your experiences together. If you remember favorite expressions, use them.

In my life, my Grandma Markham was a great influence, and certainly deserves an entire book to be written about her. This is only one small segment:

*Grandma Mary Markham
on her 75th birthday.*

After my father's death, we moved in with Grandma Markham, my mother's mother. We called her "Grams" or "Grandma", and as our own children came, she became "Grandma Mary." When we moved in, friends predicted it would "kill Grandma."

Three years earlier Grandma had fallen down the stairs, a flight of eighteen steps. Her beautiful auburn hair had turned gray overnight, I'm told. She was not well. But when we moved in, she had something to live for, and I can't remember her ever complaining about her health. She worked harder in her seventies than I did as a teenager, and she was active in mind and body until shortly before her death at age ninety-six.

Her parents, Frederick Lewis and Agnes Reid Ferguson, were Mormon pioneers who cleared a farm in Leland near Spanish Fork, Utah. Grandma spanned the century and progressed from horse and buggy to jet travel.
"Can't you drive any faster?" she would ask, as I carefully stayed within the speed limit. "You're not going to let that car stay ahead of you," she would persist. "You know I don't like any car ahead of me." I stopped at a busy intersection and waited for a break in traffic. "What's the matter with you?" she demanded. "You could have crossed that street at least four times!"

When she was ninety-two Mama took her to California. Mother was like most visitors, unused to California freeways, trying to find the right roads, adapting to the fast traffic. But Grandma was delighted. "Isn't this delightful!" she said as Mama approached a clover-leaf intersection. Grandma said, "I don't know why everyone makes such a fuss about freeways."

Later they got caught in traffic and were creeping along at five miles an hour. "Isn't this fun!" Grandma exclaimed. "Why, we could reach over and shake hands with everyone."

Because of Grandma's attitude of adaptability, she was able to bridge the generation gap. Her attitude was young, and because of that, she always had fun. Mama took her to Disneyland and Grandma had a wonderful day. She was resting for a moment in the shade of a bougainvillea bush and an older woman was sitting close by.

"Isn't this terrible?" the woman complained. "They shouldn't bring old people to a place like this. I'm seventy-five years old, you know."

"I'm having a perfectly wonderful time," Grandma replied, "and I'm ninety-two."

Grandma dated boys who called for her with a horse and buggy, later on she drove a Model A Ford and at ninety flew east in a jet to visit a grandchild. Whenever I'm inclined to complain or criticize, I remember Grandma's ability to adapt, and I decide that if I'm, going to stay young in spirit, I'm going to have to make the most of every minute. Then I'll be able to say, as Grandma did, "I'm having a perfectly wonderful time, and I'm only ninety-two."

GIVE A SENSE OF HISTORY

When the history you are living touches you personally, it is most important to record your own feelings about that happening. I wish I had recorded how I felt when the first space rocket was launched; when John F. Kennedy was killed; when the Berlin wall was built, and then years later, when it was torn down. My thoughts about these events have dimmed. They would have been more valid if I had captured my own feelings about them at the time they happened.

My sister was on the California freeway headed for the airport at the time of the 1993 earthquake. As she was in the airport limousine, she witnessed highways crumbling, electrical explosions, bridges falling. She arrived at the airport only to be told the airport was closed. So she retraced her path and saw all the devastation a second time in the light. She writes about her experiences in a vivid way.

Through television we have witnessed many things: wars, floods, sensational murders, new presidents of nations, collapse of Russia as it once was, space travel. What has touched your life personally?

The following is not an individual event but a progression of history that I know.

I learned how to type on an old Royal typewriter. It was a manual upright typewriter and I had to punch hard to make the letters hit hard enough for an impression. I wrote many stories and poems on this old typewriter. It took me through Junior High school.

I thought I was privileged when I had a portable Remington. I turned away from the old Royal and was thankful for my new machine. It was much easier to type on and most of my college papers were written on that old Remington.

You can imagine how excited I was when I bought my first IBM electric typewriter. It was so advanced that it would space the words to look good on the sheet. I no longer had to pound the keys. It was painful to go back even for a time to the manual Remington. I had an electric typewriter and it was faster and easier than I ever imagined. I typed my masters and doctoral thesis on this wonderful machine.

I started writing longer papers--whole books with many revisions. Now my electric typewriter wasn't enough for me. I discovered a class on word processing and took a class at the local college. The word processor took most of a very large room. I could write chapters in my book, and go back in and revise. It was a complicated process, but it was so much better than rewriting the entire section. Word processors were terribly expensive though, and I had to use the machine at the college, which became difficult. I was required to leave the disks in a file at the college. Then one day, someone took my disks and everything I had written was lost except the hard copy I had luckily made. When an old word processor became available I jumped at the chance to buy it. I wrote and rewrote as many times as I needed to, and the process was so much easier.

Then computers became available, and each year they became less expensive. Once I started using computers, I stored my old word processor and without a backward glance embraced the mysteries of the wonderful computer. Each month computers came onto the market with more and more memory, and more capability. There is no way I could keep up with current technology. Fax machines, graphics, E-mail, networking. The whole concept of computers is mind-boggling. As I write on my computer, it is difficult to remember back to the old manual upright typewriter.

I don't think I'm living through miracle times, and yet as I look back on the progress made in my lifetime in just this one area, I know that I'm living in a different time from the one of my youth.

NEED FOR POETRY OR OTHER WRITINGS

Poetry is sometimes the most autobiographical part of you. It gives a hint into that part of you that may be hidden otherwise. Of course, if you have a lot of poetry, it would be better to use it at the end of your book or as a separate book. But a representative poem interspersed occasionally to forward an idea or a special time in your life might add greatly.

It may or may not be rhymed.

When Mother had been a widow some forty years, she wrote a poem which no one saw until after her death. It tells how she felt about meeting Dad in the Hereafter.

Can this be I?
This gray streaked hair
This sagging cheek and wrinkled neck?
I feel so young, my spirit taut and firm
My hair is golden as when he left.

Dear Lord, when next we meet
Let my spirit self
Be what he sees.
My heart would break
If he should turn aside
And murmur, "Not that old hag!"

NEED FOR TRADITIONS

Every family has traditions or customs. These can be included in your personal history. The obvious traditions are observed at holidays. What family doesn't celebrate birthdays, Christmas or New Years in its own special way? But what about the little traditions?

> Every April 1, Grandma would pull some trick. It usually started with her announcement that Smokey had a new batch of kittens. Inasmuch as Smokey always had new kittens, we fell for it every year. We were always suspicious of the food Grandma served. What appeared to be pink lemonade was usually colored water.

Perhaps some of the most difficult times in a marriage occur when one spouse wants to break with the traditions of the other. In a new marriage, sometimes a discussion needs to be held about which traditions are going to be kept and which ones are going to be changed. It may mean establishing a new set of traditions.

For example, in our family we have always had a big Thanksgiving dinner with the Dixons. When my children married, they had to decide how they were going to handle that tradition when their in-laws also want to celebrate Thanksgiving dinners. The compromise was that every other year they would go to the Dixon dinner and the next year with the other side of the family.

Have your traditions changed or evolved throughout the years?

- What traditions are you currently observing?
- How do you celebrate the New Year?
- When do you have family outings? What do you do at those outings?
- What do you do when a new baby is born in your family?
- What foods are served for special occasions?

- Do you have a special time for sleeping in, indulging yourself?
- When do you entertain?
- What anniversaries do you enjoy?
- What photographs do you take? Are they posed or spontaneous?

The list could continue, but you know what is most important to you. Write about these traditions, especially those you would like to continue.

NEED FOR PHILOSOPHY

You have lived through many experiences and should have learned from each. Why not share these philosophies with others. You might say, "But other people know that." That may be so, but when you tell your reasons why you believe as you do, you are adding your evidence of truth to that of the wisdom of the ages. Tell your philosophy and add to it the reasons why you have come to believe and accept it as your philosophy. Back it up with your experiences. It is not enough to throw out fragments of truth without your reasons. The important thing is that, if you have learned from it, someone else also might learn from you.

Philosophy is better accepted if you include an example, either preceding or following the advice. I have many personal beliefs. Some of them I have learned from many years of experience. As I grow older these thoughts have strengthened. I don't know if they are important to anyone but myself, but in my own personal history I write:

> When I was younger and had my little ones I thought I knew all there was to mothering. And then my children became teenagers and I realized I didn't know as much as I thought. After they married, I still had a lot to learn about motherhood. My grandchildren started coming and I realized that grandmothering is only mothering on another scale.

When my own mother died and I found her letters and stories she reached back to me from her grave and gave me solace. It was then that I realized that mothering is a continuing process. It even reaches from the grave to give comfort and help. My time as a mother is then and now and even forever. It's a sobering thought.

EMERGING PATTERNS

As you look back over your written material, perhaps you will find that the philosophy of your life has emerged without your even being aware of it. Try analyzing the decisions you have made. If your book does nothing else, it should allow you to see yourself better than you ever have.

You may not even have realized it before, but you may have one theme that colors everything you have written. Is it the same way with your life? What has been important to you will probably become a major part of your autobiography.

Has your autobiography become a soapbox for some cause? Have you substituted explanations for honesty.

You may decide that your most important contribution to the world was your involvement in a cause, and you admit that everything is filtered through that one perspective. As long as you admit this to yourself, so that you are seeing your life as it really is, you will have learned much about yourself.

You may ask, "Have I tried to present a rounded picture of myself, or have I emphasized only one part of me?" To answer this, look back at your writing. How much space has been allotted to each issue? If you spend most of your autobiography talking about your career, then rightly so, this is where your greater interest lies. Or it may be your family, your ideas, or your activities.

If you look at your autobiography carefully, (if you are a daring person) you may even see yourself as others see you.

Challenge

1. If you had a pet in your childhood, include a story about that pet.

2. Write about a favorite place you enjoy?
   - Describe it. Tell why it is special.
   - Give an experience you have had there.

3. Write about a vacation that was memorable?
   - Why do you remember this vacation?
   - Write about it.

4. Talk about one person in your life who has influenced you.
   - Describe the person.
   - Give some of the person's favorite expressions.
   - Give examples of your times together.

5. Write about something that has happened in the world in your lifetime.
   - How did you feel about it?

6. If you have ever written a poem, include it?
   - If you haven't written a poem, why not start?
   - If someone else wrote a poem that is important to you, include it. Tell why it is important to you.

7. Write about one of your traditions.

CHAPTER ELEVEN

Ending Your Autobiography

Here you are writing along, adding anecdotes, telling of your travels, talking about traditions and favorite sayings, and all of a sudden you realize you have nothing more to say. Could it mean that you have come to the end of your autobiography?

I suppose that, logically speaking, an autobiography ends with your life, but that isn't the way it generally works. You could continue writing your book all of your days, of course, but you need to come to a conclusion or a rounding out of your book.

Some suggested endings include summarizing, philosophizing, giving tribute, sharing your hopes for the future and telling your beliefs. I have attempted to give a portion of each, although I prefer some more than others.

SUMMARY ENDING

As you look back over your life you can see the path you have taken. Maybe it is the way you wanted to go, or maybe you would chose differently a second time around. At any rate you may feel that you have been this way before. Try writing a summary of how you feel about your life. This is one way:

Well, here it is, family. My book, the one with all those stories that I have told so many times. Now if I start on one of my stories, you can stop me with the reminder that I've already written it.

Maybe I could have gone a different direction, but I didn't, and perhaps it is just as well. As I look back, some of the things I have done gives me great satisfaction. Other things, I can only say that it was a great learning process.

I came from a wonderful background. Mother set an example that I always tried to copy. She had high goals and reached those goals. I wish my father had been around longer so that I could have known him, but it wasn't to be. Grandma was such a strong force in my life that I find now that I have her voice and her strength.

I've had such a wonderful time with my sisters and brother. Our yearly vacations have been the best and we have never been closer.

I couldn't have asked for a better husband. He has been my companion, my lover and my friend. We counsel each other, relying on each other for advice and strength. We are always laughing together, enjoying each other's presence. Apart, I am lonely. Together, we are a team.

I have six wonderful children. Not perfect. But I have learned from each one. And as they grow older, they have also become friends. I would rather be with my family than with anyone.

PHILOSOPHY

I guess I'm not much of a philosopher, but this is what I believe:

My husband says I'm an idealist. I look at life with the greatest possible hope. If everything is falling down about me, I can still see that bright light ahead of me. I guess that is because I've been so happy. I've had my disappointments and troubles, but I know that when it's all over, that everything will be all right.

TRIBUTE TO FRIENDS

There are so many people in my life that I care about. My life has become richer because of them. I think a paragraph or two about those who mean the most to you is appropriate in your book.

I have been blessed with good friends, and to mention them all would be much too long. But there are two who have influenced me, each in a different way.

The first is my life-long friend, Marilyn Young Deem. We became best friends when I was in seventh grade at a time when I was a pathetic thirteen year-old suffering growing pains. How wonderful to find a kindred spirit. We are so much alike that sometimes people thought she was my sister. We always competed for everything, (grades, sports, contests, even boyfriends) and that was all right too, because sometimes I won, and sometimes she did. I always looked up to her as a person with the highest of ideals. She has remained a best friend through my lifetime.

My second good friend is Peggy Nichols. I met her at the University of Utah when I was working on my Masters Degree. We are opposites in everything and yet drawn together in other ways. We both love to write and I suppose that is one of our ties. She is the person I trust the most to edit my writing. She had the patience to edit this book, for which I am grateful. After thirty years she is still a strong influence in my life.

HOPES OR GOALS FOR THE FUTURE

Whether you are eighteen or eighty, it can be valuable to list your goals, just to make sure you still have them. In writing them down, you are more likely to make them definite and commit yourself to them, and to reassess your life in terms of what you want.

People who know me, or think they know me, see me as a serious person. I have been working with my husband in an asbestos testing laboratory for the last ten years. I can discuss at length the problems of asbestos containing substances in a building.

But this isn't what I'm really like. I'm a writer and I like to write humor. Deep down I know that I would be happy writing comedy again. I think that for a change I would like to write stand-up comedy or comedy sketches and after that another full-length comedy.

QUESTIONS ABOUT
AND HOPES FOR AN ETERNAL LIFE

Sometimes you have strong beliefs about what is going to happen after your death. This is personal and sometimes difficult to discuss, even with family. And yet, you could take the time to write down your beliefs or questions. Writing them down will help crystallize them in your own mind and let your family know how you feel.

I can not draw a floorplan about Heaven and what will happen to me when I get there, but I'm not afraid. I know that those who have loved me before are there waiting for me. I believe strongly that my father, who died when I was eight years-old, was looking after us for all these years, even though we were unaware of his presence.

I have felt the presence of Mother and Grandmother after their deaths. When I was writing a book about Mother, she came and gave her approval. It was as strong a feeling as I have ever had, and I know that she is alive and very happy now with my father. At my mother's death, Grandma came for her and helped her through the veil that separates heaven from earth. I know my Grandmother. Nothing would have kept her from being there. And I felt Grandma's presence.

I have also been counseled by my deceased father-in-law. Two years ago there was a question whether or not I should move in with my mother-in-law who was then 93 years old and living alone. I was happy in my own home and didn't want to move. But Dad Dixon came to me, and though I didn't see him or hear him, I knew what I had to do. Dad Dixon was always good about getting me to see things his way. We moved into her home the following week and I have felt good about living with her.

I have had the help of the Holy Spirit many times. He has given me warnings when I needed it, and help with the things I have endeavored to accomplish. When I asked for His help He has given it. I acknowledge His help.

CONTINUE WRITING. LIFE ISN'T OVER YET

I helped my mother-in-law with her personal history. She wrote what she could and then she told me her stories and I wrote them down. I gathered her precious pictures and we copied them and put them with the writing. It was important to her as well as to the rest of the family. She even wrote a final segment, a conclusion.

After the book was finished, she had a fun experience with two of her daughters and we wrote that up and put it at the end of her book. I don't think her book is really finished. As my mother-in-law says, "I'm only 94 with a lot of life left in me."

This is what she wrote, after she had finished her book:

October 4, 1996

On my birthday Portia and Linda took me sightseeing at the Gardner Historical Village. This is a place where they have a lot of old homes that have been made into craft stores. Because it involved a lot of walking, Linda went to the office to see if they had any wheelchairs for me to use. They didn't have any wheelchairs, but the lady said I could use her motorized cart.

The cart was hard to drive, and one time I nearly drove it into the water. Sometimes I went fast and Linda and Portia had to run to keep up. We went into one of the stores and while we were there a policeman came up to us and asked who was driving the cart.

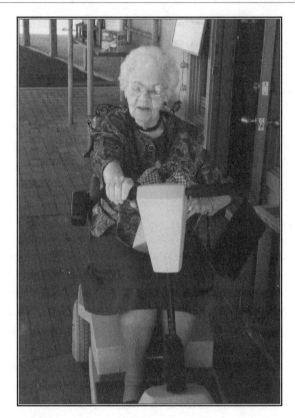

*My mother-in-law, True Call Dixon, October 4,
1996. Sightseeing at Gardner Historical Village.*

"I'm driving it," I said.

"Can I see your drivers license," he asked

"I don't have it with me, but I have one. And its legal too!"
Linda took out her purse, "I have my drivers license," she told
him.

"Were you driving the cart?" he asked.

"No," Linda said.

"What's wrong?" Portia asked.

"It's parked illegally. I'm going to have to give you a ticket."

I felt awful. "I didn't know!" I started to say. And then I looked at Portia and she had a grin on her face. I knew she had put him up to it.

"Happy birthday," the policeman said. Later he came by and gave me a candle as a gift.

CONCLUSION

There are as many ways to conclude your autobiography as there are people. And I might add, there are as many ways to write your autobiography. That is what makes your autobiography uniquely yours.

Your autobiography is finished. Your life continues. I hope you have been gentle as well as thorough with yourself. You have been probing into your past, into your emotions, like an analyst and have found areas of tenderness. You have looked at yourself as a child, as a young person, and each succeeding year.

What a marvelous thing it is, this life, which allows you to grow physically, morally, intellectually and spiritually. You are allowed experiences to help you grow. These "turning points" test you and you are strengthened or weakened, depending on your responses. You reflect back on these experiences and understand, in perspective, things that at one time were incomprehensible.

You are the child, the young person, the adult, and you take each part of yourself and hold it closer with love, insight, tolerance and understanding. When you completely accept yourself, then you can accept others.

Your life continues, perhaps now with greater self-love and self-knowledge. Now that you have written your story, remember that this is just a beginning to what you can do and what you can write. Try to look at this as a close of the most recent chapter or volume and not as an end to your autobiography.

Tomorrow you will go on to a new day with more skills and self-knowledge.

Set your goals a little higher, realizing that no matter what your age, you still have turning points to meet. It would be nice to add an epilogue to your autobiography by saying:
"Where I once was weak, now I am strong...because I know myself."

Challenge

1. Try ending your book using suggestions from this chapter.

2. Try a second ending and compare the two. Which do you prefer?

3. Continue adding stories. Each day is a new adventure.

Section Two

Writing Your Family History

CHAPTER TWELVE

Families are Important

In November, 1989, my mother, Lucile M. Thorne, died. She left us with boxes filled with newspapers, personal papers, letters, diaries, photographs and more memories than can fill many books.

Mother inherited all of the papers, photographs, diaries and letters written by her parents and grandparents, as well as everything from my father's family.

All of this was stored in boxes in her basement. Nothing was filed or organized.

I had never been so inundated with such a wealth of material before. As I gathered the material I knew that I would write Mother's story and it would become my story as well.

I used to know the difference between personal and family histories. Now, I'm not so sure that there is such a distinct line. My family and I are linked in many ways. Heritage is only one link. We are linked in interests, friends and experiences. We are alike in our mannerisms, preferences in food and clothes. Our laugh, our voices, our appearances are all similar. We are a family and as far back as I can discern, the decisions made by the previous generation have a direct influence on me, through me to my children, and on through my grandchildren.

Finding all the family stories and photographs is an over-whelming task, but it is most important. I want first of all to let my children and grandchildren know me, know my mother and father and to understand who we are, what we stand for, and what we expect of them.

Now that Mother is gone, all that we have left are memories and stories of her, and these will fade with time. Some of Mother's stories are already forgotten. I have tried to capture her life on paper, and it has been easier because she took the time to write letters, stories and poetry and entries in her diary.

What she has written is her gift to us which will never be lost. She is the only one who could tell about herself. I only knew her as a mother. And there are so many other personali-ties in her. One day, I said to Mother, "Oh, Mother, why don't you write your personal history."

"I should, I suppose," Mother answered. "I do think I have a story inside me." I didn't know then that she was doing just that.

As with Mother, you are the only one who can write your life. You have a story inside you. Sometimes you have many stories: Stories that happened to you, to your family, to your parents or grandparents that are waiting to be told.

As I looked at all of the boxes containing the papers, my one outcry was, "Where do I start?"

And that is the biggest question everyone has.

If you have gone ahead and written your personal history, you have started the process of writing a family history, because you are number one in a long line in your family.

To say you are writing a family history is almost over-whelming in itself. It is almost as overwhelming as to say you are writing your personal history. As in writing a personal his-tory you don't write a book, you write a sentence at a time. It is the same with writing a family history. You start with one person, one incident, one story and go from there. It is not dif-ficult if you break it up into segments.

WHAT IS A FAMILY HISTORY

In the library, there are many biographies of famous, and not-so-famous people. They are written by professional writers who have had training in historical research and in writing. Usually they bring to the book their own interpretation and often will fictionalize parts. They do this in order to make the characters live for the reader. Sometimes they succeed in their aim and sometimes they completely fail.

The purpose of a family history book is to give as accurate a look at a family as it possibly can. You are not required to fictionalize your material, only present the facts.

In a broader overview, a family history is the story of a family's heritage. It is not simply a collection of names, dates and facts, but the story of a person's ancestors written in such a way as to recreate a glimpse of humanness from the past. It touches on the areas of history, sociology, biography, psychology, genealogy and creative writing. It is a part of each field and yet distinctly different because specialists aren't the ones who are writing these histories. We are.

All over the country we are searching for family Bibles, long-forgotten diaries, letters, scrapbooks, the remembering of family stories and traditions, and the quizzing of all those who remember the past.

IMPORTANCE OF FAMILY HISTORIES

Our children need to know our parents and grandparents and beyond, as we know them, not as names and places and unsmiling photographs, but as warm, real people.

When you gather mementos or spend an evening with a brother, daughter or aunt enjoying and sharing memories, this is a part of family history, but when you take the time to write down those family stories you have something far more lasting, something tangible, like a photo, that you can remember. This is a beginning of family history.

When a neighbor boy was suddenly killed in an accident last month, instead of sending flowers or a card, a neighbor wrote a letter to the parents telling them of the boy coming to her home early one Saturday morning and mowing her lawn and trimming some bushes without ever being asked. She tells about inviting him inside and talking with him about school. The neighbor liked the boy and told the parents why she liked him. The parents treasure this letter because it holds a moment in the life of their son that they might not have known otherwise. I know that my neighbor has written other letters, and in a small way she is writing segments of many family histories. A memory then. But much more.

No longer is the practice of tracing families limited to the elite few whose parents founded the country or those who were trying to trace their families to royalty. Each one of us is uncommon or unique in his own way. As we write we discover that special quality.

A young child, whose parents both work, has been going around the neighborhood telling anyone who listens that she is adopted, which she is not. The parents have been so busy working that they have only provided her with beautiful clothes, the latest toys, and a competent baby-sitter. There has been no time for unposed photos of her at the zoo with daddy or with mama going shopping, or with her first birthday party. Her photographs are formal, taken alone. And that is how she pictures herself...alone. There are no scrapbooks she can look at, and no stories she can remember. Essentially, she is an orphan even though she isn't adopted. She has no touchstone with her own identity.

It seems a simple enough thing to tell this child about what she did when she was a baby, but evidently these parents have not realized its importance.

A friend has a troubled grandson. She worries about him and the fact that he seems so aimlessly lost. Recently she has taken the time to talk with him about family. She started by gathering all his photographs that she has of him. "Do you have a photograph album?" she asked.

"No," was his reply.

Together they started to put photos in his album. Then the friend found letters and stories which talked about the boy. These were also added to the album. She is gradually going back into the history of the family, telling about the boy's father and some of the stories about him. She may not be able to help her grandson, but this is her way of giving him a sense of belonging.

After a speech I gave recently, a woman came up to me and told the following story.

Every week for over a ten year span of time, Emily had picked up Marjorie and taken her shopping and to the doctor. While they were in the car, Marjorie talked about her life. Marjorie had married Arthur when she was in her 60's and they had had a good life. She regretted not having children, but her life had been happy, and she talked about growing up, and her parents, and the things she had accomplished. She especially liked to talk about Arthur and their life together. Arthur had died a few years before so now Marjorie was pretty much alone.

Suddenly Marjorie had a stroke and she was put in a rest home. Emily went to visit her friend.

"Tell me about Arthur," she said.

Tears filled Marjorie's eyes. "I've forgotten," she whispered.

Emily hesitated a moment, then put her arms around the frail woman. "Let me tell you about Arthur," she said, and started to repeat back to Marjorie all the stories she had been told.

A short while later, Marjorie died, and Emily went to the viewing. There were few people there. A niece was at the mortuary.

"How did you know Marjorie?" the niece asked.

"I was her friend."

"Did you know her well?"

"Very well."

"I hardly knew her," the niece said.

"Let me tell you her story," Emily said. They talked for over an hour.

"Oh, I wish I had known her," the niece said. "Would you write down these stories for me. It's all I have of my aunt."

Emily isn't a part of Marjorie's family, but she is a part of Marjorie's family history.

When my youngest son was five years old he never got tired of watching home movies of himself as a baby. I told him simple stories of his first words, how he ate everything on the floor and how he pulled the cat's ear. A few minutes later I heard him telling a friend the same stories. He was delighted in things he did even as short a time ago as yesterday.

Willard told him stories of a pet lamb that he raised, and I tell him about wandering away from home when I was his age and getting lost. Grandma held him captive for as long as a five-year-old was able to sit with her stories of mine shafts, rattlesnakes sleeping on railroad tracks and lizard pets named Jack and Jill, all stories from Grandma's past.

DIFFERENT WAYS
TO WRITE A FAMILY HISTORY

There are many ways to write a family history:

• You can write about one person at a time with a personal sketch of each. This means that you are writing many sketches, but each one in depth. Be sure to write about one time period at a time. Suggestions on how to do this are included in the personal history section. Time periods may include: childhood, youth, young adult, married life, children, career, hobbies, retirement.

• You can write about each parent, and then as a couple as their lives join.

- As children join the family, their stories are also included.

- You can go back and write about the extended family, which will include grandparents, great grandparents, and as far back as your history will allow. This history can start with the "revered grandfather" and come forward in time, or can start with you, your parents, grandparents and back to the "revered grandfather."

STARTING YOUR FAMILY HISTORY

Before you start your personal family history, you should decide whether you are going to write a one-generation or multi-generation family history. Unless you are an expert in family history, it is better to start a one-generation history beginning with your parents' generation.

The easiest way to start a family history is to write about your parents first. You know your parents better than you know any of your other ancestors. You have more of their papers, mementos, diaries, letters, etc. You also know many of their friends and can talk to them. If you have written your personal history, then perhaps you have already started writing about your parents. Chapter Four gives additional help on writing about your parents.

Concentrate on one person at a time. Make it easy on yourself by choosing someone who can supply the necessary information about himself, preferably someone close. If you have a family member who is in poor health or advanced age, you may have to start with that member first, however. Common sense will dictate which direction you will go.

Directions will be given how to proceed in the writing. For now you need to focus on how much you want to do and where you want to start.

If you decide to start with your parent, the next step would be to write about the other parent. And then a grandparent.

Take it sketch by sketch, generation by generation. As you go further back in time, less will be known, and the research will be of greater challenge. But you will learn how to research, organize and write with each portrait that you finish.

These are more than stories. They are part of a heritage which helps establish our identity. As we search our past we discover special qualities that reinforce our own individuality.

Frank Smith gives a challenge which I think is an excellent way to start a family history. He suggests that you write a letter to those who will follow after you.

> ...First you could write a letter to present and future generations. Call it a preface if you wish, but write to those future generations. Tell them how proud you are of your ancestors and how proud you are to be their ancestor. Tell them they are an important link in the chain of excellence. Without being overbearing or lengthy tell them of your own convictions, the things that you have found in life to be most worthwhile, how, by writing this history, you have gained a tremendous regard for your ancestors.[1]

There is a searching out by many who feel the need of finding their roots. They find it necessary to trace their ancestry and to search out truth. This search can provide an identity for the young, a sense of meaning and continuity in the hectic middle years and a strength in the mature years. Once you understand your need for this truth, you will discover an added bonus of finding strength

Your family can become closer and more unified when you search out your family stories by asking family members what they remember, when you share the information you gather, and when you gain strength from establishing your own ties with your ancestors.

NOTES

[1]Smith, Frank, *Toward Preserving Our Heritage*, World Conference on Records, 1980, Salt Lake City, Utah, Volume 1, page 3.

Challenge

1. Write a foreword or letter to present and future generations as suggested by Frank Smith.

2. Make the decision how you are going to proceed. Focus on one ancestor.

CHAPTER THIRTEEN

Interviewing
and
Gathering Records

$\mathcal{W}$hen I was newly married, we lived with my husband's grandmother who had suffered a stroke and needed someone in the home to help her. She was eighty-three years old and in poor health and her family came often to visit her. I should have kept a record of the stories they told in reminiscing with her, but I didn't. As each one came, they asked for certain parts of her family history, and she promised it to each one, but added that they couldn't have it now. They must wait. Sometimes the same history was promised to more than one member of the family. I realized then that she had a valuable record, and started to copy all of Grandmother's family records and stories as a Christmas present for my mother-in-law. This took a lot of typing, as there were no copy machines in those days. When Grandmother died, family members came and each took the portion of the family history and records he wanted. It was scattered. My mother-in-law's copy and its carbon are the only complete records we have. We did sort it into somewhat of an order, but it was not organized into one complete record. When photo-copying became available we had it reproduced and gave it to close family members as wedding presents.

Here in the United States and in Europe, we have not realized how vital it is to remember our own family stories and traditions. Other areas such as Hawaii, New Zealand, and Africa have captured their histories in chants, songs, artwork and stories. Alex Haley, in searching out his heritage, discovered that in Africa some men, called griots, are specifically trained from childhood to remember the history of families or tribes.

Alex Haley, in a speech at the World Conference of Records in Salt Lake City, said:

> What we have now is an urgent need to collect as much of the oral history that remains as we possibly can. The greatest part of the history of this country is in the memories and minds of older people. Every year in this country about two million people who are sixty-five or older pass away, and with them goes a great big chunk of this country's history. That history is irretrievably lost unless those older people have been interviewed and their memories recorded by members of their family or others who are interested. We are now in a position to do something about family histories.[1]

WHAT SHOULD WE COLLECT

We have many ways of gathering and storing information, but we may not even be aware of it. In my own files and drawers I have documents and information not only about myself and my children, but also about parents and grandparents. They are all jumbled together, like families.

We all live with our parents for twenty years, more or less, and during that time the lives of each are separate, but still meshed with those of the others. Brothers and sisters become a part of that pattern—grandparents, aunts, uncles and cousins fill out the design—each one separate and yet fitting together like a picture puzzle. Each fragment is separate and yet incomplete without the others. A family is like that puzzle. When you open up a puzzle box and see the many pieces, you might sigh and wonder where to start. As you begin, you find it intriguing and return time after time to fit a section together or fit in another piece. Some pieces of the puzzle are recognizable and you quickly grab the easy ones.

With family histories it is much the same. Some of your family members you know well, such as your own parents. Like a puzzle you start with one piece at a time.

THE GATHERING PROCESS

There are three major types of information that we need to gather:

- The written record. This includes legal documents, certificates, diaries, letters, histories, newspaper clippings, journals, written accounts, genealogy records, school records, church records, employment records, etc.

- The visual record. This includes photographs, drawings, maps, slides, video recordings.

- The spoken record. This consists of the unwritten stories and accounts that is within each individual person and are recorded in tape recordings, video tape.

Put all of these together and you have the essence of what is most important in your life and theirs. Obviously, all of these sources are not available to everyone, especially if the subject of your research was born earlier than 1900. This is one reason that it is better to start your family history with those still living.

Modern technology has cooperated with us in giving us aids to gather, store, and copy needed information:

- The first is the copy machine. It is within the financial grasp of the average person to take a written record and copy it within minutes at a copy center.

- The second is the availability of quality tape recorders. These cassette recorders are small enough to carry around without straining a back or a budget.

- The third is the video recorder which can capture the family as they are speaking and moving. These recorders are available for rental, if they are out of your price range to purchase. These recorders make video history within the budget and reach of everyone.

- The fourth labor saving device is the computer which can help a person write and rewrite histories without the painstaking drudgery of retyping entire document.

- A fifth device is the use of computers for researching genealogy records. This will be covered in a separate section, but the field is growing so fast that what I say today is going to be outmoded by the time this book is printed.

PREPARE A FAMILY HISTORY SURVEY

You will save yourself and your family member time if you will prepare a list of dates and places. This list should also contain information of where your records are kept. If one spouse has all the information and doesn't communicate it to anyone else, it can be devastating to try to find needed information especially in a time of stress, such as a death.

If you are doing research on a family member, this is a quick way to get all the information in front of you and let you access exactly what information you have about this family member. This way you can refer back to this list easily without having to stop and look up the needed information. It will also save you time if the work has already been gathered or printed.

A family history survey is included in Appendix B of this book. It is a questionnaire on material to ask yourself or others, and documents to research. As you begin your search, you may wonder what you are looking for. At first you may feel unsure of what you need. This survey will guide you. You may not be able to fill in all the facts, but do not overlook the obvious. Be sensitive to feelings, and if certain questions are touchy, you may have to wait.

Filling in the information on these sheets may be the most difficult part of your family history. If you can get through this simple survey, the rest is fun. Many people love to fill in statistics, but I would much rather be listening to family stories.

When you have finished filling in the information on the survey, you will probably find that you can't answer some of the questions. Perhaps someone else in your family would have those answers, so make a visit or write a letter. You may even have to go to public or church records for your information.

Take the survey sheet and see how much is filled in. Does the person you have chosen to write about have a diary, journal, writings of any kind?

Take a three-ringed notebook and place all the information about this member of your family in the notebook.

On a separate sheet, remember as many of the stories as you can and list them. These are favorite stories, and you want to get it right. Try to remember the stories you have heard and facts you already know about that one person and write what you can. After you have written the stories to the best of your ability, it is time to visit with that family member. Call or write and tell him you are coming and why, so that he can be looking for his diary, scrapbook, documents, etc.

Decide how long you will be interviewing and let your relative know in advance. Usually an hour to an hour and a half is plenty long. After that he may get tired, especially if he is older. It is better to come back a second day. Be careful not to tire the relative.

Make a list of photographs you have. You may want to categorize them in time periods, i.e., baby pictures, youth, wedding, older years, etc.

Be sure that you protect your photos. Refer to Chapter 18, the Photograph Section of this book, for suggestions on preserving your precious photos.

SPOKEN HISTORY

Spoken or oral history is a fancy name for sitting down with a family member and talking about the things that person knows. In order to remember everything that is said it is best to use a tape or video recorder.

People who are taking taped interviews should use a simple form which is an agreement between you and the person you are interviewing. This will protect both of you from a misunderstanding, and gives you the right to use the taped material. With law suits as prevalent as they now are, you would be wise to follow this counsel. The agreement which you may alter or append is as follows:

Narrator Agreement

In view of the historical value of this oral history interview, I _____ knowingly and voluntarily grant and assign all my rights of every kind whatever pertaining to the tape and transcription resulting from this interview to _____
for the furthering of historical studies, in return for which I will receive a typed/taped copy of the interview.

Narrator _____ Date_____
Interviewer_____ Date_____

Tape Recorder

If you are using a tape recorder, the ideal would be to get a recorder with a digital counter. That way you can find the information faster when you want to go back and retrieve a certain section. After the interview, document when specific events occur on the tape. Be sure to buy the best quality tapes at a music or stereo store rather than the inexpensive discount tapes found in grocery stores or discount centers. Your quality tapes will last longer and you will have better quality if you want to copy them for relatives.

On each tape be sure to include the name of the person being interviewed, the date of the interview, and the person doing the interview. This information should also be labeled, so that you know exactly what is included on each tape. Take extra tape and any necessary supplies with you so that you can be prepared. Know how to work your tape recorder before you get there, and check it out in advance to know if it is in working order. Take an extra blank, just in case. If you are using a computer, carry extra disks and a power supply. You may want to include an extension cord.

Video Recorder

Some people like to video the interview. This takes added preparation. Set up your camera about five feet away from the person being interviewed. Use a tripod so that your picture will be firm. Keep the lens level at the face of your subject. Find a brightly lit room with a neutral background. Do not include windows as part of your background. If the room is poorly lit you may have to add some lighting. Ask at a photographer shop about a clip-on reflector light for video recorders. The same preparation that you have made for a tape recording is necessary for the video recorder. Bring extra supplies including extension cords and video tapes.

Room Preparation

Make sure the area is as quiet as possible. Talk indoors, as sometimes traffic noises will interfere with the interview. I did an interview on the front porch of a home and did not realize that even a car going by on the highway created background

noise.   Television, toilets flushing, dishwashers, washing
machines, radio sounds or people talking in another room are
distracting and may make it impossible to distinguish words on
a tape. If there are other people in the house, see if you can find
an unused room away from them. If the person is uncomfortable or distracted with others around, you may need to find
another place to conduct the interview.

For an audio tape, sit about four feet apart facing each other
and place the microphone on a table or magazine between you.
Don't put the microphone on anything electronic.

Beforehand Preparation

Know as much as you can about the person before you
arrive at your interview. Know how this person fits into the
family. A quick look at his/her basic genealogy helps.

Preparation before you arrive at the interview is almost as
important as the interview itself. You will be able to make the
best use of your time as well as theirs if you take a few minutes
to put the physical helps (tapes, recorders) and the background
information together.

Preservation of tape

When you have finished your interview, be careful with the
tape. Do not place it in the sun or in a warm place. Be careful
that you don't place it on a television set or a video recorder.
Keep them away from magnets or anything magnetic.

The Interview

There is only one thing more devastating than saying, "Tell
me about yourself," and that is, "tell me about your family."
The subject is overwhelming unless you can break it down into
segments and ask specific questions.

Ask first of all if he remembers his parents. Ask him to tell
about one of them. This gives you vital information, and gets a
person started talking easily.

Ask about his birth.

As you interview a person, ask him what is the most important thing that has happened to him. There are turning points in every person's life, and these are the ones that should be covered first. If you don't cover anything else, let the turning point story be a part of your interview.

I have found that many people try to cover too long an expanse in a person's life at a time. Ask the person what is the most important time that he would like to talk about. Don't hurry to finish as much as you can. Be relaxed and give the person time to talk, even if there are silences. The focus should be on the person being interviewed.

Don't interrupt. Give him time to finish what he wants to say. You can go back later and ask further questions. Keeping the flow of conversation going is most important.

After you have covered the turning points in a person's life, then you can go back and fill in with stories of the person's life cycle, starting with birth, childhood, adolescence and through to old age.

There is controversy among professional historians about whether looking over photograph albums or scrapbooks with the person is a good idea. It may help the person relax as well as to jog the memory, but it may also serve as a distraction. You may finish the interview and then look at the photographs later. If anything comes up that you want to record, then you can turn on the recorder again.

Listen to all the stories. Later on, you may decide that part of the information is inaccurate. For now, accept everything.

When you talk with him, try to ask questions that can not be answered with a "yes" or "no". Don't interrupt the person or contradict, even if you are sure the answer is incorrect.

If the person has genealogical records, or printed matter that you need, ask him to accompany you to a copy center, so that you can make a photocopy of the information. Most people do not want precious records out of their possession, but may be willing to go with you, so that you may copy them. Be willing

to share some of your information with him. Your other alternative is to hand copy the information. It is also possible to
photograph important documents or records. Refer to the
Chapter 18, Photography, of this book.

Be friendly and cooperative. Be careful you do not offend
him. Be genuinely interested in him.

When you start to put the history together, remember that
time is the organizing factor in all of our lives. As he tells you
his stories, ask how old he was at the time of that event. Try to
follow his life chronologically.

You will probably need more than one interview time.
Don't try to hurry the story, but keep to one designated period
in his life. You are looking for quality memories, not an
overview. On the second interview, try for a second turning
point.

After you have talked to that family member about himself,
find out how much he knows about others. You may want to
spend another time talking about his parents and grandparents.
Be sure to ask who else could supply you with the information
you need. Perhaps there are family records, letters, autobiographies, diaries, or other written material available. Ask who has
that material.

You may not be a trained interviewer and you could make
all the mistakes in the book, but if you are genuinely interested
and considerate you will find a wealth of stories, anecdotes and
personal feelings that become a part of your heritage.

As you can see you are working backward in time from
yourself to your parents to your grandparents. Discover each
preceding generation, not only facts and dates, but the richness
of character and color of personality that give pictures value and
worth. Stories, traditions and personalities fill in missing segments to make your history as interesting to a teen-age son as it
is to you, the researcher/writer.

If you decide to tape your interviews, label the tapes and file
them so you can find them easily. An identifying sentence at
the beginning of each tape will identify the person speaking,

date and subject. You could also slip the tape into an envelope giving the same information and perhaps a summary of the type of information contained in that particular tape. At this point, don't try to transcribe these tapes, but jot down key information on paper, so that you will know where to look for that material when you are ready for it. This can go on the envelope.

When you have finished interviewing the person, make sure that you leave the door open for future visits.

You may want to interview other people who may live a distance from you. You may be able to get much of the information by letter.

Writing Letters

A carefully written letter may be the best way for you to get needed information. In writing, make sure your letter is easy to read. This means that it is typed or written legibly with pen. Don't overwhelm the person with too many pages or too many requests. It is better to have everything on one or two pages, if possible. If you have several questions, it is easier to read if you number the questions.

The relative may have much more information, but if you limit yourself to a few questions, you will be more likely to receive an answer.

They are doing you a favor by taking the time to respond to your letter, so be friendly, appreciative and concise in your requests. Form letters tend to be cold. However, you may decide to send a brief questionnaire for family information.

Leave the door open for a follow-up letter or visit.

ORGANIZE YOUR RESEARCH

In order to keep your information straight, organize your research. You may want to expand your 3-ringed looseleaf notebook with a section for each member of your family or you may decide to dedicate this notebook only for one family member. This notebook is your traveling family history to be taken with you when you talk to family members, so don't stuff it full of pictures, newspaper clippings or rare documents. Leave those at home in file folders or labeled boxes.

The first page of your notebook should contain your name phone number and address. This is only a precaution in case you should lose it or leave it someplace.

One of the best organizing devices is a Pedigree Chart (see illustration in genealogy chapter, page 231) that shows relationships and gives vital statistics. This should be on your second page. A quick look will refresh your memory and give direction to your research. The third page will be your survey questionnaire found in Appendix B of this book. Other pages will include notes you have taken about the family member, and stories you have written about him.

Look through this chart and prepare a section or separate notebook for each family member. Dividers can be purchased at any stationery and in most variety and grocery stores. Starting with your parents, label each section or notebook for each individual member. If your survey questionnaire has been filled in accurately then you can cross-check all the other information you receive against this. A survey questionnaire should be filled out on each member of the family. As you question your first member of the family, you will likely find information that you can fill out on other members of the family. This is why the 3-ringed binder is important to carry with you whenever you visit with family members.

As you interview family members, write the anecdotes and facts on separate sheets. You may find your material in different places, so be sure to give the source of your material on each sheet. As you interview your family members individually they may give you information about another family member. If you write your information down on separate sheets, you can slip it into the appropriate section.

PERSONAL VISITS TO
OTHER FAMILY MEMBERS

Now that the basic facts are gathered and carefully recorded, we can start remembering stories, retelling family anecdotes
and talking to friends and family.

In the gathering process, you may have to visit other family
members in order to ask questions. Personal visits are usually
more productive than writing letters because you can get a better feel about the personality and life of the person you are
researching. The personal touch comes with visits. If these relatives live a distance from you, sometimes you can plan family
vacations in the area. Family ties can be strengthened with
these visits.

As you proceed from family member to family member
gathering your information you will find that family stories are
handed down from generation to generation. The ancestors of
Alex Haley passed the stories over and over again until sometimes his mother objected. Then his grandmother would retort,
"If you don't care who and where you come from, well, I
does!"[2]

You will discover that some family members have taken a
deeper interest in the family stories than others. My mother
always had an interest in gathering and retelling family stories.
She tells of the time when newly married, she helped in the
kitchen in her new in-law's home preparing for a party. All the
women mingled together and told stories as they worked.
When the time for the party came, Mother knew more about
some of my father's family and history than he did. She could
tell stories of many ancestors on not only her own side of the
family, but on my father's side as well. In her way she was our
family griot—a special and honored member.

It's time we search for those family members who are willing to admit, like Grandma Haley, "If you don't care who and
where you came from, well, I does!"

NOTES

[1]Alex Haley, *Perserving Our Heritage*, World Conference on Records, held August 12-15, 1980, Salt Lake City, Utah, Volume 1, pages. 8-9.

[2]Alex Haley, *Roots*, page 566.

Challenge

1. Choose one family member to write about.

2. Start to fill out a Family History Survey on this one family member.

3. Make contact and interview a family member. Cover the following:
   - His birth
   - His parents
   - One turning point

4. Make plans for a second interview.

5. Review your tape and/or interview notes.

   - Make notes on any questions.

CHAPTER FOURTEEN

Setting the Scene

A story has been handed down through our family, a story about my great-grandmother Lewis. It seems that she was cooking a big pot of soup one day and an Indian chief came and looked into the pot. He decided he wanted a taste so he took his hunting knife and stuck it into the pot to spear a morsel of meat. My great grandmother became angry and said, "No, no, no," and shook her finger at him. The chief raised his knife and was going to kill her. She screamed and nearby men grabbed the chief and took away his knife.

This is the beginning of a family history. It is a story handed down by a parent or a grandparent. Some of these family incidents are written down. Others are passed on to the next generation by word of mouth. Sometimes the stories are embellished in the telling, others have important parts missing. Unfortunately, this is where most of the stories stop.

I asked Everett Cooley, a librarian in charge of family histories at the University of Utah, what was the element in family histories that was usually missing. After thinking about it for several days he gave his answer. "Most family histories are sterile," he told me. "They don't give any background." As I studied, I could see that he was right. Most histories present families living in a nebulous world, not eating or sleeping, or making decisions. The families don't worry about war, money, food on the table, wayward children, unfaithful spouses, floods, crop failures, leaky roofs, social obligations, failing grades, polio, dysentery, a lame horse, or the nature of God.

Like my story about my Grandmother Lewis, they are presented without background of any kind. If you are going to write a family history, you need to know about conditions that existed at the time your ancestors lived in order to understand why they lived as they did and what prompted their decision.

"The past is a foreign country," said C.P. Hartley. "They do things differently there."

When you started your family history, you probably had no idea how far into the past you were going. Perhaps you were only going into your parents' lives, or maybe you were going to record the lives of your grandparents. Now that you have searched out your information you have a better idea just how far back you really are going. The question now is, "How well are you going to know this foreign country of the past?"

Travel tour companies take travelers to most of the countries of the world. They might stay a day or so in selected metropolitan cities flying between stops. When the travelers return, they brag that they have seen the world...and they have, from 35,000 feet. A friend sails on freighters and spends six months traveling. At each port she stays two or three weeks and takes the time to explore the country at her leisure. Other people spend a year or more in a different country, living with the people, knowing their customs, and facing the same problems they face.

In order to write about the past you have to do more than fly 35,000 feet above. Your visit to the past will not cost money, but it will take time for research.

Frank Smith, in an address at the World Conference on Records, said:

> Knowing who your ancestors were, what they did for a living,
> how they dressed, where they lived, why they moved, what they

ate, their living conditions—this is the stuff that family histories are made of.[1]

Remembering your own childhood days is a beginning. When you look into yearbooks and discover old letters, it will all come back quite vividly. If you have already finished your autobiography, you will have an idea how to start. You must do the same for each family member. First you need to establish the dates you will be working with. Birth and death dates are the most logical. If you are working with someone still living, then you will only need the birth date. If a grandmother was born in 1875 and died in 1934 then you are interested in the period of time within those dates.

What are you looking for? I have listed some information that would be helpful to know. You may not be able to find out everything, but what you do learn will give you a better feeling about the era and the area. If your ancestor (mother, grandparent, even great grandparent) is still living, start taking pictures of homes in which she has lived, schools she attended, friends, workplaces, tools and anything that was important.

Maps

Look for maps of the country in which your ancestor lived. Maps were being made by the nineteenth century, and some were made even earlier. Compare them to today's maps. See if you can find the area in which your ancestor lived.

Politics and Economics

Which President most affected the nation during those years? What policies affected your family? Were there racial problems? Which war or wars were being fought? What involvement did family members have in the military service?

During this time was the country in a period of inflation or depression? What was your family's business or vocation? Were there any natural disasters and did they affect your family (droughts, hurricanes, earthquakes, fires, floods, disease)? Look for general history books, but if possible, look for local histories to help you find what was happening in the locale in which your ancestor lived. What were your family's finances?

Religion

What was the general religious climate? Were there any religious problems or harassments? What were the specific family beliefs? Was your family divided in their religious beliefs? Did they take an active part in their church? Did they hold any offices or positions?

Culture

In the fields of music, theater, dancing, art and literature, can you find out what type of art was popular or appreciated, how much it affected your family, and famous artists of the day in each of the fields especially as it influenced your family members.

Home, Clothes and Food

What was the location? City or farm? How were the homes heated? Plumbing? Electricity? How was the cooking done? Stove? Ovens? Did your family have hired help? Were children born at home. What were responsibilities of the children?

Were clothes and shoes homemade, or store-bought? What material was used? What was the style...men and women's? Look for books that show the kind of clothes used in different periods of time. The library has several resource books that depict clothing worn from different eras and countries.

Was the food simple or fancy? Scarce or plentiful? Did your family prefer food originating in a specific country (Norwegian, Mexican, Italian, Chinese)? Do you have any recipes that were passed on to you from ancestors?

Transportation

How did the family travel (bicycle, walk, horse and buggy, car, bus, trolley)? For long distances, did the transportation change (bus, train, covered wagon, horse)?

Schools and Vocation

Were the schools private or public? Were they large schools or one room school buildings? What subjects were taught? What were the educational theories of the day? What education did your ancestor have?

What did your ancestor do for a living? What tools did he use? Did his vocation affect his physical appearance? A four-volume series entitled, *A History of Everyday Things in England,* is an excellent book on occupations and the tools used in England. Ask the librarian for a similar book relating to your ancestry.

Newspapers

Look in local newspapers and see what was happening that would have affected your ancestor. She may have even been mentioned in the newspaper. Most papers are copied on micro-film or microfiche.

Once you have found the geography, time span, vocation, etc. of your ancestor, go to a library and look for pictures, census returns, tax lists, typical houses of the area, anything that can help you to understand your ancestor. Now it is possible to put a CD in your computer and have an entire library on your own computer.

You may even plan a vacation to the family spot (or area). A friend of mine spent a few days with her sisters in New England. They walked the area looking for the family home (which had been torn down). They took pictures of other homes built at the same time as their home. They asked questions, went to the local library, and finally discovered that the hotel in which they had been staying was built on the land that had once belonged to their ancestor. It gave them such a wonderful sense of "returning home."

Take photographs, or if you can't vacation or travel to the place, find other photographs in books that would be typical of the places and scenery of your ancestor. Be sure to include maps, transportation, tools of the trade of that time. You might even want to include poetry or writings of the day from this location. Be selective, however.

It would be difficult to fill out all the categories listed and you probably wouldn't want to either. Take notes about anything that might have affected their lives. For example, your parents were married December 4, 1941. It's just a date until you realize Europe was at war. Hitler was on the march, and three days later Pearl Harbor was attacked. Some honeymoon! For those family members who are still alive, ask them about their memories of home and town as a youth, but don't expect them to remember everything. Go to a library and ask for help from the librarian. They have been trained to help and can save you hours if not days of work by finding the right book. Look in general books first, encyclopedias, yearbooks, or magazines of the day. You can even check out some of the books to read at home, or to show your grandparent and refresh his memory. Other sources are listed in Appendix C. Use the encyclopedias or yearbooks as a reference as you write your stories. When I write my family histories I try to keep a reference book close by, because I am always wanting to recheck different points.

If your family moved from one country to another, you would want to compare and research both countries. It will give you a much better background into their lives and decisions.

Remember that people live through a period of time and they are constantly meeting new changes.

When I was a young girl, we would spend our evenings listening to the great radio dramas of the day. Television was still in the future. Now we have television, VCR's, and video games.

There are many sets of books out that cover several time spans. *This Fabulous Century*, put out by Time-Life Books, gives the history of America with lots of pictures and is enjoyable to read. It starts with 1870-1900 and proceeds in ten-year time spans to the present. The *Album of American History* is another encyclopedia, this one starting with the colonial period and covering the material chronologically with lots of pictures.

The more you know about the time and place, the more accurate you become. Without this awareness of the past you become like the *Connecticut Yankee in King Arthur's Court*, an intruder into the past. In order that you see Grandma in her youth, with her beaux calling for her in horse and buggy, you have to move to the country of her youth. Unless you do some background searching, you place your ancestor in a vacuum. She will exist without the politics, economics or geography of her own time. Gather as many family traditions and stories as you can about one family member.

Let's take the simple story of my Grandmother Lewis and the Indian Farm and develop it.

First of all, if there is anyone who knows anything about this ancestor or this story, go to him or her first. In my case I went to my mother who was the one who told me the story. She told me that her grandma was asked to help teach the Indians how to cook and sew. Mother added, "At that time there was an Indian Farm."

"Where was that?" I asked her.

"Near Spanish Fork, Utah. I remember once as a little girl, riding west toward Leland and Grandma pointed to a hill by the old sugar mill and said, 'This is where the Indian Farm was.'"

An Indian Farm! This gives credence to the story and makes it much more interesting.

I checked other sources—the family writings—diaries and accounts already written. I needed facts. My great-grandmother was named Agnes Reid Ferguson Lewis, and for convenience, let me call her Agnes. She was born in 1843 and died in 1920. This establishes a time period in which we can work.

At the time that her family came to Spanish Fork, the family consisted of her father, her stepmother, Elizabeth, her twin sister Barbara; Elizabeth, 12; Eli, 10; William, 7; and Andrew, 3. Agnes and Barbara were 15 years old.

I found two sources that told about the Indian Farm reservation. One was *The History of Spanish Fork* and the other was a pamphlet telling about the historical monuments located in or near Spanish Fork, Utah.

While you are writing your family history make use of source books such as these. Go to your historical societies and ask for information about the city or town of your ancestry. Go to your library and ask for help.

In the two books I found about Spanish Fork, I discovered that the Indian Farm Reservation was set apart by Brigham Young in 1854, but it didn't get off to a good start until 1856. The farm was twenty square miles and extended from the state highway and the Spanish Fork river to Utah Lake. Governor Young promised the Indians that the pioneer settlers would teach them the art of farming. Men were called from surrounding settlements and about one hundred men responded to the assignment. They tilled the land, built a dam on the river, and dug an irrigation canal to channel the water. They raised twenty-five hundred bushels of wheat in 1859, only three years into the project.

In the early 1860's, more troubles began with the Indians. The Ute Indians were unhappy about the number of settlers taking over their lands, killing their deer and catching their fish. They started making demands on the settlers, asking for sheep and cattle. The more warlike Indians raided the settlements and in 1865 a family was massacred. It was at this time that a new treaty was signed with the Indians and the farm was no longer in existence.

This is the background for my great-grandmother's story. During the time of the Indian Farm Reservation there was a period of uneasy peace with the Indians, but generally they were considered as savages, ready to turn on you at any time.

Agnes and her family moved to Spanish Fork in 1858. Agnes was fifteen years old. She was unmarried at this time, a young girl of Scottish descent. She married in 1865, so this incident happened sometime between her fifteenth and twenty-fourth year. She was small, about five feet tall, but held herself erect and straight. She had brown hair and light blue eyes. In fact, the Indians called her "Sarapouche" which they told her meant "white eyes." Her photograph shows a short woman with firm-set jaw. From stories about her, I must assume that she was outspoken, determined, and rather stubborn. She had a sense of humor and a strong sense of right and wrong. She was also compassionate. One time, according to family tradition, she went to the river for water and found an old Indian woman left there by her tribe to die. At first Agnes gave her a cup so that she could drink from the river. Later on she brought her food to eat. Gradually, through Agnes' help, the old woman recovered and crawled up to the farmhouse.

My Great Grandmother,
Agnes Reid Ferguson Lewis

Here was a young girl cooking soup. The Indian chief, on the other hand, probably considered his knife as clean. He only used it for killing and eating. When Agnes reprimanded him, it was a great blow to his pride. He did not like being reproved by a woman, especially one as young as Agnes. His reputation was at stake.

As we write this story, as we write all of our family histories, we must remember the culture of the people involved.

Try to mingle the history from the books with the stories told by our traditions. Agnes tells about living in a dugout. As we study the history of Spanish Fork, it appears that the people started to settle there in about 1852 and because of the scarcity of wood, they were forced to make shelters in the ground. These dugouts were usually dug four or five feet deep with steps leading down into the room from one end, and a roof of willows and mud. Family records corroborate this description. They tell us that their first home was a dugout and wagon-box which had been previously constructed by Duncan McIsaac, Agnes' stepbrother. The dugouts were quite warm and comfortable during the winter with a fireplace in the end opposite the entrance.

Food at this time was in short supply. In 1855, crickets ate the crops and for several years after that famine faced the entire territory. The next year the settlers ate lambsquarter, another word for pigweed. A few potatoes were raised and some grain. They dug roots and gathered greens and caught fish in the streams. In addition to the grasshopper plague, in 1862 a flood washed out the lowlands in Spanish Fork, ruining the early crops and flooding fall-planted grain. So at the time that this story must have happened, food was scarce, and yet the settlers were neglecting their own farms and the building of their homes to establish a farm for the Indians.

While we are researching background, we cannot forget the compelling force that brought the settlers to this area, forcing them to accept a culture alien to their previous ways of life. Their religious beliefs must be brought into this story or you have left out the whole reason for their being there.

These people believed that God had spoken to their prophet and that they had been led to a land away from persecution by their enemies. This is why they accepted dugout homes and starvation diets. Brigham Young told them that the Indians were their brothers, that it was better to feed them than to kill them. This is why they left their own fields to till, cultivate, water, and develop land for their Indian brothers.

What about the national politics of the time? Even this far away from Washington they were still affected. Buchanan was the President of the United States and in 1857 he sent an army into Utah to invade the settlers. The men of the territory stood ready to defend their lands as the threat of war hung over their heads.

As I continue to research background for this story, I am finding material not only for one story, but for many of the family tales that have been told.

All of this seems like a lot of work. It isn't. I was able to find most of my information in one book in a few hours. My problem is that it was so interesting that I wanted to find out more.

So far, I have been discussing researching your family's history. Research is the great iceberg that often is never seen, but must be there. Now I'd like to talk about the part of the iceberg that does show—the written part of the family history.

How do you organize a history? Separate the times in a person's life according to the background changes. For instance, in Agnes's life she first lived in Scotland. I need to present her background there and then give any instances that occurred. Then they boarded a ship in 1855 and were eight weeks crossing the ocean. I need to research the type of ships used at that time. They crossed the plains in a covered wagon arriving in 1856. Another background for her. They stayed in the Cottonwood area near Salt Lake for two years. More research. When they moved to Spanish Fork in 1858 I need to add information about the specific area.

In order to develop the story about the Indian Farm Reservation I would carefully outline the story giving background material first. In giving the background to this particular story, what would be the important material that should be covered?

- The date they arrived in Spanish Fork.
- What was Spanish Fork like at that time?
- The type of homes and where they lived.
- The members of the family at that time and the ages.
- The personality and nature of the person involved.
- A background of the Indian Farm Reservation: what was its purpose and where was it located?
- The tribe of Indians involved and its nature.
- The feeling of settlers and Indians toward each other.
- Economic conditions.
- Religious climate.
- Political climate.

After setting the scene and using this information, you are ready to tell the story about the Indian and the soup. Now your reader appreciates the story more because he can understand the situation. You are also better able to go on and tell other family stories that occurred in this period of their lives.

As Agnes grows older, her background is going to change. She marries and after a few years in a dugout home, moves into an adobe home. I have stories about Indian raids and how she bars the door of the home with scissors and forks stuck in the door frame to keep out the marauding Indians. She doesn't move from this home until just a few years before her death, but her circumstances have changed. I need to show some of those changes.

As you go back in time trying to recreate a history of your family, you will find that you are less likely to judge your ancestor. Your job is to present facts and stories and not to praise or condemn. Often facts become colored by emotions, and bitterness can exist for generations. "I don't want to write about my grandfather on my mother's side," someone might say, "because he was a terrible person." Have you stood in that person's shoes? Do you really know why he made the decisions he did? On the other hand, when someone says, "my grandmother was a marvelous person," then he is also judging, and frankly I don't always believe him. Give the facts and the stories and let the reader make his own decisions.

Write an outline. Sift out the significant points, and include anything applicable to your ancestor.

As you research and gather the material, be careful about documenting your sources. Be accurate and thorough. Photocopy pictures and maps. Today's photocopying is improving each day. You may not find your sources a second time around. The energy you have today to do this work may not reoccur. Take pride in doing the job the best you can, so that you never need to redo it.

The past is there, waiting for you to discover it. Each venture is a new experience and an exciting one. As you start filling in the puzzle pieces of your ancestors, you discover the mystery of the past. That mist which has surrounded them is dispelled and you find people with problems, with decisions to be made, and with emotions and character.

NOTES

[1]Smith, Frank, *Toward Preserving Our Heritage*, World
Conference on Records, August 12-15, 1980, Volume 1,
page 1.

Challenge

1. Find a resource book that gives the history of your
   ancestor's country.

2. Decide the time element you will be covering.

3. See what you can find out about:
   - Politics at the time
   - Religion your ancestor believed
   - Type of home your ancestor lived in
   - Style of clothes
   - Transportation
   - Food (include family recipes)

CHAPTER FIFTEEN

Links to Your Past

*W*hile you are discovering that, indeed, the past is a different country, what you are really trying to find is that sameness that has carried through from generation to generation, that allows you to relate to the past and to your family for as many generations as you can recall.

Marbles, jump rope, hide and seek, dressing up in old clothes are all activities that can be traced a long time. When my own daughter, Lucy, was thirteen years old she loved to dress up in her grandmother's clothes. Grandma rewarded her with stories of her own youth when she wore those same dresses for special occasions. Grandmother and granddaughter were pulled closer together as Grandma told about her dates and dances and Lucy looked forward to that time when she could have the same privileges.

The whole idea is to bring the past closer through familiarity with the time and area and to find that material from the past that will relate to the present.

By placing your ancestors in a historical background you have added another dimension to them and have also given the reader a second link with which they can relate. There are other ties as well.

TIES TO THE COUNTRY'S HISTORY

Many families proudly trace their ancestors through actions and deeds performed in the building of this country. Sometimes this becomes a link from generation to generation.

These ties have carried on in many cases for several generations. But what happens when that link is broken? The very fact that it is broken can sometimes be a link in itself.

My husband's grandfather served in the Spanish American War and was very patriotic. When his wife had a child, he was in the Philippines. But he wrote home and instructed his wife to call his daughter Liberty. After he returned home he was filled with pride in his country and so another daughter was named Unity and a third daughter, my husband's mother, was named True.

There are other families serving the country through the military. These families move from base to base but they have a common link in the service. Sons and now daughters are raised knowing they will enter the Army, Navy or Air Force and continue in the family tradition.

If your family has served the country in political, military or other service, these links strengthen the family as well as our country and can be used in writing your family history.

TIES TO YOUR HERITAGE

Elly Card has ancestors two generations back who migrated from Czechoslavkia. Elly's mother was a great storyteller, and told Elly stories about the homeland all the time she was growing up. This so influenced Ellie that she has returned to Czechoslavkia many times for visits and has become involved in the country there, teaching and working with the people. When Communist Russia was overthrown, Elly returned to take American flags to the Czechoslovakian schools. She also gathered books in America, especially children's books, and has sent them to their schools. She has not let the link of her ancestors be forgotten.

My brother-in-law, Roy Samuelsen, came from Norway shortly after World War II. His parents did not sever the ties with their family in Norway and Roy grew up still involved with family there as well as in America. As an opera singer, he has returned many times, singing concerts in Norway and visiting with aunts, uncles and cousins. He has not forgotten the foods, traditions, celebrations and especially his extended family.

Our families extend beyond the borders of this continent. These are links in our lives. Some of our links are many generations back, but others are more recent. Some remember still the discriminations pushed upon us and our parents. Some struggled with a foreign language, others with new customs and traditions. Some found problems adjusting to the old and new ways. Remember these ties as you write about your family.

Use these links to recapture your past. Get a map that shows your origins. Find histories of the land of your heritage and look for similarities in your own life.

TIES TO FAMILY HEIRLOOMS

In many homes, heirlooms are passed down from generation to generation. These heirlooms tell stories of many owners. These heirlooms may or may not have monetary value, but they all have sentimental value.

As a young girl my Grandmother Markham gave me a yellow flatiron candy dish which she received as a young girl. She told me that this candy dish was the only present she received for Christmas one year. I was most impressed. Grandma was born in 1860, so this dish dates back many years. Just looking at the dish brings back many memories.

A friend of mine, Joyce Crystal, has a doll that was brought by the pioneers across the plains in a covered wagon in 1850. It still wears the original clothes. This was given to her by an old friend of the family. The doll has a wonderful history and is an honored part of her home. My mother has given me some of her old dolls, some dating back to 1920.

Quilts have wonderful histories, telling much about the women who spent hours designing and quilting them. They tell about hardships, barn raisings, deaths in the family, hopes and dreams. If you have old quilts in your family, you have a wealth of history.

Many vases, goblets, figurines, dishes are products of times past. These are treasures of the women of our past. Books, magazines, calendars give us a peek into the years when we weren't there. They let us know some of the objects that gave our ancestors pleasure.

TRADITIONS THAT LINK US TOGETHER

One time as a child, I was riding in a car with the windows open and a bee flew in and stung me. My mother stopped the car, found a patch of dirt and made a mud poultice for me to draw the poison out. This was one example of a home remedy she had when she was a girl. She also made sure we had an aloe vera plant in our home to take care of minor burns. To this day I keep an aloe vera plant for that very reason.

Other home remedies that I remember are mustard plaster poultices which mother put on my chest when I had a bad cold and cod liver oil for my vitamins. These are not traditions I have pushed on my children. Home remedies may or may not be carried down to the present, but they present memories to be explored.

Foods and recipes are also passed down from generation to generation. These recipes are brought out and tried again and again and with them come memories of special occasions from years past.

TIES TO BUSINESS, CAREER OR VOCATION

In nearly every city, town, or spot in the road you will see signs proudly displayed on top of buildings announcing the name of the establishment and then the term "and son." It has been a common practice for families to follow in the tradition of their fathers. This practice, however, is not as common today as it was a generation or more back, and it is causing sadness and a breakdown in families as a result.

Families have carried on the business for generations, and customers have traded there because they "know the name and what it stands for." Farmers have worked their lands, with their sons working beside them. Children inherit the lands and their own children follow in the same tradition. Families are close knit because they have worked together in a common cause.

Today "big businesses" seem to be taking over family businesses. Large conglomerates can buy in quantity, advertise better and sell cheap. Students going into colleges have difficulty planning for a career because by the time they finish four years of training, the career may no longer be needed.

The traditions of the past have, in most cases, tied families together and can add continuity to your history.

Your family might not have owned a business, but might have had professional or skilled trades in common. You might note that many of your progenitors were doctors, lawyers, policemen, or teachers. In my family my mother and grandmother were both teachers and as a result my three sisters also followed this profession. These vocational ties can make you feel closer to your ancestors.

There are many families who can boast of generations of sheet metal workers, carpenters, or other skilled trades. This probably stems back to the apprentice programs in which a young boy was apprenticed and learned the trade from his father or other close relative. In the early days, the father had the shop close by and taught his children the trade. Now the father works away from home, and often the children have no idea what their father really does. This is another breakdown in the family unit. But some traditions carry on, especially if the father loves his job and transfers that enthusiasm to his children.

A neighbor told me that he wanted to be a doctor. He put in his application to the School of Medicine, but was told he had to wait, that the school was filled with other applicants. So he

made a second application to the School of Law while he waited for an opening. He was accepted in the School of Law and
continued his schooling, all the time waiting for his time in
Medicine to open up. During the summer he took an internship
with a law firm. He was most surprised to find in the old books,
that his grandfather had started the law firm many years ago.
This had a deep influence on him and he changed his mind
about being a doctor. This last year he wrote a history of his
law firm, and his grandfather.

RELIGIOUS TIES

Families often take on the same religious attitudes of their
parents. If a parent is devout, attends church, and has a strong
belief in God, then usually the children develop those same attitudes.

We can find this link with the first Charles Dixon in my husband's family who tells of several religious experiences. He
feels that he has not worked in the service of God and repents
and prays for an entire year for the spirit of forgiveness. He
then tells us:

> At length on Wednesday, September the 21st, 1759, while seek-
> ing and striving on my knees, the Lord proclaimed his name
> merciful and gracious to forgive my iniquities, healed all my
> diseases, and set my soul at liberty.[1]

In the history of our family we can find many men and
women who have devoted their lives with the same kind of ded-
ication as did this ancestor. This is another unifying link in our
family history. You will find that you can bring the past and
present closer by showing these reappearing links. In them is a
key and a guide to the future.

Catholics, Protestants and Jews each have religious traditions tracing back for as long as anyone can remember. The
Jewish pilgrimage back to the Holy Land is an excellent example of religious unity for a cause they believe in. These beliefs
tie families together.

If you are able to say, "My ancestors were searching for the truth even as I am today," it would strengthen your ties with the past.

GEOGRAPHICAL TIES

My brother-in-law complains each year, "Why do we have to come home *every* year! After a day of visiting family he is ready to hike the mountains, boat the lakes, and explore the deserts. But my sister is content to visit and reestablish family relationships.

Even though some people establish themselves in another community they still consider the place in which they were raised as home. As families become more mobile the family ties with a specific place are broken. If you do have one home where the family celebrates births and marriages, compares children and lets cousins become acquainted, where deaths are mourned together, then this home is a link with the past.

My grandmother, in her ninety-sixth year, often wanted to go home. She didn't mean the home she had lived in for sixty or more years, but the home of her childhood.

Sometimes a city, town, or state can be that link with the past. Sometimes ancestors have built the community or have been leading members from the beginning. In the West, a few families sometimes colonized an area which became a town.

One writer I know, left her home and community because it was too "regional." She traveled far and lived in the great metropolitan areas all over the world. At first she wrote well, and then she reached a slump and couldn't write at all. Finally she realized that she had lost her identity and had to return home. Now she returns every year or so "to find her roots."

Many naturalized Americans have a need to make a pilgrimage back to their homeland. They spend many years saving for the trip even though they are perfectly happy where they are. We have Vietnamese friends who have lived in the United States for seventeen years. But, much as they love their new home, they are saving to return "home" for a visit with friends and family left behind.

The traditions of celebrating Christmas, Easter, and other holidays have often come to us from other lands. These traditions are another tie to our past and should be included in our histories.

TIES OF RECURRING TALENTS OR INTERESTS

Certain talents seem to run in families. If one person has a musical ability, often you find that several in the same family have that same ability as demonstrated by the musical ability of the famous Osmond and King families. The same is true with art, writing, dancing, and drama.

Interest and appreciation in the home has much to do with the development of that talent. Mothers or fathers who love music will teach their children the piano or other musical instruments. Perhaps your ancestors weren't famous, but the fact that they enjoyed singing, painting, writing, or any of the arts can be a link that has been traditional in your family.

Story telling is a part of my heritage. I remember my Uncle Fred Markham walking in the front door of our home with the announcement that he had a "good story" to tell. All of my siblings have the gift of storytelling although my sister, Joyce, and brother Jim have excelled in the art.

Education is of great importance in many families. In addition to having teachers, lawyers, or doctors in a family, you also find that some families put education as a first priority and so each member has obtained a high degree of education.

Many times a hobby such as gardening, cooking, crafts, sewing, knitting, quilting, carpentry, or painting has interested family members for many generations. This is also a genuine link. My sisters-in-law all have a great interest in dancing, particularly folk dancing and ballroom dancing. This interest is being passed on to the next generation.

TIES OF FAMILY RESEMBLANCE

It seems that a baby is hardly born before it has everyone commenting on similar features. "He has Dad's ears, Grandma's eyes, Mama's mouth and, of course, my good looks."

In addition to family resemblances, it is important to account for family illnesses, weaknesses or strengths. Cancer, heart problems, strokes, diabetes, or other genetic problems should be noted. This may be important in saving or explaining a life in future generations.

WE KNOW OURSELVES THROUGH OUR PAST

As you research your family, keep an eye on your ancestral chart. If you find any of the mentioned links appearing in your family, make a note. You might even prepare a separate chart with names and links which have carried down through the generations. These links should not be forced. You are not forging links, only trying to uncover them.

These family similarities run through families tying generations together because the past is part of us and so is the future.

Americans are beginning to talk about their ancestors and to write about them and to gather their stories and their strength. We are discovering that we are unique and special. We know where we're going because we see where we've been.

NOTES

[1] *History of Charles Dixon,* compiled by James D. Dixon, (Rockford, IL, Forest City Publishing Co., 1981) page 2.

Challenge

1. Choose one of the links mentioned.

    * Trace the link to at least one other generation.
    * Write about that link.

2. Choose a second link.

    * Trace the link to at least one other generation.
    * Write about that link.

CHAPTER SIXTEEN

$\mathcal{G}$etting to $\mathcal{K}$now $\mathcal{Y}$our $\mathcal{A}$ncestors

$\mathcal{O}$ne well known biographer studies for several years about the life of each person he writes about and then doesn't start writing until, as he puts it, "I hear him speak to me." All the time that you are researching the background of your ancestor you are getting to know him better because you are understanding his problems. By now you are getting to know your ancestor better and before long perhaps he will "speak to you." You have the advantage of knowing many of your family members personally, and you are probably still learning about others.

Archibald Bennett says:

A well written family history should be brightened and enlivened with human interest by the introduction of bits of biography and character sketches of the individuals in the pedigree. A dry catalog of mere names and dates and places is most forbidding and lifeless. There is no excuse for leaving any genealogical record in such an unattractive guise, valuable though these facts are, for all human lives are interesting, if properly delineated, fairly pulsating with heartthrobs and romance and dramatic elements.[1]

One of the first things to do is to place a photograph of the person about whom you are writing in a prominent place where you will see it often. If you have more than one picture, that is even better. Try to obtain a picture of the person in the three main periods of his life—youth, middle age, and old age. This will remind you that the person didn't remain static, but changed and grew. The more you see those photographs the better acquainted you will become with him. The farther back you go in time, the more difficult it will be to find photographs or paintings.

You can include in your family history selected pictures of your ancestors as you tell of their lives. It is expensive to print these pictures, however, so if you do include them, try to put the pictures together on a few pages rather than scatter them throughout the history. Before you have many copied, check the quality to see if you are satisfied with the reproductions. (See Chapter 18 on Photographs for additional information.) Be sure to date and identify each photo. You may know which photo is which, but others may not. An ancestral photo chart is fun to study. There are several different kinds of charts available.

PHYSICAL DESCRIPTION

Without a photograph or painting we have to rely on a written physical description. If you are writing about a close family member, such as a parent or grandparent, try to give a description of him in his prime as well as his old age. For earlier ancestors the problem becomes more difficult, especially if no likeness has been preserved. In this case you will be searching the written record for any information and be happy for anything that you find.

A great-grandfather on my mother's side was very shy. Although he was a leader in many ways, he never wanted to be praised or noticed, and refused to have photographs taken of him. In fact, every time a family portrait was to be taken, he

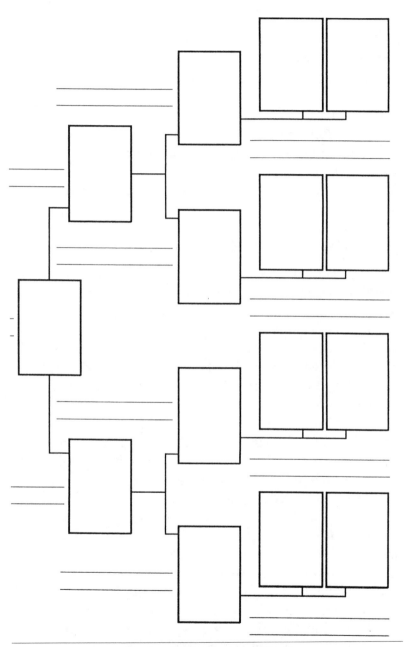

Portrait Pedigree Chart
© Copyright Stevenson's Genealogy Center, 230 West 1230 North,
Provo, Utah 84604 (801)374-9600

disappeared, and as a result, his physical likeness is unknown except for chance remarks, such as "Grandpa looked a lot like Frederick, only his face was thinner," or "He was tall and slender, like his son, Joseph." This year an artistically inclined uncle took all the photographs of Great-Grandfather's brothers and sons and constructed a composite portrait based on comparative descriptions. Inasmuch as there is a close family resemblance among family members, the portrait is probably close to his likeness. Composites are useful, but often inaccurate. Use them only as a suggestion, not as an identical likeness.

DESCRIBE THE INNER MAN

A physical description or photo of a person is extremely useful to have, but the inner quality of that person is more important than the outward appearance.

In telling your story put the emphasis on the human qualities of that person, and the accomplishment will speak for itself with out overwhelming either the subject or the reader. Find the description that is typical. This is a vital clue for you in deciding which stories to choose.

Earlier I suggested that you list the highlights of each ancestor's life. Now take a good look at those highlights. Have you listed only his accomplishments? Although it is impossible to divorce what a person *does* from what he *is*, it is also important to realize there is a difference.

Several years ago, I was asked to be president of an organization. I hesitated, knowing how much time it would take. They pressed me further, adding the bait, "Think how it will look in your obituary!" After a good laugh I accepted the position in spite of the bait and not because of it. Accomplishments are inescapable and do become part of our biography and eventually our obituary. There are many dimensions to every person, and what a person accomplishes is only one small part. Too many times a list of accomplishments, such as "My father was president of the Junior Chamber of Commerce, a successful businessman and a member of the Board of Education" is substituted for your father's real qualities. It is much easier to summarize a person with long lists of accomplishments than to give examples of his personality traits.

"But that is what he did!" you might object. And you're right, of course. We can't dismiss his accomplishments that easily. So let's take that list of accomplishments and do something with it. Fact without the human element is mighty cold and impersonal. On one side of your paper make a list of the accomplishments of your ancestor in chronological order.

- Lawyer
- Teacher
- Farmer
- Church Member
- Politician
- Parent
- Businessman
- Boy Scout Leader
- Volunteer

Beside that list, can you remember any stories that might be typical? Use a few words to recall it to your mind. The more stories you can remember, the better, even though you may decide to delete some of them later on. Try to find contrasting stories.

Find both the human stories and the success stories. In your writing remember that your subject is or was very human. The minute he starts becoming perfect, your readers will start doubting your story.

My great grandmother Lewis does not have a list of accomplishments. What I do have is an assortment of stories about her.

- Great Grandma, the Indian and the soup. She shows great determination, perhaps stubbornness. She is not timid. (Age: about 16-20)

- Great Grandma finding the old Indian woman dying. Shows compassion. No prejudice. (Age: 16-20)

- Great Grandma has a home in a dugout in a hill in Spanish Fork. One day a snake falls down and lands in the baby's crib. Great Grandma moves the family out of the dugout and refuses to go back inside. She insists that Great Grandpa build her a real home. Great Grandma is determined. (Age: early 30's)

- Great Grandma putting forks in the doorjambs to hold the door shut to keep out marauding Indians. Shows bravery. (Age: ? must check to see when there was an Indian uprising.)

- Indians coming to ask for Great Grandma and sitting in her cabin. Shows that she has great love for Indians and they for her. They call her Sarapouch which they tell her means pale eyes. She probably feeds them. (Age: 20-35 because her children are still young.)

- Great Grandma has five children: Priscilla, Agnes, Mary (my grandmother) Adelaide and John.

- Great Grandma's twin sister, Barbara Ellen, dies in childbirth when she is very young. Her husband marries another woman who was (in Grandma's words, "a bitch"). Barbara Ellen leaves a young son, Johnny Koyle, who is hated by the stepmother. One day the stepmother throws a knife at Johnny and it lodges in his back. He runs to Great Grandma who saves his life and refuses to let Johnny return home. Great Grandma raises Johnny with her own children. Shows righteous anger, compassion, follow-through. (Age: 30-40)

- Grandma went to work for the railroad as a cook when she was 16. She gave all her wages to Great Grandma who bought a sewing machine, and then didn't let Grandma use the sewing machine. Maybe a little selfish. At least she was stubborn. Grandma says that was the "Old Country Way" of doing things. Maybe its true and maybe Grandma is trying to rationalize. (Age:40-60)

- Great Grandma in her old age having a tea party with my mother. Shows love and tolerance of children. (Age: 50-70. I think I can narrow that age better.)

These stories are about my ancestor three generations back. No one is around now that can verify them. Mother and Grandmother are the ones who told them to me and to my sisters. I will need to talk to my sisters to make sure that I tell the story as accurately as I can.

Actually these series show Great Grandma with many different characteristics, ranging from selfishness, bravery, determination and compassion.

As we go back further in time, we may not be able to find so many stories. Trying to keep the human part of an ancestor is even more difficult to do when you go back many years. No one wanted to say anything bad about the dead and so they tended to enlarge the virtuous.

RELATIONSHIP WITH OTHERS

Very seldom is a person seen alone. Each of us interacts with family members, friends, business associates, and even enemies. As you are telling your stories you are including those relationships with other people. In doing so, you are showing other dimensions.

With Great Grandmother Lewis we see her with the Indians in four different circumstances; we see her with a step son, with her own children and her grandchild. Each story paints a more colorful picture of this woman.

FAMILY PETS

To many, the mention of a family pet immediately brings a smile. Mother had a genuine fondness for her cats. Before her death she had Dolly, a Siamese who thought the house belonged to it. Before that, it was Baby, an alley cat that I rescued from an old tom and stitched back together with an embroidery needle and dental floss. Smokey was the cat of the family when I was a girl. It sucked its claw the same way a child sucks its thumb. My son, Dan, is positive that our old dog, "Uncle", is waiting in heaven for him, and will be among the first to greet him when he dies. In your family you may have your stories of favorite horses, dogs, lambs, pigs, or whatever. In some families the pet becomes a part of the household and stories about them become almost legendary. Mother tells the story of her old cat, who, after catching a mouse, would transport it to a special tree. There it forced the mouse to run in circles around the tree until the mouse dropped in exhaustion, at which time the cat finally ate it. I'm sure the story became enlarged with time, but it became part of Mother's repertoire.

DEATH INFORMATION

Death is a major fact of life that influences all of us. No one can escape death, and we should not avoid discussing it. Although it may not be pleasant to write about the death of one of your family, especially someone who may have been close to you, it is most important to know certain facts about it. You should include these facts for the sake of posterity as well as giving a final statement to your sketch. You should include the date and place of death, age, and reason for the death which might include part of a medical history. It is also vital to know if your ancestor had cancer, diabetes or heart problems. This information is often needed for medical reasons. Perhaps in another generation the same problems might arise. Other health information that might prove useful to include would be data on respiratory illnesses, circulatory problems, blindness, deafness, deformities, epilepsy, or mental illness.

Beyond that, you might include the emotional or philosophical feelings by telling how the person felt about dying. Did he accept death, fear it, or fight it? Such information may be found in letters or personal papers.

What you are trying to do is to walk in another person's shoes for a short time. You are stepping into his past, telling his stories, meeting his friends, feeding his pets, accomplishing his deeds, and finally, reporting his death. And perhaps, when you have finished, you will understand and appreciate the person your ancestor really was.

NOTES

[1]Archibald Bennett, *Out of the Books*,Deseret Sunday School, Salt Lake City, 1940.

Challenge

1. Find a photograph of your ancestor.

2. Give a physical description of ancestor.
    *   Include photograph, if possible.

3. Describe the inner qualities of your ancestor.

4. List accomplishments.

5. Give death information.

CHAPTER SEVENTEEN

Pulling It All Together

The difficult part of your family history is finished. You have researched the time and place of your ancestors, found a common tie among family members, told stories of each of your progenitors and discovered their personalities. Once all this is accomplished, the writing is easy, especially if you write accurately and clearly. No matter how much you have researched, if it isn't presented well, no one will read it.

Writing skills include what you say, how you say it, and how you present it.

All the research material you have collected, the stories you have chosen and the details you include will make up what you say in your family history.

WHAT YOU SAY

Say It Accurately

In history writing, the material must be accurate. Your family history must contain the truth in as complete, unbiased, and objective a form as is possible for you to write. Many years ago the most important part of a biography was proving that you and your progenitors were faultless. Luckily we have progressed beyond that concept. The worth of early religious leaders was measured in the miracles performed and in a perfect image. Ninth century Agnellus, Bishop of Revenna, did a series of sketches about his predecessors. He must have found it difficult to find all the necessary material and admitted,

> "In order that there might not be a break in the series, I have composed the life myself, with the help of God and the prayers of the brethren."[1]

Sometimes you think you are writing accurately and do not realize you are being tested. The material you choose to omit is that subtle test of your accuracy. Obviously you can't include everything in your history, but the material you leave out as well as the material you put in can distort the true picture. No one can be completely objective, of course, but be careful not to let personal biases color your writing. For example, if you are writing about a favorite grandmother or a hated uncle don't choose all the warm, fun stories of the favorite grandmother and all the underhanded stories of the less-liked uncle, unless, of course, that's all there are.

Think of one person whom you dislike (it doesn't necessarily have to be a relative). Would you be able to write about that person without your own prejudices showing through? The tendency of most people would be to vent their antagonism and tell about every fault and bad deed. Others (there aren't many) feel they should never say anything bad about anyone and so they give a one-sided picture of everyone. Another group of pacifists either ignore problem subjects or write as little as possible to avoid controversy. In all three solutions, the truth is being stretched, avoided, or compromised. The best way, is to be aware of your limitations and prejudices, realize how easy it is to distort the truth, and be on guard to try to write as objectively as possible.

Once you have decided what material you are going to include, and have been as objective and careful as you can to give an accurate picture of the situation as you understand it, the next problem you face is proving whether your material is truth or hearsay. In your writing you may find stories that are lively, fun, and have been told in family gatherings for as long as any-one can remember, but you have no way of knowing for sure how to go about proving the accuracy of that story.

In our family folklore is a story about Grandfather Stephen Markham. It seems that a group of Indians ride up to Grandfather who is plowing his fields. They have a young Indian girl of a warring tribe. They try to trade the child for Grandfather's horse. "No trade," Grandfather says. So the Indians take the little girl and start swinging her by the feet. They threaten to bash her head against a tree if Grandfather doesn't make the trade. Grandfather relents and trades the horse for the young child. They raise the little girl and name her Julia. In time she marries a Mexican fellow. She returns many years later to introduce her children and husband to the family. When I went to a family reunion, the story of Julia was told again. The basic story was the same, but her name had been changed, and it was no longer a horse that had been traded. There were about three different versions of the story. Until I can find proof I will continue with my family's version, but prefaced with the words, "According to family tradition..."

Alex Haley, when faced with this problem, tests the legend of his family and discovers its truth. If it is possible to prove the accuracy of a story such as Haley did, it is much better. Whenever possible, check the facts. Be as accurate as you can and when you can't prove your facts, at least be honest in admit-ting your doubt.

There will be many times in your writing when you come across anecdotes and there will be no way to verify the facts. If you decide to use the story, you should note that it is a tradi-tional story that may have been altered in the telling. This way you are alerting your reader to the fact that it is a family folk story and not necessarily true. The other alternative would be to leave out those folk stories, but usually family histories are richer if you do include them.

Using Quoted Material

One of the most difficult choices you have to make is in deciding how much you are going to use from your ancestor's source
material. Should you quote that diary...and how much? Some
authors quote the most pertinent parts, summarize events and
quote again in a series of quotes and summaries. This is difficult to do and not always successful. You will be better off summarizing most of the material you want to give and then use the
quote as the high point or final statement. Build your material
so that the words of your ancestor become the most significant
part of the section. Giving the quote the most prominent place
is like placing a frame around a photograph to make it stand out
or draw attention to it.

We are still faced with the problem of how much to include.
One historian gives this help:

> Most novices at historical writing quote too often and at too
> great length putting too much burden on the work of others.
> Remember that for the reader a quotation is a kind of interrup-
> tion. Keep it brief and urgent unless you are presenting it as a
> document you wish to analyze for the reader...Yet a well chosen
> quotation can add liveliness, flavor on conciseness where noth-
> ing else will do as well.[2]

In theory this works well. It is more difficult when you are
faced with the actual material. Sometimes when you find writings of your ancestors, especially from one who lived a long
time ago, you are so delighted that you want to include every
sentence. If this is the case, try typing the quote on a separate
sheet of paper. Now take a yellow felt pen or crayon and cross
out anything that can just as easily be summarized. Keep cutting the quote until you have only the most forceful, interesting
and pertinent material. Summarize, give background material,
and start to build a frame in which to display that quote.

Are you still having difficulty in cutting the quote? Let's
face it, there will be some material that is written so well that
you would destroy it if you changed anything. This is the case

in GreatGrandfather's (back six generations) autobiography. He gives advice to his son, and it is so concisely written that it can't be changed without destroying the value of the quote. You may find similar quotes. In this case prepare the quote for the best presentation you can. The following excerpt from my family history contains background material showing the religious climate in Sackville, Grandfather's reaction, and finally the letter to his son:

> When Charles arrived in Sackville with his family he sought out other members of the Methodist faith. There was already a group of Methodists who met each Sunday. At that time no church was built and Charles Dixon took it upon himself to help build the first Methodist Church in Sackville.
>
> He was disturbed, however, because the members were divided into factions all ready to say to each other, "I am holier than thou." Because of this he was prompted to write a letter to his son warning him about pride and vanity. The advice still is valid two hundred years later:
>
> "This, my son, Charles, is written for thy and thy little sisters' instruction, that thou be not high-minded, but remember the rock from whence thou wast hewn, and in the future time when I and thy mother shall be called home, and rest in the silent grave, you may remember, that for your sakes we crossed the ocean. See that you outstrip us in purity of heart and holiness of life, and always let your words be the picture of your hearts. Study to adorn the doctrine and Gospel of God your Savior, and acquaint yourselves with God and be at peace. At peace with yourselves and with all men, and may the God of peace be with you evermore. Amen."[3]

When you have finished with your quote be sure to give the proper source and where that source may be found. If the material is printed and available in a public place such as a library or bookstore, then follow any of the stylebooks in presenting your source. Include title, author, publisher, publisher's address (city), copyright date, and page number. Unpublished sources should trace that material to the owner. Include identifying information. In my grandfather's autobiography, the book is published, but is a limited edition, and this is the only available copy that I have found. In this case, I would include both the material for the published book and then tell where it is available including name of owner, address, and date.

It is a simple thing to check back on the accuracy of a quote, and yet easy to become careless. If you can photocopy those letters, personal papers, or whatever information you might have, you have an advantage. If this is not possible, copy the quote carefully, read it aloud to someone else for errors, and send a copy back for verification. Both the quote and source must be accurately recorded. If a simple mistake is discovered, your entire work is challenged.

Adding Dialogue

If you look at biographies, you will notice that most of them contain direct quotes used as dialogue. What does dialogue do for your family history? For one thing, it gives the illusion of reality to your writing. When you read dialogue you often feel that you are right there listening to events as they occur. If the dialogue is characteristic of a person, you may even receive the compliment, "I've heard Grandpa say those exact words!" The personality of a person is revealed better through dialogue than any other means. If, however, you are not accurate in the dialogue, your family will immediately criticize.

Dialogue takes the past and brings it to the present by making your scenes vivid and direct. Those words within the quotation marks are present tense whereas the section leading to it and after the quote are past tense. "Don't give up the ship," the captain said. "Give" is present tense and "said" is past tense.

Another value of dialogue is that it gives variety to a page. As you look at a printed page, if it is nothing but long paragraphs your eyes become tired before you even start. Each time you use dialogue start a new paragraph.

"Make your dialogue short," he said.

You can see how this one sentence, set apart from the others, gives variety to this page.

There are some helps and warnings in using dialogue which you should remember. In telling a personal story it is often easy to remember what was said. At least you can remember generally the words. As long as you can capture the feeling and truth of the occasion you will probably be free to put quotation marks around it. Don't try to remember a long speech, however. A sentence or phrase will often be sufficient if you have prepared the reader for the quote. In order to do this, you build with a summary of what has gone before and then use the quote as the high point of the story.

Very often, a person has a pet phrase. These pet phrases should become a part of his story, if you don't overdo it. Once or twice should be sufficient to let the reader know the flavor of the speech without wearing out the taste. Overdoing any phrases, defects, or dialect tends to turn a real person into a caricature or comic character.

Try to use natural conversation when you quote someone else. Contractions such as "don't," "isn't," "I'm," "aren't," sound more natural than spelling such words out, unless, of course, your subject is very correct in his spoken language and would not use contractions.

Sometimes a person uses language that may not be grammatically correct and it is tempting to correct his English. Correct some grammatical errors in order to make it more readable, but be careful not to change the personality of that person. If Grandpa says "ain't" all the time and you change it to "isn't," then Grandpa "ain't" going to sound like Grandpa. Rather than do a lot of correcting, carefully select the quotes you are going to use.

If your family has come from another country, especially one which speaks another language, there will be language differences. Use this dialect sparingly. It is like spice. A little adds taste, but a lot is difficult to digest. A picture records the physical likeness and dialogue records the speech. Try to capture that speech that will depict your family member best.

When you have no memory of a person, it is difficult to put words in his mouth. Some biographers do give dialogue to their subjects, but others feel that in doing so they are writing fiction. If you are going to be accurate, record only that dialogue you have heard.

Quotation marks may cause a problem because they are used for dialogue as well as longer quotes from diaries, biographies, letters, and other sources. To make clear which is which, many writers solve the problem this way. If you quote from a diary or book, cite your source first: Charles Dixon told his son these important words, "See that you outstrip us in purity of heart and holiness of life, and always let your words be the picture of your hearts."

AVOID A SUPERVIEW

As you write, remember that you are looking at that individual with all the hindsight that time allows you. You can see his complete life even while you are writing about his early years. As you look at your own life, you cannot see into the future, and there is that uncertainty or suspense as a result. As you write about your ancestors, try to give that feeling of suspense.

To do this, try to recreate in your mind the circumstances surrounding the event. This is where a good background of the time is valuable to you. During the time of the Revolutionary War, the patriots had no idea that their words would be reverently handed down through the ages. They could just as easily have been hung as traitors. You need to show their fears and other possible consequences of their actions. When Grandfather Dixon arrived in Nova Scotia in 1772, he had no idea what his future was. This feeling of uncertainty needs to continue through the family history.

Beware of such phrases as, "if he had known what the future would be, he might not have..." or, "later on, John would laugh about his misfortune, but now..."

Try to pretend that you are a reporter on the scene recording an event. Give all the pertinent facts. Then show the results of those actions as they naturally occur. Often you want to give the ending of a story, but you add suspense and interest if you unfold it chronologically as it occurred in the life of your ancestor.

HOW MUCH TO TELL

There will come a time when you will have to make a decision on how much you are going to tell about a person's life. If you have an abundance of material, it is obvious you can't use it all. On one side of my family everyone kept journals and wrote sketches of family members. I can choose my material from a wealth of sources. You may have the same problem in writing about a parent or close grandparent. The other problem of how much to tell is an ethical one. How much are you going to probe into private lives? Let's consider each problem separately.

Perhaps you aren't worried now about having too much material, but it can become difficult to handle. Remember that some members of your family are going to accomplish more than others, or they are going to keep better records. Somehow you are going to have to decide which incidents to use and which to cut. Opposite to this, you may have to fill out and search for more material. Some kind of balance must be established. If you have too much material, you will have to choose incidents in their lives that are representative of others. You will have to decide on the basis of relevance. Does it really matter that he prefers roast beef to leg of lamb?

The other problem in deciding how much to tell concerns the private aspects of a person's life. It may not be pleasant to mention that your grandfather had a mistress with an illegitimate child or that your great Uncle Thomas was an alcoholic, or Aunt Lily was twice-divorced, but these are facts in your background whether you like it or not. Whether or not you use embarrassing bits in your history is up to you, but do not tamper with your source in case in the future this information is needed. That illegitimate child also has a right to a heritage.

James Clifford, a professional biographer, says:

> It is all very well to describe a man's bad temper, or his silly foibles, or to point out that occasionally he drank too much, but what about secret love affairs, illegitimate children, or the subject's syphilis? Or that he had been a very clever thief, who fooled all his reputable friends, while at the same time he was in the forefront of liberal causes? One may answer, "It all depends..." But on what?[4]

He doesn't give an easy answer. Instead he asks himself the following questions, which we might also ask:

- Why did the subject try to keep this a secret?
- Will this information embarrass anyone living today?
- If I put the information in, or if I leave it out, will it distort historical truth?

It all boils down to a simple question, "Does it really matter?" And only you can decide. After all, it's your family.

Divorce, annulment, separation and desertion can happen in any family. In 1890 one out of every eighteen marriages ended in divorce. By 1965 that figure had risen to one in every four. Today it is even higher. These statistics do not include those marriages that have ended in annulment, separation, and desertion. Statistics, however, only show that others have the same problems. We don't always want to include unhappy or difficult times in our family history, but when they happen we can't close our eyes and hope they will go away.

The causes of the breakup of a marriage are many. You may or may not have all the facts. Even if you did know all the problems involved from both points of view, you may wonder how much you should include. Before you write anything, ask:

- How much is necessary to tell in order to preserve the truth?
- Would my family history sound like gossip if I included it?
- Do I really know the facts?
- Do I know both sides of the story?
- Would I hurt anyone by telling everything?

Often the facts become colored by emotions, and there is always the tendency to place blame. Often bitterness can exist for generations. In time, the causes of a marriage breakup become history and the effects become the real issue. Emphasize the results of a marriage breakup rather than the causes.

- What was the legal settlement in the case of divorce?
- Who took care of the children?
- How did the children adjust to the divorce?
- What housing arrangements were made?
- Did the wife have to work outside the home as a result of the breakup?
- How often did the children visit the other parent?
- What relationship did the children have with each parent?
- Did it cause remarriage problems?

In divorce, annulment, separation, live-in arrangements and desertion, the effects are handled differently. Desertion takes on additional problems that must be faced by the remaining partner, such as: Is the other partner dead or alive? Will the partner return? How long before I can remarry? What legal problems must I face? If there has been a divorce, you should include the names of subsequent marriages and additional children born of those marriages. This may be all you would want to include. Use tact, consideration, honesty and relevance in your writing.

What you say about your family includes many things: their anecdotes or stories, their achievements, problems, personalities, human qualities, background, vital statistics, dialogue, and quotes. Your attitude and honesty will also become a part of your family history. Treat your family well. Be objective, careful, and accurate. Remember that someone in the future may update the work you have done and you may find yourself in a family history as written by one of your descendants. How would you like to be presented to your posterity?

HOW YOU SAY IT

All this material accurately gathered and presented is the clay or basic building blocks with which to work. The next step is to write it so clearly that you communicate to your readers what you have to say. How you say it then becomes as important as what you say. The two must work together.

When I first started writing this section on writing clearly, I was tired. Everything I wrote was correct, but somehow it didn't hold together. All the right words were there, but it didn't say what I wanted it to say. Finally, one of the statements I had written took on a personal meaning, "In order to write clearly, you have to think clearly." I was not communicating because I wasn't taking my own advice. When you become tired you should stop your work for a while. Your eyes scan over material and your words and sentences may become vague and unfocused. After resting, ask yourself the question, "Just what is it I am trying to say?" and then, start over.

Sometimes this is not easy to do. When you are having trouble with a section of your family history, examine your material. Perhaps you haven't thought out the material carefully enough. Analyze it and ask yourself:

- Do I have enough material? Should I fill it out
  more, find more details, give more background?

- Am I trying to say too much? Instead of lumping this together, maybe I should separate the ideas and spend more time on each thought or story.
- Is this section necessary? Maybe it doesn't belong and I am trying to force it in.
- Is this material in the wrong place in the book? Maybe it should come earlier—or later.
- Have I approached the material with the right attitude? Am I antagonistic when I should be sympathetic? Am I flippant when I should be serious?

When you write clearly you are creating a bridge from your mind to that of your reader, allowing him to share your understanding, knowledge, and enthusiasm.

CLARITY THROUGH CONTINUITY

Because your family history involves many people it is important for you to present each member clearly. The lives of children, parents, grandparents, and great grandparents intermingle, and yet in a family history there must come a time when you focus on each individually.

Many historical biographers solve this problem by devoting a chapter or section to each generation. This would include husband, wife, and children in one section. The beginning paragraph and heading would clearly designate which time segment and family members you are going to include. When children reach maturity start a new section or chapter for them. Another way would be to divide your book into sections with several chapters in each section:

Section One: Great, Great Grandparents

Chapter 1, Their Lives

Section Two: Great Grandparents

Chapter 2, Youth and Adventures
Chapter 3, Mature Years

Section Three: Grandparents

Chapter 4, Youth
Chapter 5, Middle Years
Chapter 6, Mature Years

Section Four: Parents

Chapter 7, Youth (Father)
Chapter 8, Youth (Mother)
Chapter 9, Marriage and Middle Years
Chapter 10, Politics, Business
Chapter 11, Mature Years

Section Five: Autobiography

Chapter 12, Youth
Chapter 13, Middle Years
Chapter 14, Mature Years

Section Six: Your Children

Chapter 15, Oldest Child
Chapter 16, Next Oldest Child
Chapter 17, Youngest Child

Section Seven: Your Grandchildren

Chapter 18, Oldest Grandchild (etc.)

As the children marry you will need to include the name of the spouse. For the sake of continuity give a brief summary of each partner. Sometimes this continuity can be made more clear by the inclusion of the ancestral chart focused on these two individuals. At this point you might also want to include pictures which relate directly to these ancestors. These might include individual or group pictures, photographs of the family home or business, a copy of the ancestor's handwriting, or any other material you have that would be of interest. Even though you focus on the husband and wife, these individuals will also be included in other chapters as children or grandparents.

In writing your family history you will notice that time is the major unifying factor. After you have traced your ancestors and gathered their stories you have a choice as to which direction you wish to go. You can write your family history from the present into the past or you can choose one ancestor in time and follow his descendants to yourself. Either way, you are writing chronologically and this unifies and makes it easy to follow. Alex Haley searched out his ancestors from himself through his Grandmother Cynthia and back to the "African." But when he wrote the story he began with the story of Kunta Kinte and followed those descendants to himself.

When you are writing you may find that there are gaps in a person's life. These gaps may be time or geographic lapses. Let your reader know about these breaks in time or place so he won't become disoriented. For example, you may be writing about a person who is twenty years old and living in New York. The next entry might be when he is thirty and living in Mississippi. Sometimes the technique of leaving extra space between paragraphs gives variety to a page and lets the reader know that it is another time or place. White space coupled with a word of explanation is the safest, however.

Another technique of keeping the continuity between generations is to use family links as suggested earlier.

Universal Link: John had the same taste for adventure as his Great Grandfather Benjamin. Only this time instead of homesteading a plot of land in Wyoming, he became an geologist with the hope of exploring other continents.

Geographic Link: After living in nearly every state in the United States, Richard and Ellie moved back to the state of their grandparents and into the old family home.

Career or Talent Link: Marty wanted to dance. Her grandmother had been in the Royal Academie Ballet until she had married Grandpa. Grandmother hadn't been a star, but she had told Marty stories about dancing for the Queen, and Marty wanted to dance more than anything.

Historical Link: Great Great Great Grandfather Stephen Jones had fought in the Revolutionary War. He had been proud of helping to form a new nation. Great Grandfather, Stephen Everett Jones had fought in the Civil War. He wrote letters that sounded as if he had single-handedly freed all the slaves. His father, Stephen Everett Hadley Jones, had fought in World War I. He helped keep the Kaiser from taking over the world. Steve was drafted into the Vietnam War. He wasn't quite sure what it was all about, but he would serve bravely, like all those in the family before him.

These links refer us back to another time and give us a feeling of continuity.

HOW YOU PRESENT YOUR MATERIAL

How you present your material is a technical process. It means making your material easy to read by following the rules of correct grammar, by typing it free of errors for duplication, and by binding it securely so that it won't be separated and scattered. The following writing rules can make a fun checklist for you. The error is contained in each sentence.

- Subjects and verbs has to agree.
- Don't use no double negatives.
- In autobiographies diaries and family histories use commas to keep lists of words apart.
- Don't mispell words.
- Don't abbrev.
- Be sure you don't any words out.
- Its necessary to know to use apostrophe's correctly.
- When you write sentence fragments.

- Each pronoun should agree with their antecedent.
- When dangling, don't use participles.

When you are writing, make sure your pronouns are clear. Ask someone else to check over your writing for misspelled words, awkward sentences, punctuation problems and, generally, for technical errors you might have made. Most professional writers regularly employ this check on their work even before they send it to the editor. My sister, Sally, who is an English teacher at the University as well as an author, always asks someone else to check her work before sending it to an editor. Often we are so involved in *what* we are saying that *how* we say it suffers. An outside reader will help you catch those minor errors. Make sure you say what you really intended.

You have finished writing your family history. You have spent time and energy researching, writing, and preparing your manuscript. You have gained a greater interest in history because now it has a special meaning to you. You have become acquainted with some very interesting people, your ancestors. You have a better understanding of your own heritage and why it is significant to you. Perhaps you have even clarified your own goals. You can leave a memorable record for your descendants. Your record tells about the lives of your people, who they were, and what they accomplished. You have become a link between the past and the present. Your history will help weld families closer together.

A family is a very special organization. It is the basic unit of all human life. It is more than biological. It embraces the physical, mental, moral, and spiritual training of every person on earth. Some parents ignore these obligations and the family pieces scatter and become lost. A family history gathers up those pieces and places them where they belong. Guard it well for a family history is not only your past, but your future.

NOTES

[1]Coultron, G. G., *Medieval Panorama*, The Macmillan Co., New York, 1938, page 439.

[2]Felt, Thomas E., *Researching, Writing and Publishing Local History*, American Association for State and Local History, Nashville, 1967, page 71.

[3]Dixon, *History*, page 5.

[4]Cilfford, James, *From Puzzles to Portraits*, University of North Carolina Press, Chapel Hill, 1970, page 120.

Challenge

1. Check your writing for accuracy and prejudice.

2. Check your quotes.
    *   Too many or too few?

3. Do you use a superview?

4   Have you said too much or too little?

5. Is your writing clearly written?

Section Three

Photographs, The Images for our Words
Genealogy, The Organizer

CHAPTER EIGHTEEN

Photograhs, The Images for Our Words

COMBINE STORIES AND PICTURES

About a year ago a friend sent me a copy of her personal history to read. It was a wonderful history of a fascinating person. My main suggestion was that she include photographs and I told her how to copy her photographs on a color copier and put them in protective sheet protectors in a three-ringed binder. Last week I called to congratulate her on her 50th wedding anniversary. She had spent the year gathering mementos, photographs, certificates, etc. She had copied her photographs and included them in her personal history. The book was twice the size and filled with mementos and photographs, each picture illustrating her writing. She had displayed the book and it was the hit of the day. She had made copies for her children and they were as excited about it as she was. She had given a copy of her personal history to her children a year before, but it hadn't been read. Now with illustrations, everyone wanted to read it.

A student of mine wrote her stories for my class and included photographs. She put it all together and was delighted with the response. Even her teen-age brothers and sisters wanted a copy. Now they want her to help them with their books. Sometimes she wrote about the photographs, but usually she wrote the stories she wanted to tell, and then included a photo of her at that age.

The combination of stories and pictures is electrifying. It draws people in to read the stories and to look at the pictures. Don't think that you have to write about every photograph. That is not the purpose. Write about something that happened to you during that period of your life, and then include the photograph. Of course, if the picture caught a moment of special significance, then you should write about that.

As my children were growing up, I would write stories about what they did and then I included it in their scrapbooks along with their photographs. This made their books more valuable to them. In fact, when my daughter was a little girl, she was in class and a member of the fire department was giving a presentation on fire safety. He asked, "If you had a fire in your home, what is the first thing you would do? My daughter answered, "I would grab my scrapbook and get out of the house." I don't know if this is the answer the fire department wanted to hear, but it did show how important her scrapbook was to her.

As you work with your personal or family history, seriously consider including representative stories along with your pictures. It will make your histories come alive to those who read them. I have included some of my photos in this book as an example of illustrating your writing with photographs.

Go through your photograph albums. How many of your photographs bring memories to mind? Enhance your personal history and your photographs by putting them together.

Our words and images merge to become what we present to our future. Our stories are wonderful, but a personal history is incomplete without photos.

This section on photographs includes information on preserving your photographs and presenting them in the best way. It will also include a section on family photographs. It is not intended to give lessons on photographic artistry, restoration of old photographs, developing negatives, or anything required of a professional photographer. However, I will list several source books which do cover this information.

A BRIEF HISTORY OF PHOTOGRAPHS

A photograph is made up of three parts: an emulsion, an adhesive, and a base. The emulsion contains light-sensitive silver salts suspended in a gelatin layer. When the silver salts are exposed to light they turn dark and this is what forms the image. The base is usually a fiber-based paper, resin coated paper, polyester film or plastic film, although sometimes the base is glass.

Historically, the first photographs were made by the Talbotype method, also called Calotype, which was started in 1835 followed by daguerreotypes which were introduced in 1839 and used through 1850. The Talbotype prints were grainy and not accepted very well. The daguerreotypes were a better quality, but they were very fragile and could not be duplicated.

The Albumen process was developed in 1847 and used into the mid 1890's. To take a picture using this process meant long exposures and usually they were used in landscapes. It was difficult for a person to stand still long enough for a portrait photograph to be taken.

The Collodion process, introduced in 1880, included the Ambrotype (backing on glass), tintypes (backing of metal) and wet plate negatives (on glass). These photographs were a wet plate process and had to be completed within fifteen minutes. They had good contrast and detail.

The dry gelatin process was started in 1871 and is basically the type still used in photographs today. It was started with the emulsions put on glass, but then later put on paper or celluloid film.

Cellulose nitrate film was used from 1888 until 1951, but this film is chemically unstable and is highly flammable. Cellulose acetate film replaced the cellulose nitrate, but it will also self destruct. It is recommended that negatives made of cellulose nitrate or cellulose acetate be duplicated and disposed of. The fire department considers them hazardous waste.

Cellulose triacetate in 1940 and polyester film in 1960 replaced these chemically unstable films.

In 1935 Kodak introduced color film with Kodachrome and it was followed by other color films.

Polaroid film was brought out in 1947. These photos will probably not last too long. Please have copies made of your most treasured photographs, if you want to save them.

Presently, digital cameras are within the financial reach of many and will be the cameras of the future. Digital cameras are a cross between polaroid and 35 mm cameras. You can see what you are shooting and once you take a picture you can erase it if you don't like it. Pictures can be downloaded on a computer and printed in color if you have a color printer. They eliminate the need for film and film processing.[1]

KNOW YOUR CAMERA

Disposable Cameras: Know your camera and what it will do. If focusing and setting your lens are confusing to you, then you are best off to buy a "point and shoot" camera. I tried the disposable kind when I was white-water rafting and found that they give a sharp picture. And I didn't have to worry about ruining my better camera. The important thing is to have fun taking your pictures and enjoy looking at them later. You do have to have good light in order to have success with these photos.

35mm Cameras: There are other 35mm modern rangefinder cameras which will do the same functions as the disposable cameras, but will also include other functions, such as allowing for different shutter speeds, aperture selections and built-in exposures. Get someone to work with you to let you know what options your camera has. A trip to a good photography shop, or a quick class at a local community college or school district night school will help immensely.

Rangefinder Cameras: Once you have confidence with these cameras you may want to try a modern rangefinder camera which will allow a selection of shutter speed and aperture. These cameras allow you to take better pictures at medium and long distances, but will not allow you to take close up pictures. Anything closer than four feet does not give clarity of picture.

Single Lens Cameras: Most people don't need to photograph anything closer than four feet. However, if you do get into genealogy functions, such as photographing names and dates on tombstones, or a sheet from a family Bible, then you will need something with a Single Lens Reflex.[2] There are many options you can choose, but make sure that yours has a built-in metering or exposure system. Make sure that the viewfinder is the same as the lens. A macro lens can help you focus down to a few inches. This is important for genealogy functions. Some functions that are available include aperture priority, shutter speed priority, program mode and manual mode. The fancier the camera, the higher the price. Some of the newer models include automatic focusing.

You will want to have lenses for more than one focal length. Most genealogy lenses require a 50-55 mm lens. A book, *Focus on the Past, a Genealogist's Guide to Photography*, by Kenneth Smith, goes into detail on cameras, lenses, filters, flashes and other equipment. He also discusses film, developing and other necessary information which is important for those who want to focus on genealogical applications.[3]

Digital Cameras: In 1990 Eastman Kodak Company developed the photo CD which looks like a CD or CD Rom. It can take photos and put them on your computer for use with your genealogy data base. This means that you can put your family photos with your stories or genealogy. This technology is revolutionizing photography.

Digital cameras range in price from $500 to many thousands of dollars. Prices are coming down on these cameras and new models are constantly being introduced on the market. Basically, though, you can take a picture using a digital camera by pressing a button on your camera. Images will be stored on a small hard disk or battery powered memory chip. They can then be downloaded onto your computer. If you have a good color printer, the pictures can be printed out. There is no film involved, no processing and no chemicals. You can take up to 300 pictures, download it on the computer and choose which of the pictures you want to print. The Apple Quick Take Camera is a lower-priced digital camera which retails for less than $800. It probably doesn't give a good enough quality for professional photographers, but is good for most uses. Kodak put out a series of cameras which can be used for professional photography and is more expensive. Because the whole market is changing so fast, it is best to search the market for your personal needs.

With a digital camera, a good computer and a color printer you could put family photographs, captions and stories all together and see what you have. It would make your newsletters, family letters, personal and family histories come together without the cost of copying photographs and pasting onto sheets. Adobe ScreenReady is a software program which takes desktop publishing programs such as Adobe PageMaker, Illustrator Photoshop, Freehand or QuarkXPress and puts everything together including text and photographs.

FILM

When you are taking your photographs be sure to include some black and white pictures. Black and white photos last longer than color photos. The amount of time a color photo will last is still an unknown factor. I have some photographs hanging on my wall that are starting to fade. My color photographs are not nearly as sharp as some of my much older black and white photos. Direct sunlight, florescent or incandescent light will also fade your photos.

Henry Wilhelm[4] suggests that some films lasts longer than others. Kodak Dye Transfer, and Kodak Kodachrome will last greater than 50 years. Kodak Ektachrome (E-6) will last 20 to 50 years, Kodak Ektachrome (E-4) will last 10 to 20 years; Kodak Ektacolor will last 6 to 10 years. Kodak Vericolor, Kodak Ektachrome (E-3) and Eastman color negative will all last fewer than 6 years.[5]

DEVELOPING FILM

It takes time and money to take family photos. Make sure that when you develop them or have them developed, that you take the best care of them.

There are three types of developing centers:

- Mass developing centers found in grocery stores, drug stores or shopping malls.
- One-hour photo centers
- Commercial photography shops

The mass developing centers offer specials such as two prints for one price, or larger size prints if you come in on a certain day of the week, or some other special. They are also less expensive. They can process your film while you are doing your grocery shopping. These centers can put out film as fast as two prints a second. Your photos are not going to last as long or have as good a quality print because there has been no special consideration for them. The chemicals used on them are usually not fresh and often there is chemical residue left on the photos that will cause them to deteriorate. Some mass photo developing centers go for months without changing chemicals or doing any kind of a quality control on them. These are the photos that are going to fade. Mass photo developing centers use a resin-coated paper which is mostly plastic, with very little paper.

The one-hour photo shops usually have the same problems as the mass developing centers, although there may be some centers that do take care with their developing procedures.

The commercial photograph shops take more care when they develop your photos, especially if you ask for archival quality because they run quality control measures on their machines and processing procedures. If you need special work on your photos, they will do that.   However, you need to shop around and find the commercial shop that gives you the best service. Get to know the people in the shop, so that you know what their standards are. The commercial developing centers cost more, but your prints will last longer. The best photos will be printed on a paper base instead of the resin-coated paper. Ask what your prints will be printed on, and request archival prints.

Whatever photo center you patronize, ask them when the chemicals were last changed. You could also ask if they do a quality control on them.

If you aren't developing the prints yourself (which I would never attempt), look around for a photographer who does it the best. One of the reasons I am losing one picture on my wall, is because of the poor quality of developing.

The factors that determine an archival print include the quality of the paper and chemicals used in developing and printing the photo and the time spent in developing the print. Chemical residue left on the prints will cause deterioration.

SUBJECT CHOICE

My sister Joyce, who always exaggerates, tells me that she has the best photo of the inside of my nose.

"My nose!" I exclaim. "Why would you want a picture of my nose?"

"I don't," she says, "but when I asked you to take a picture of me, you held the camera wrong."

Some people are better with words, while others have the knack of placing people, setting the focus and taking each photo with an artistic touch. Each family has the family photographer whether professional or delegated.

Just how creative are you in taking your photographs? Do you always stand your family just outside the front door, or in front of a bush. Year after year, do you always have the same picture with the subject a year older and wearing different clothes. Let your family members do something a little different. Take a picture of Mom in the kitchen taking out the Thanksgiving turkey. Photograph Dad in his workshop or when he is fishing or bowling. Try to vary their activities for more interesting photographs. Let your photos tell a story. Posed photos do not show the interaction of people.

Have you a good photo of the family home, both back and front? Have you moved to different homes? Do you have photos of each of your homes? How about the first apartment after your marriage? Or that terrible place you stayed while you were waiting for your new one.

Do you have photos of your school building? My high school has now been torn down and the only photo I have of it is in the school yearbook. How about elementary school, junior high, special schools. Give us a sense of belonging even in your photos. You didn't exist in space. You lived in homes, schools, work places. Let us see you in your settings.

How about your family pet? How about sister holding a favorite kitten or brother with his guinea pigs. You could even have a close-up of the family dog. Remember the time Fido chased the skunk and you had to clean him up with tomato juice. Wouldn't it be fun to have a photo of Fido in the tub with tomato juice all over him. What memories that would evoke!

Another point to consider, do you have pictures of all the family members, or only the most available ones? How many photos do you have of the family photographer? You know, the one behind the camera. Make sure that in all your picture taking, you suggest that the family photographer be included in some of the photographs. Usually a bystander can be requested to take a picture of family groups.

While on a family vacation in Calgary, Canada, we asked a bystander to take a family photo, which she did graciously. Then she requested that we take her photo. "Of course," we said and waited for her to supply the camera. We were most surprised when she posed for us and wanted us to take her picture on our camera. She did give us a name and an address.

Do you have any photos of your family cemetery or grave side plot? What about tombstones of Grandpa, Grandma or any of the Greats. Which cemetery? Of course you know. But do your children?

If you are visiting any of the distant relatives, take their picture. If they have family records which you don't have, ask if you can photocopy them. Another alternative is to photograph those records. This is one way to get the records without taking them out of albums.

PHOTOGRAPH COPYRIGHTS

If you have a photograph taken by a photography studio in the last few years, they own the copyright to that photo and you can't copy it without their permission. This is not true of old photos or snapshots.

SCANNING PHOTOGRAPHS

It is now possible to scan photographs into a computer, save it onto a disk which can then be sent by E-mail, or printed. These scanners are becoming more sophisticated and less expensive all the time. Once into the computer it is possible to retouch, crop and enlarge your photos by using software packages which will help you. Some of these software packages include Adobe Photoshop, PhotoStyler, Window Paintbrush and HSC Live Picture. The most popular among desktop publishers is Adobe Photoshop. Many times it is possible to clean up the original photo and make a copy which is better than the original. This is especially important if the original has been damaged. When you buy a scanner, see what software packages come with it.

Handheld Scanners: These scanners are less expensive, but are not able to do as much as other scanners. They can only scan a photograph up to four inches wide. They are not advised.

Flatbed Scanner: There are different kinds of scanners. For home use, the most popular model is the flatbed scanner. The scanner will scan old photos, digitize them and put them onto your computer without causing damage to the photo. If you are going to buy a scanner, do not consider one unless it will scan color into your computer. The most important factor to consider when buying any scanner is to look for the resolution. There are low-end scanners, mid-range scanners and high-end scanners. The difference is the cost and the quality. You get what you pay for. If you have a Windows program, you might also investigate Storm Technology's EasyPhoto Reader which costs at this time about $250. Before you buy any scanner, however, it is best to investigate what is available, what quality will satisfy you, and what will be compatible with your computer.

SlideScanners: This is similar to the flatbed scanner except that it scans slides rather than photos. Slides often give better pictures than photos since they are more translucent. For this reason, if you are only working with slides, a slide scanner will often give better digital images than a flatbed scanner but it requires more upkeep. However if most of your photographs are prints, then a slide scanner would not serve your purpose.

Rotary Drum Scanners: These scanners give the best quality, but they are out of the price range of most people. However, you could take your photos to a prepress house or service bureau and have them scan the picture for you. They are expensive, however with a price range between $50 to over $100 per scan on these photos.

There are companies who have access to the Kodak Image Digital Enhancement Station 100. This system will scan your photo into the computer, clean up the photo by taking out flaws and give you a quality photo on archival paper. Some companies may even have a do-it-yourself unit with the Kodak Image Magic Creation Station. When you have photos developed, some companies can provide a photo CD or photodisk. When you use this format, photos can be sent over the internet to family members.[6]

Mary Curtis Markham

Before computer correction   *After computer correction*

My friend, who is now divorced, is considering replacing her former husband's face with her current husband's face in a family portrait. I don't think it will improve the photo, but she is convinced that it will. This kind of action, should she do it, would be falsifying her family records. The fact that it can now be done, is a tampering with history, and should be avoided.

The quality of the photo will depend on the DPI (dots per inch), printer, and expertise of the computer programmer. Some mail order photo companies advertise that they will put your photos on disk for you. The price of about $10.00 will not include retouching and the pictures will be about 1 1/2x2 inches. You are probably better off paying a higher price and going with a reputable company. The amount of retouching done will increase the price. They will charge for the time spent.[7]

LABELING

A family story we have is that in the late 1800's Jenny, a happy-go-lucky spirit, talked a boyfriend into having their picture taken together. They posed as husband and wife and she grabbed as her bridal bouquet some carrots, corn and various weeds. She stood behind him with her hand possessively on his shoulder. It was done spur of the moment and forgotten about, except that the photograph was discovered after Jenny was long dead. The family had no picture of her real husband, the patriarch of the family, and so it was assumed that the man in the picture was her husband. Family histories have been printed and distributed with Jenny and her so-called husband. Of course there was no label on the photograph, and hence the confusion. Luckily, Jenny had told her grandchild about the prank, and the truth was disclosed.

As soon as you have your photographs developed, be sure to label them. Include who is in the photograph, when and where it was taken. Ideally, you could write about each photo, giving the occasion, background and reason for it. That's a lot to put on one photograph, and most people are lucky to get the who, when and where. You can write the name, place and time on the back of the photo, but be sure to use a graphite pencil or a photo film marking pencil. All pens can damage your photograph. The ball point pens make an impression on the photograph. Felt tip and roller-ball marking pens bleed through.

Do not use labels as they fall off. Labels have an acid adhesive which can destroy your photo. You can also buy photo inventory pages. These would be handy for your negatives or slides. Another way would be to mount the photograph on an acid-free sheet (single-sided) and write the material underneath the photo. If you aren't going to get to the mounting part of your photographs for a while (sometimes "a while" can stretch into years) it is better to get the information of the photo while it is still fresh in your memory. Write the information on a separate piece of paper and put with your photographs. Try to keep everything together.

Some cameras include the date on the face of the print. Make sure the camera date is correct. When I bought a new camera I didn't check for this feature and took the first set of pictures and dated them incorrectly.

For a group photograph make a photo copy of the photograph, then cover the copy with a clear paper. Put light behind it and trace the outline of each person. Number the people and then on a separate sheet of paper give names and other information necessary for identification. You may even want to give family relationships (Jen is the second daughter of Sam and Dora Jones).[8]

PRESERVATION

What fun it is to get your photographs back from the photo center and to look at them, share them with the family or friends, and to enjoy the occasion a second time.

As you are looking at those photos, touching them, pointing to special parts of the picture, you are leaving oils from your fingers, maybe food particles, dirt or sweat. You may even scratch these photos unknowingly, and not realize it for many years. If you use hand creams or lotions, these oils can also be transferred to your photographs. Wash and dry your hands before touching photographs.

After the initial joy, what do you do with the photographs? Most photos are stuffed back into the envelopes and put in a box or drawer for future use. Some are even put into albums.

Buy a pH-balanced storage box to store your photographs. These boxes will help protect your photographs until you are ready to put them in a more permanent place.

If you take care of your photos immediately, then you will be saving them for enjoyment throughout the years. If your hands are moist, oily or sweaty, you may want to buy a light cotton glove from a photography store. These are inexpensive and can save your photographs.

Your photographs will not look dirty, but if they have been handled, they do have oils and dirt on them. Buy Kodak Film Cleaner and carefully wipe with a Q-tip or cotton ball. Do not immerse your photo in any fluid, just wipe the photo side carefully. Brush the back with a soft brush. Do not clean any photographs taken before 1900 as it might destroy them.

PROTECTIVE SLEEVES

Place photos in a protective polypropylene or Mylar sleeve. These sleeves are clear and you can enjoy your photographs without damaging them. There are many of these sleeves available. Make sure that the plastic is of archival quality, which are products made of polypropylene, polyethylene, or Mylar D. Use the "clear" sheets rather than the non-glare type. Non-glare sleeves have a rough texture that may scratch the emulsion layer on photos.

Do not use plastic which is made from polyvinyl chloride or PVC. For a long time photograph albums were produced that had a self-adhering back. These were called "magnetic" albums. You could peel back the plastic, place the photos inside and then replace the plastic. It was extremely fast and easy. These were made of PVC, and they are ruining the photos. After a few years, the photos are sticking to the plastic and being ruined. This damage is irreversible.

The first five years of a photograph is the time when most of the damage will occur. If you used these photograph albums, please take them out immediately. The magnetic adhesive attacks the photo image chemistry and the paper support.

By enclosing your photos in a sleeve you are sealing them from the atmosphere. Moisture, dirt and sulphides in the air will cause your photograph to deteriorate.

Whatever the size of your photographs you will find a sleeve to fit. If you don't have time to mount them at this time, you can slip the prints into the pockets right after picking them up from the photo center. Then you wouldn't have to clean them first. Make it a practice of labeling new photos and putting them in the sleeves immediately. You can sort and mount them when you have the time.

NEGATIVES

Be sure to care for your negatives as carefully as you do your prints. They should be labeled and placed in negative holders. You can purchase negative envelopes with individual pockets. These negative holders can also fit in a three ring binder. Be sure they are acid-free and lignin-free. There are a variety of these envelopes to choose from. I like to have my negatives separate from my prints in case something destructive happens or I misplace some of my photos. Again, it is better to have archival binders for storage purposes. You can also buy a negative storage box. Do not cut your negatives apart.

PRINT AND NEGATIVE ENEMIES

In addition to making sure your photographs are kept clean, there are some other factors that should be considered: rodents, fungus, molds, insects, humidity, temperature, air purity, light, string, paper clips, tape and rubber bands.

Insects

These pests can ruin photographs. The most common insects are the cockroach and the silverfish. They like to eat the photo emulsion. To prevent this from happening, keep food away from your papers and photographs so that you are not attracting insects.

Rodents

If you see small holes or dark spots this could mean that rodents (mice, rats, squirrels) have left their droppings. These droppings are acidic and destroy your photographs. The animals also use the paper and photos for nesting materials.

Fungus & Molds

High humidity accelerates chemical reaction in the film. It can cause fading and discoloration. It also allows fungus and mildew to grow on your film. Try to keep your photos away from areas that have humidity higher than 50%. Ideally, the humidity should be kept at about 35%.

High temperatures are associated with high humidity. The rate of deterioration is doubled with every 18 degrees F. The lower the temperature, the longer your photos will be preserved. Try not to keep your photographs in attics where the temperatures will soar, or in basements where it will become damp. Don't hang your photographs in bathrooms, on outside walls or over heating vents. Try to keep your negatives in a closet, drawer or cabinet with controlled temperatures. By placing your photos and negatives in protective envelopes you are helping to maintain constant temperature control.

Air Pollution

Dirt, grease and chemicals in the air can ruin photographs. It is best to store your photographs and negatives in a metal cabinet or container. Wood containers generate gases which can ruin photographs. Keep your photographs away from fresh paint fumes, plywood, chipboard or janitorial supplies.

Light

Light can also destroy photographs. It can cause your photographs to become brittle, yellow or faded. Direct sunlight or florescent lights will damage them. If you want to hang some of your photographs on the wall, try to place them so that they won't have direct exposure. Tungsten lighting is preferred for photos. You could also have your photos framed using ultraviolet filtering Plexiglas.

Mechanical Devices

Paper clips, rubber bands, string, pressure-sensitive tapes can cause permanent damage to your photos. Paper clips can oxidize and leave dark stains, or tear your photos. Rubber bands dry hard and leave dark stains. Strings can be acidic and can leave brown stains. Pressure sensitive tape (like cellophane tape) dries and also leaves stains.[9]

PHOTOGRAPH ALBUMS

A photograph album should be one that is acid free. I personally like a three-ringed album with a matching slipcase that contains 8 1/2" x 11" pages. The slipcase slips over the end of the album protecting it even more from invading dust. It is easy to buy polypropylene sleeves to fit the album, and you can fit pages in easily. I like the freedom of adding a sleeve of pictures to an album, or putting it in a different place in the album. A three-ringed album gives this flexibility. The D-rings (as opposed to the round rings) allow the pages to lay flat. Other archival albums use the screw posts and they offer flexibility in adding pages.

There are many sizes of albums. Try to find one that has room for insert pages. A good place to look is at a quality photography store. They are more difficult to find and more expensive, but your photographs will last longer in an acid free album.

Don't paste photographs on both sides of a paper because sometimes a photograph needs to be removed. If photos are pasted on both sides of one sheet the photograph on the other side of the paper could be destroyed. Many photos from old albums were ruined for this very reason. The black paper found in old photographic albums is acidic.

ACID FREE MOUNTING PAPER

Be sure to mount your photo on a heavier acid-free paper. Do not use the black mounting paper found in some albums on the market. These are usually highly acidic. Ask for heavier quality archival paper.

ADHESIVES

To mount photographs on your acid-free sheets, be as careful of your adhesives as you are with your paper and your polypropylene covers. Make sure your adhesive is acid-free.

One of the best ways to mount your pictures is to use mounting corners. Make sure these corners are of archival quality. Another highly recommended method is to use a small piece of 3M double-sided tape on the back at the top and bottom of your photo. This brand of double-sided tape is an archival product.

You can use Dennison glue stick. This is acid-free, but sometimes the photos don't adhere too well. You can also buy acid-free adhesives. White Neutral pH adhesive is one brand that was made for preservation materials and doesn't become brittle with age. Other adhesives are available at photographic supply houses. You can also use photographic film tape, Grippit Glue or Uhu (white, not colored) or mounting corners. The new mounting corners are clear or see-through with self-stick adhesive on the back which have been approved for archival mounting.

I have been using photo sticker squares to adhere my photos to the backing sheet. These come in a box of 250 squares with pressure sensitive mounts. You have to peel off the protective backing, put the sticky side on the photo and the other sticky side on the backing and you can place the photo anywhere you want on the page. Do not use rubber cement or cellophane tape.

CARING FOR OLD PHOTOGRAPHS

As you go back to old family photos you will want to keep them in as good condition as is possible. If you see that some of them are deteriorating, it is best if you have a copy made of them immediately. After that take them to a specialist who knows how to care for old photographs. If you need references for a photo center who can do this work, you can contact:

The American Institute for Conservation
AIC National Office
3545 Williamsburg Lane, NW
Washington, DC 20008

International Institute for Conservation
Canadian Group
IIC-C6
PO Box 9195
Ottawa, Ontario KIG 3T9

Unless you know what you are doing, you are better off taking rare or precious photos to photo centers that specialize in cleaning and caring for old photos. Siegfried Rempel gives good advice in his book, and there are other books with suggestions on caring for your old photographs.[10]

MOVIE FILM OR SLIDES

Old movie film and slides all need the same care as your black and white or color photographs. Make sure that they are kept in a cool place and away from light. Any film that was made before 1951 was made from cellulose and nitrate and is highly flammable. Make copies of this film and then destroy it.

I had an old home movie that was taken prior to 1940 and showed rare footage of my father who died young. This film was extremely valuable to our family. However, we found that it had shrunk and the sprocket holes no longer fit any movie projector. We had it copied at a center that specialized in old movie film. Later we had it copied onto video tape.

Make sure that you periodically show your home movies, if for no other reason than to check and see if it is in good condition. Movie film also can get brittle. It is also a good policy to video tape your old home movies.

Store slides in an acid-free container. You can obtain boxes made for slides from an archival supply company. You can also store slides in page protectors made for slides.

VIDEO TAPES

The first thing to consider when you buy video tapes is to get good quality ones. Do not try to save money by buying cheap grade tapes. Inexpensive tapes will not last and can ruin your camera and your VCR. A rule of thumb is to look at the VHS insignia on the package. If it is circled, then it means that it is a better quality video tape. Usually the tapes come in regular grade, high grade and premium grade. You are better off choosing premium grade video tapes even though they will cost more.

Moisture

Keep your video tape away from humidity and avoid spilling anything on the tape. Keep it at room temperature for at least an hour before playing. This will keep condensation from ruining your equipment.

Heat

Heat will also ruin video tapes. Keep them away from radiators, heater vents, or direct sunlight. Do not let them stay in cars for a long time. Be careful with your video cassette. Do not drop or jar it.[11, 12]

Magnets or Magnetic Fields

Video cassettes can be destroyed by magnetic fields created by stereos, television sets, VCR's, electric motors and especially from magnets.

Cold

Do not leave videos in your car overnight in the winter. Also make sure you do not store them in unheated areas of your house such as attics or basements.

Dust

Return video to its box to prevent dust. Never touch the tape with your fingers.

Do not leave your video on "Pause" for any length of time. When you have finished watching a video, be sure to rewind. Videos will last longer if you store them in an upright position, never laying flat. Because of the magnetic fields associated with the VCR, do not leave your video in your VCR after you have watched a film. Review your videos at least once a year and check for obvious damage. However, every time a video is shown, the magnetic particles on the tape fall off and actually damages the video tape. Most video tapes do not last more than ten years so it is best to have your precious videos transferred onto compact disc.[13]

If your video tape breaks, becomes tangled or is dropped hard enough to break the case, take it to a video repairman. Often they can repair the damaged tape. Do not try to fix it yourself.[14]

VIDEO TAPE YOUR PHOTOGRAPHS

Another way to make copies of your photographs, slides and home movies is to video tape them, creating a family video album. This is inexpensive and can be copied and sent to family members at a reasonable cost. Some companies specialize in putting photos, slides or home movies onto tape. Be sure to get a quote before going ahead with that project.

Photos

Organize the photos you want to video tape into sections. Weed out dark photos or extremely light colored ones as they will not video well. Your best pictures will be the ones with good contrast. Your horizontal photos fit the size of the video screen better than vertical ones. Use a close up lens on your recorder and focus for the clearest picture. You can put your video on "pause" but keep the pauses relatively short, under five minutes. If you have all your photos ready before you start, you can cut your pauses to a minimum.

Slides and Home Movies

Again, organize your slides so that you present them in a logical order. It will be easier for everyone if you keep a list of the slides in the order they are being presented. Whether you send the slides to a company to be videoed, or decide to do it yourself, this organization needs to be the first part of your project.

One of the best ways to keep an extra copy of a home movie is to video tape it. Most people find it easier to slip a video tape into the VCR rather than getting out the movie projector and setting it up. You may also find that your home movie equipment may become obsolete or broken. Parts for old equipment is becoming more difficult to replace.

If you do choose to video tape it yourself, project your slides/home movies on a white poster board for a better picture.

Other Material

Other material that you can use for your family video could include maps, certificates, artwork, pictures of hobbies or talents. I did a family video of an historic home where a relative lived. It included going from room to room and showing family furniture and prized possessions.

Sound

There are many options on the sound you use for your photos. You can dub in music of the era or you can have a family member narrate the pictures as they show on the screen. The narration needs to be planned in advance with one person narrating rather than a group narration. Names and dates should be at hand so that the narrator can supply this information without hesitation.

A video is available for further help if you decide that this is a direction you want to pursue.[15]

NOTES

[1]Greenburg, Seth & Adele Droblas, *Digital Images, A Practical Guide,* McGraw Hill, Berkeley, CA, 1995.

[2]Smith, Kenneth L., *Focus on the Past, A Genealogist's Guide to Photography*, AGLL, Bountiful, UT, 1994, pages 5-6.

[3]Smith, Kenneth L., *Focus on the Past, A Genealogist's Guide to Photography*, AGLL, Bountiful, UT, 1994.

[4]Wilhelm, Henry, *Photo Communique*, 3:1, 1981.

[5]Rempel, Siegfried, *The Care of Photographs,* Lyon & Burford, Publishers, New York, NY, 1987, page 73.

[6]Greenburg, Seth & Adele Droblas, *Digital Images, A Practical Guide,* McGraw Hill, Berkeley, CA, 1995.

[7]Miller, Ilene Chandler, *Preserving Family Keepsakes,* Shumway Family History Services, 5041 Stone Canyon Avenue, Yorba Linda, CA 92686, 1996, pages 90-96.

[8]Miller, Ilene Chandler, *Preserving Family Keepsakes,* Shumway Family History Services, 5041 Stone Canyon Avenue, Yorba Linda, CA 92686, 1996, pages 27, 95.

[9]Tuttle, Craig A., *An Ounce of Preservation,* Rainbow Books, Inc., P.O. Box 430, Highland City, FL. 33846-0430, 1995, pages 46-47.

[10]Rempel, Siegfried, *The Care of Photographs,* Lyon & Burford, Publishers, New York, NY, 1987.

[11]Williams, Gene B., *Chilton's Guide to Using and Maintaining Home Video Cameras and Equipment,* Chilton Book Company, Radnor, Pennsylvania, 1988.

[12]*Film Maker's Guide to Super-8,* Septow Publishing, A Division of Litton Educational Publishing, Inc., 135 West 50th Street, New York, NY 10020.

[13]Miller, Ilene Chandler, *Preserving Family Keepsakes,* Shumway Family History Services, 5041 Stone Canyon Avenue, Yorba Linda, CA 92686, 1996, page 113.

[14]Huberman, Ron & Janis, Laura, *Video Family Portraits,* Heritage Books, Inc., Bowie, MD, 1987, pages 38-39.

[15]*Make a Family Video Album,* Christopher Stanton/Edgewater Productions, St. Paul, MN 55112, 1989.

Challenge

1. Check your photo album. Replace any albums that are magnetic.

2. Look for photos that are not identified.

   * Identify photos according to instructions in this chapter.

3. Go to an office supply store.

   * Find archival polypropylene, polyethylene or mylar sheets to store your photographs.
   * Look for acid free 3-ringed notebooks.

4. Choose a photograph.

   * Remember the circumstances around this picture.
   * Write it down.
   * Put the photograph and writing together.

CHAPTER NINETEEN

Genealogy Basics

Genealogy is a systematic method of studying, organizing and recording family ancestry. It studies the relationship of one ancestor to another. By taking one person's line of descent, you trace the ancestry of that person. It isn't even necessary to trace dead relatives. You can often simply find those closest to you, most of them still living. However, many like the challenge of finding ancestors from years back. Tracking and recording this information can be a fun hobby, like tracking down a mystery that needs to be solved.

My brother, Jim Thorne, was able to tie in our genealogy with 875 pages of 5-generation charts. We end up with Clodius II, King of the Franks, born 0006 AD, who seems to have fathered his son, Marcomir III, King of the Franks at the ripe old age of 14. My brother also penned this poem:

Old King Coel
was a merry old soul,
and a merry old soul was he;
Find this ancestor, droll,
On the pedigree roll,
On chart eight hundred, seventy three.

I had always thought that Old King Coel was simply a nursery rhyme. It comes as a whimsical surprise to find him as part of my own pedigree.

Usually the goal of genealogy is not to see how far back in time you can trace your ancestry, or to see how many illustrious ancestors you have, but merely to try to link together the information you have and put it in a logical and organized order. The easiest way to do this is to compile charts of relationship.

The basic genealogy charts include the pedigree chart and the family group record. There are many variations of these charts.

PEDIGREE CHART

The most basic of all of the charts is the pedigree chart which starts with yourself and your mother and father. This sounds easy if you have strong family ties, but if your family is scattered, this may be difficult.

A pedigree chart allows you to look at the whole picture of your family. It lets you know at a glance what is known about your family, and what still needs to be discovered. In addition, it shows the direction in which you are going. It shows how the family comes together and how the branches fit together.

Organize your pedigree charts by assigning numbers to each name.

A three generations chart, sometimes called the Family Tree includes your grandparents. There are charts available which include this three-generation pedigree, or you can easily make one yourself. Try to include birth dates, marriage dates and, if applicable, death dates. If you have any question about a place or date, add a ?.

The full name of each person should be recorded. In the older genealogical records, you were supposed to put the Surname first, (DIXON, Willard) but in the newer computerized version, you write it as Willard DIXON. Dates are written with the day first, then the month and finally the year written in full,

Number 1 on this chart is the same as number _____ on chart number _____

Use the back side to create an alphabetical index of all individuals on your
pedigree charts. Include name, birth year,
chart number, and person number on that
chart. (ie: Smith, John (1855) chart 5 #14)

8
Born/Chr   Cont. on chart ____
Place
Married
Place
Died
Place

4
Born/Chr
Place
Married
Place
Died
Place
Bur
Place

9
Born/Chr   Cont. on chart ____
Place
Died
Place
Bur
Place

2
Born/Chr
Place
Married
Place
Died
Place
Bur
Place

10
Born/Chr   Cont. on chart ____
Place
Married
Place
Died
Place

5
Born/Chr
Place
Died
Place
Bur
Place

11
Born/Chr   Cont. on chart ____
Place
Died
Place
Bur
Place

1
Born/Chr
Place
Married
Place
Died
Place
Bur
Place

(spouse of #1)
Born/Chr
Place
Died
Place

12
Born/Chr   Cont. on chart ____
Place
Married
Place
Died
Place

6
Born/Chr
Place
Married
Place
Died
Place
Bur
Place

13
Born/Chr   Cont. on chart ____
Place
Died
Place
Bur
Place

3
Born/Chr
Place
Died
Place
Bur
Place

14
Born/Chr   Cont. on chart ____
Place
Married
Place
Died
Place

7
Born/Chr
Place
Died
Place
Bur
Place

15
Born/Chr   Cont. on chart ____
Place
Died
Place
Bur
Place

Pedigree Chart

© Copyright Stevenson's Genealogy Center, 230 West 1230 North,
Provo, Utah 84604 (801)374-9600

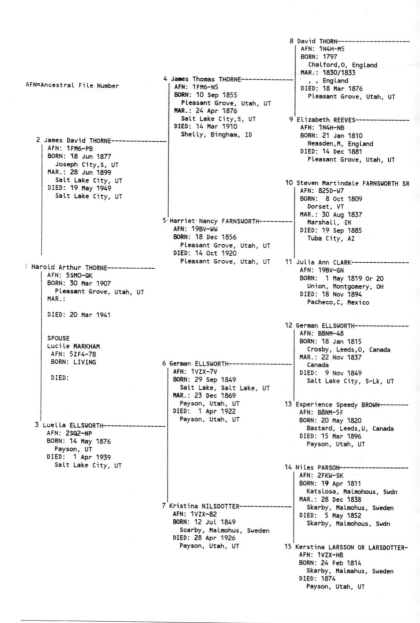

AFN=Ancestral File Number

8 David THORN--------------------
  AFN: 1N4H-M5
  BORN: 1797
    Chalford,O, England
  MAR.: 1830/1833
    , , England
  DIED: 18 Mar 1876
    Pleasant Grove, Utah, UT

4 James Thomas THORNE-------------
  AFN: 1FM6-N5
  BORN: 10 Sep 1855
    Pleasant Grove, Utah, UT
  MAR.: 24 Apr 1876
    Salt Lake City,S, UT
  DIED: 14 Mar 1910
    Shelly, Bingham, ID

9 Elizabeth REEVES----------------
  AFN: 1N4H-NB
  BORN: 21 Jan 1810
    Neasden,M, England
  DIED: 14 Dec 1881
    Pleasant Grove, Utah, UT

2 James David THORNE---------------
  AFN: 1FM6-PB
  BORN: 18 Jun 1877
    Joseph City,S, UT
  MAR.: 28 Jun 1899
    Salt Lake City, UT
  DIED: 19 May 1949
    Salt Lake City, UT

10 Steven Martindale FARNSWORTH SR
  AFN: 825D-W7
  BORN: 8 Oct 1809
    Dorset, VT
  MAR.: 30 Aug 1837
    Marshall, IN
  DIED: 19 Sep 1885
    Tuba City, AZ

5 Harriet Nancy FARNSWORTH---------
  AFN: 19BV-WW
  BORN: 18 Dec 1856
    Pleasant Grove, Utah, UT
  DIED: 14 Oct 1920
    Pleasant Grove, Utah, UT

11 Julia Ann CLARK----------------
  AFN: 19BV-GN
  BORN: 1 May 1819 Or 20
    Union, Montgomery, OH
  DIED: 18 Nov 1894
    Pacheco,C, Mexico

1 Harold Arthur THORNE-------------
  AFN: 5SMO-QK
  BORN: 30 Mar 1907
    Pleasant Grove, Utah, UT
  MAR.:

  DIED: 20 Mar 1941

  SPOUSE
  Lucile MARKHAM
    AFN: 5ZF4-78
    BORN: LIVING

    DIED:

12 German ELLSWORTH---------------
  AFN: B8NM-48
  BORN: 18 Jan 1815
    Crosby, Leeds,O, Canada
  MAR.: 22 Nov 1837
    Canada
  DIED: 9 Nov 1849
    Salt Lake City, S-Lk, UT

6 German ELLSWORTH-----------------
  AFN: 1VZX-7V
  BORN: 29 Sep 1849
    Salt Lake, Salt Lake, UT
  MAR.: 23 Dec 1869
    Payson, Utah, UT
  DIED: 1 Apr 1922
    Payson, Utah, UT

13 Experience Speedy BROWN--------
  AFN: B8NM-5F
  BORN: 20 May 1820
    Bastard, Leeds,U, Canada
  DIED: 15 Mar 1896
    Payson, Utah, UT

3 Luella ELLSWORTH-----------------
  AFN: 2SQ2-NP
  BORN: 14 May 1876
    Payson, UT
  DIED: 1 Apr 1939
    Salt Lake City, UT

14 Niles PARSON-------------------
  AFN: 2FKW-SK
  BORN: 19 Apr 1811
    Katslosa, Malmohous, Swdn
  MAR.: 28 Dec 1838
    Skarby, Malmohus, Sweden
  DIED: 5 May 1852
    Skarby, Malmohous, Swdn

7 Kristina NILSDOTTER-------------
  AFN: 1VZX-82
  BORN: 12 Jul 1849
    Scarby, Malmohus, Sweden
  DIED: 28 Apr 1926
    Payson, Utah, UT

15 Kerstina LARSSON OR LARSDOTTER-
  AFN: 1VZX-H8
  BORN: 24 Feb 1814
    Skarby, Malmahus, Sweden
  DIED: 1874
    Payson, Utah, UT

Thorne Genealogy

© Copyright The Church of Jesus Christ of Latter-Day Saints

Husband's Name		
Born	Place	
Married	Place	
Died	Place	
Father		
Mother		
Wife's Name		
Born	Place	
Died	Place	
Father		
Mother		

Child 1		
Born	Place	
Married	Place	
Died	Place	
Spouse		
Born	Place	

Child 2		
Born	Place	
Married	Place	
Died	Place	
Spouse		
Born	Place	

Child 3		
Born	Place	
Married	Place	
Died	Place	
Spouse		
Born	Place	

Child 4		
Born	Place	
Married	Place	
Died	Place	
Spouse		
Born	Place	

Family Portrait Chart

© Copyright Stevenson's Genealogy Center, 230 West 1230 North,
Provo, Utah 84604 (801)374-9600

i.e., 9 May 1932. For the place you should record the smallest geographical area first, town, county, state. You should use the postal abbreviations for states, i.e. Provo, Utah County, UT.

The pedigree chart most often used is the five-generation pedigree chart. However, I have a 20 generation chart that folds out and is very large. You can purchase one at any place that has genealogy supplies.

Even more interesting is the Portrait Pedigree Chart, (see sample chart on pages 175, and 233) which shows the photos of your ancestors. These pictures should be reduced to a 1" x 1 1/4" size to fit onto the chart. With the color copier available you can have many of your photos copied and reduced at a minimum cost. Or you may decide to have a negative made of your old photos and then printed at the size you prefer. You may decide to make your own pedigree photo chart and have the photos larger than the 1" x 1 1/4" on the printed charts.

Some computer programs have photo input. Make sure you have enough memory to use the program. If you have Photo CD-compatible genealogy software you might consider these programs:

- *Family Tree Maker for Windows* by Banner Blue Software[2]
- *Visual Family*, A Windows Shareware Program
- *Cumberland Family Tree for Windows*

FAMILY GROUP RECORDS

The Family Group Records chart takes a single family and lists the father, mother and children of a family. Information included on this chart lists such information as birthdate, birthplace, baptism or christening information, death date and place, marriage date and place. It may include other religious information. It also includes the name of grandparents and children. On one chart will be listed all the information pertaining to one family.

Organize your family group records in alphabetical order, with the husband's name first.

Husband's name		
		Sources of Information
Born	Place	
Chr.	Place	
Mar.	Place	
Died	Place	
Bur.	Place	
Father	Mother	
Husband's other wives		

Wife's name		
Born	Place	
Chr.	Place	
Died	Place	
Bur.	Place	
Father	Mother	
Wife's other husbands		

Children List each child (whether living or dead) in order of birth

1 Sex Name		Spouse
Born	Place	
Chr.	Place	
Mar.	Place	
Died	Place	

2 Sex Name		Spouse
Born	Place	
Chr.	Place	
Mar.	Place	
Died	Place	

3 Sex Name		Spouse
Born	Place	
Chr.	Place	
Mar.	Place	
Died	Place	

4 Sex Name		Spouse
Born	Place	
Chr.	Place	
Mar.	Place	
Died	Place	

5 Sex Name		Spouse
Born	Place	
Chr.	Place	
Mar.	Place	
Died	Place	

Other marriages and necessary explanations

Family Group Record

© Copyright Stevenson's Genealogy Center, 230 West 1230 North, Provo, Utah 84604 (801)374-9600

A Family Group Sheet should be started for the marriage of every person on your Pedigree Chart. That means that if there was more than one marriage, then you would include a sheet for each marriage.

Put an X on the name of your direct ancestor.

In addition to the various pedigree charts and family group records charts is a research log in which you keep a record of what records you have, where you found the record and the date. Basically it tells you where you found the data and how to return to that data if you need to find it a second time. List books by author, title, publisher, page number, library or genealogy society.

To help you find the data you need, list in alphabetical order with the surname first. Try to keep generations together as much as possible. If you have followed a lead and it turns out to be a wrong direction, list this also, so that you won't be tempted to follow that lead a second time. When you find material you need, write it down immediately before you forget your source. If the material cannot be documented, note "family tradition," or "not verified."

COMPUTER-BASED GENEALOGY PROGRAMS

Genealogical research can be expedited by using a computer based genealogy program.

Family Tree Maker: The best selling genealogy program is *Family Tree Maker* by Broderbund which includes two CD's and contains more than 6 million names. This program has records from 1937-1993. You can write Broderbund's Banner Blue Division, 500 Redwood Boulevard, Novato, CA, 94948-6121 or telephone (415)382-4770. Internet address is http://www.familytreemaker.com

Family Origins: This program sells for about $30.00 and has programs in Windows and DOS. Internet address is http:/www.parsonstech.com/software/famorig.html. Write

Research Log

Ancestor's name

Objective(s)

Locality

Date of search	Location/ call number	Description of source (Author, title, year, pages)	Comments (Purpose of search, results, years and names searched)	Doc. number

PFGS3082 5/88 Printed in l.

Research Log

Stevenson's Genealogy Center, 230 West 1230 North, Provo, Utah 84604
(801)374-9600

Parsons Technology, One Parsons Drive, Hiawatha, IA 52233 or telephone (319)395-9626.

The Master Genealogist: This program tracks conflicting data, contains a database of libraries and courthouses. It is considered one of the best programs. Internet address is http//:www.WhollyGenes.com. Write Wholly Genes, Inc., 6868 Ducketts Lane, Elk Ridge, MD 21227 or telephone (410)796-2447.

CommSoft's Roots IV: This program takes a genealogy program and follows it through from start to finish including a printed report. Write CommSoft, Inc., 7795 Bell Road, Windsor, CA 95492-0310 or telephone (707)838-4300. Internet address is http:/www.sonic.net/commsoft.

Reunion: In addition to having a first rate computer program this program also can produce printed charts and oversize wall charts. Write Leister Productions, Inc., P.O. Box 289, Mechanicsburg, PA 17055 or telephone (717)697-1378. Internet address is http:/www.LeisterPro.com.

Personal Ancestral File: This computer program is produced by the Church of Jesus Christ of Latter-Day Saints (Mormons). This is a program designed to record basic genealogy data. No internet address, but you can contact Salt Lake Distribution Center, 1999 West 1700 South, Salt Lake City, Utah 84104-4233 or telephone (801)240-1378).

There are other computer based genealogy programs available. Check at a computer store, genealogy store or even some bookstores for names of available genealogy based computer programs. Try to find one that is compatible with the FamilySearch file.

THE FAMILYSEARCH CENTER

The FamilySearch Center is a software program developed by the Church of Jesus Christ of Latter-Day Saints (Mormons) to access all the files that they have gathered. They have the world's largest collection of genealogical information, and each year they are adding about 100 million new pages of historical documents. Their records date from 1550 to 1920. The FamilySearch Center includes the Ancestral File, the International Genealogical Index (IGI), the U.S. Social Security Death Index, the Military Index and the Family History Library Catalogue.

Ancestral File: Contains data collected by Mormons and non-Mormons which links parents, children and/or spouse. This program often links many generations. By using a GEDCOM file you can down-load material onto your own computer.

International Genealogical Index (IGI): Contains millions of names of deceased persons from around the world. As new names are located they are added to this file. It contains pedigree and family group records submitted by people throughout the world.

U.S. Social Security Death Index: Contains the names of deceased persons who have been reported to Social Security and whose records have been computerized. This information can be downloaded to disk or printed out.

Military Index: Lists those who died in the Korean or Vietnam wars with records covering 1950 through 1975.

Family History Library: This is an electronic card catalogue of material found in the Family History Library in Salt Lake City. Information is found on microfilms.

Information found through the FamilySearch files may be accessed by using a local Family History Center of the LDS Church. Small branches are located in the United States and overseas and have access to all the same records through CD's, microfiche and microfilm as those found in the main library. You can find the closest Family History Center by calling

(800)346-6044 or (801)240-4085. These centers are usually located in the Mormon Churches, but not every church has a Family History Center in the building. The information contained in FamilySearch is not available on the internet at this time. The main FamilySearch Center is located at *The Joseph Smith Memorial Building* at 15 East South Temple Street, Salt Lake City, Utah 84150

The nice thing about computer-based programs is that if someone else has done research for your family and has submitted it to the genealogical library, then it is available for your use. This means that you don't have to duplicate work already done. These files can be transferred onto disk. My brother put all the work he had been doing on disk and by using a system called GEDCOM I was able to put it on my computer.

By using a computer, you can find information in much less time. The computer will allow you to group your family easily, search for pedigree, display and print them on a chart, print out any information you need, and sort alphabetically or by the RIN number (the number assigned each ancestor). You can also put your notes on the computer.

WHERE TO START

Before you start doing genealogy, do a family search on the computer and find out what has already been done. This way you don't spend a lot of time doing work that is readily available. Once you have established what has been done, then you have a better idea where to start.

- Focus first on one line
- Search available datebase files
- Evaluate what has already been done

Once you have documented the work already in the records, then you can go look in other compiled sources:

- Other genealogies.
- Biographies and autobiographies

- Periodical Source Index and other periodical indexes
- Family Group records collections and newsletters
- Local histories

When you have looked into these compiled sources, then you may want to go to original documents. There are many places you can look. These include:

- State and local Records
- Vital records, (birth, death, marriage, divorce)[4]
- Probate records
- Land records
- Naturalization records
- Legal suits
- State census reports
- Tax records
- Public school records
- Welfare records
- Census records[5,6]
- Passenger arrival lists
- Military records[7]
- Federal records[8]
- Church records
- Social and fraternal organizations
- Business and labor records
- Gravestones

ADDITIONAL HELP

Additional organizations have records and trained personnel available to provide assistance. Several are listed as follows:

Church of Jesus Christ of Latter Day Saints (Mormons)

In addition to the Family Search Center, the Mormons maintain one of the best genealogical libraries. This organization opens its doors to anyone and is not limited to the members

of the LDS faith. The library is located at 35 North West
Temple, Salt Lake City, Utah, 84150. There is no charge to use
its services.

National Genealogical Society

The National Genealogical Society is located at 1921
Sunderland Place N.W., Washington, D.C. 20036. This organization is open to the public for a nominal fee. You can obtain
membership in this society for $20.00 per year. They publish a
Quarterly and a Newsletter. You can borrow by mail many of
the published works for a small one-time enrollment fee.

National Society of the Daughters of the American Revolution

This society is located at 1776 D. Street, N.W. Washington,
D.C. 20006. It has excellent genealogical records for colonial
American including Revolutionary War pensions, federal cen-
sus, and index of patriots.

National Archives and Records Center

Washington, D.C. 20409 has a vast amount of federal
records. You can go to the regional branch closest to you.

In addition, there are Genealogy Libraries and Historical
Societies in almost every state. The *Directory of Historical
Societies and Agencies* published by the American Association
for State and Local History, 1400 Eighth Avenue South,
Nashville, Tennessee 37203 contains a current list of these
addresses. Your local library may have a copy of this book.

WPA List of Vital Statistics—published by the federal government—is a state by state compilation of vital statistic
records and where they can be found. See Appendix C for state
records.

U.S. Government Printing Office

This office has several pamphlets available. You may obtain the following pamphlets from U.S. Government Printing Office, Superintendent of Documents, Washington, D.C. 20402.

- *Where to Write for Birth and Death Certificates*
- *Where to Write for Marriage Records*
- *Where to Write for Divorce Records*
- *Where to Write for Births and Deaths of U.S. Citizens Who Were Born or Died Outside of the United States*
- *Birth Certificates for Alien Children Adopted by U.S. Citizens.*

INTERNET

It is now possible to access more and more genealogy research by using the Internet. Many public and university libraries have computers available that are linked to the Internet, so even if you don't have internet capabilities on your computer, it is still possible to gain information by finding a library in your vicinity. Some of the providers are America Online, CompuServe and Prodigy. These providers also have a Chat Room and Forums so that you can contact others interested in the same areas as you. Some of the general sites include:

- *Matt Helm's Genealogy Toolbox*, genealogy.tbox.com/
- *Stephen A. Wood's Genealogy Home Page*, http://www.genhomepage.com/
- *Everton Publisher's homepage*, http://www.everton.com/
- *National Archives*, http://www.nara.gov
- *The Library of Congress Homepage*, http://lcweb.loc.gov/homepage/lcph.html
- *National Genealogical Society*, http:www.genealogy.org/~ngs

Search Engines

Search Engines help you to find information on the Internet that is difficult for you to uncover. Some of these Search Engines will link you to other Search Engines. Three of the Search Engines with their web-sites are included here:

- *Yahoo*:http:/www.yahoo.com/search.html
- *Lycos*: http://lycos.cs.cmu.edu
- *Ancestors*: http:www.kbyu.byu.edu/ancestors.html

Public Libraries Access to the Internet.

- *Cyndi's List of Genealogy Sites on the Internet* - Over 17,3000 links, categorized & cross-referenced, in over 60 categories.
- *Genealogy Home Page* - A source that links to the many genealogy resourced on the Web.
- *Genealogy SF* - Particularly deals with software currently available but also covers many useful items about genealogical research and genealogical information as well.
- *GenServ* - This site charges a small fee to search more than six million names.
- *GenWeb Site Index* - Site offers 50 GenWeb databases with over 100,000 names.
- *Roots Surname List Name Finder* - A searchable list of thousands of last names that were submitted by genealogists.
- *The U.S. Civil War Center—Researching People of the Civil War Era*

NOTES

[1]All charts are from Stevenson's Genealogy Center, 230 West 1230 North, Provo, UT 84604 (801)374-9600

[2]Eastman, *Your Roots: Total Genealogy on Your Computer*, Zeff Davis Press, Emeryville, CA , 1995, page 193.

[3]Richard, Jim and Terry, *Ancestors, A Beginner's Guide to Family History and Genealogy*, Houghton Mifflin Company, Boston, New York, 1997, pages 105-109.

[4]U.S. Goverment Printing Office, Superintendent of Documents, Washington, D.C. 20402.

[5]Federal Population Censuses, 1790-1890, booklet, National Archives, Washington, D.C.

[6]National Archives and Records Service, Publications Sales Branch, Washington D.C. 20408. (Ask for publication and price list.)

[7]National Archives, Washington, D.C. 20408, ask for a copy of GSA Form 6751.

[8]Regional Branches of the National Archives, National Archives, Washington, D.C., a pamphlet.

Challenge

1. Buy or make a three-generation genealogy sheet.

    - Fill in information about yourself
    - Your parents
    - Your grandparents

2. Place as many photos as you can on a photograph pedigree chart.

Section Four

Writing Diaries, Personal Letters,
Family Newsletters

CHAPTER TWENTY

Writing Your Diary

A diary or journal is written soon after the event takes place. It is not written to be read by others, except at your invitation. It is impulsive, and though honest, is incomplete. In a diary you catch the excitement of each event because the emotion is fresh. The diary is spontaneous, uncalculated, and persuasive because the event has just occurred. This sense of immediacy is the value of a diary and gives the feeling of newly discovered truth. Facts are more likely to be accurate because events are happening with people you know, and the time is now and the place is here. A diary records your story as it is happening without your analytic comment and critique as distanced by time.

But diaries have an additional value far beyond the recording of facts. You can write to someone who listens patiently, never condemns, allows you to rationalize, and never gives advice (your diary). This process of "getting it off your chest" has proved to be a safety valve for many people. For my mother it was a healing device, a way of sorting out her feelings.

Nearly every person has at least started a diary. Perhaps you started one when you were thirteen or fourteen in one of those five-year diaries that gives you the amazing space of one inch a day to record all your thoughts, actions, and dreams. But perhaps you gave it up and didn't even fill up that limited space. Some have written faithfully for many years. Others have begun and stopped, perhaps losing the book or even throwing it away when they were in one of their "cleaning up" moods.

You might say, "Diaries are important if you are an important person doing important things, but I go about every day and one day seems like the rest. What could I possibly write about myself?"

But each person is important to himself. And that is the purpose of a diary. It captures your thoughts, records your worries, questions your actions, and allows you to brag and whine and laugh about yourself. It is not written for anyone else to read. That is where it is different from any other kind of writing. It's very private nature is its strength. Taking the time to write in your diary is taking time out for yourself.

Each diary has its own power and personality as each person has his own power and personality. The outward appearance of a person is not necessarily the person himself. My giggly, out-going teenage daughter shared her diary with me, and it revealed a serious, thoughtful young adult. To hear her talk you would not have had any idea that she had a serious thought in her head. Anne Frank mentions in her diary that "the more quiet and serious I feel inside, the more noisy I become on the outside."[1]

WHAT SIZE OF DIARY DO YOU WANT?

There are as many sizes of diary as there are books available. First of all you need to decide when you are going to be writing your diary. Are you going to keep it in one place or carry it with you? Are you going to type it or write it by hand? Decide what your needs are first of all. Some options which might be considered are:

- A large or small bound book with lined or unlined pages.
- A loose-leaf notebook that can have pages added as needed. Individual pages can be typed or handwritten. At the end of the day, these pages can be added to the permanent notebook.
- A small notebook that can be slipped into a pocket or purse. Notes can be added throughout the day.

Many people think that to write a diary you need a special book printed for that purpose, but it isn't necessary. I prefer a notebook with lined pages and no limiting factors to tell me how much I have to write. Some days I feel like writing three or more pages and the next day maybe I'll feel like writing a paragraph. I find it most annoying to be limited in how much I am going to say. If you do use a notebook, though, be sure to date your own entries. Write with a permanent ink pen rather than a pencil. My grandmother's diary was partially written in pencil and was smudged and difficult to read. A Uniball pen is better than a ballpoint pen which may fade or smudge. You don't need to rewrite, so you won't be going back to correct or erase anyway. For those who type, you might want to use a 3-ringed notebook so you can add typed pages daily. Choose a book with heavy enough paper, so that when you write with a pen, the ink doesn't bleed through to the other side.

Bound or unbound, lined or unlined, written throughout the day or at a quiet, unspecified time, a diary has no rules, no guidelines, except imposed by you.

WHY DO YOU WRITE?

We write with as many motives and needs for a diary as there are diaries. Perhaps you write because you:

- need a friend
- need to explain your actions or ideas

- might need to ask yourself those questions that no one else could hear
- need to feel your way into your fears or doubts or questions
- are afraid you will lose your identity
- might feel that the events or trials you are now going through will be lost if you don't record it
- have a need for self-expression
- need to write so that you can understand yourself better
- need to heal yourself.

But perhaps you are like Francis Kilvert who wrote in the mid-1800s that he kept his journal because life was such a "curious and wonderful thing."

In your diary you can be very practical and present the facts in a no-nonsense way, or you can tell how you feel about a situation. It is easy to categorize them into these two classifications but not so easy to draw the line between the two. Usually diaries are written with no thought to their purpose. They are divided now only to show the wide range of possibilities and open a new vision to those who want to start.

A good example of a practical and complete diary comes from a friend of mine, Doug Snarr. In the upper left-hand corner of a standard-size diary he writes his goals for the day, which are crossed off as he accomplishes them. Phone calls and interviews are summarized; brief accounts of current events are pasted in his book; small photos of friends, family, business associates, places, or events are placed on each page, important graphs and tables are folded to fit inside; social, business, religious, and civic events are all included. In other words, everything that is significant to him for that day is written in minute handwriting into his diary. It includes international, national, family, religious and local information. It is the world for him in capsulized form on each particular day. He considers his diaries so valuable that he keeps past diaries locked in a safe when not in use. Because of his thoroughness he has been able to use material recorded in his diary in court cases. It is a valuable record, which he uses for practical purposes.

Most of you will not be as organized as Doug. Instead, you might be like another friend who has kept a diary since she was a child. I asked her what she did with her diary.

"I write in it every night."

"Do you ever reread what you have written?"

"Oh no. I never look at it again."

For her, the diary is release of tensions, an unwinding of a day's happenings. There is nothing wrong with this. Perhaps someday she will want to go back and read it. Maybe she will even use it for reference. When she does, all the basic material is there waiting for her.

RESPOND TO YOUR NEEDS

In Chapter 5, *Turning Points in Your Life*, I mentioned that everyone has a time when life is peaceful, and then suddenly everything changes. Decisions must be made. This can happen when you get married, change schools, change careers, have a death or serious illness in the family, retire. Anytime you take hold of your life and examine it carefully is a turning point. And this is a time when a diary is especially important to you.

ADDING THE HUMAN ELEMENT

How many times have you read entries such as "Got up, went to school, came home, went to bed," or, "went shopping, met a friend?" What is the difference between these entries and those that are interesting? Often it is as simple as adding a few details.

You need to train yourself to see in specifics instead of general terms. If you meet a friend, give the name; if you attend a party, tell about it; if you are bitten by a dog you ought to tell us if it was a German shepherd or a miniature poodle. In other words, use specifics instead of classifications—Aunt Gladys

Smith instead of aunt; Macy's instead of store; Girls Preference
Ball at Skyline High Gym, instead of dance. Observations
include using all your senses. Tell what you see (four-point
buck standing not more than thirty feet away); smell (crispness
in the air, autumn leaves decaying underfoot); hear (rifle shot so
close you can't tell the direction); taste (mouth felt sour, as
though you were trying to hold onto your stomach and hadn't
quite made it); feel (confused, life is so precarious!). Using
your senses can help you describe the events that are going on
around you.

In your writing, don't say, "I'm so unhappy," or "something
strange happened today" unless you are willing to give examples. You will find that your diary will be more interesting and
valuable if you include names of people and places and stories
of what you do. Doug Snarr's diary, mentioned earlier, is
packed with specific details complete with pictures to illustrate
visually as well as verbally.

From the moment we wake up until we fall into bed at night
we cry, laugh, yell, hug, love, advise, scold, spank, gossip, listen, and occasionally think. Emotion fills our days; even when
we are sitting watching television we are reacting in some way.
Even lack of reaction is a reaction itself.

In every diary, the reactions of the person to his situation are
most evident. The diarist was worried, upset, angry, happy,
bored, afraid, confused, or a combination of several emotions.
When Anne Frank writes we see the gamut of emotions. We are
drawn into her life, seeing her life through her eyes and feelings
and made a participant for a short time.

The statements, "President John F. Kennedy was shot
today," or "Today the first astronaut walked on the moon," show
us nothing of your feelings about these events. They could be
interpreted, perhaps, as numbness, grief, extreme emotion of
some kind that prevents you from telling how you felt.
However, how much more valuable if you had said how you felt
at the time, and wouldn't it be interesting to go back and reread

your observations at that time and compare them with how you feel today.

Emotions are the common bond between the past, present and future. How you feel about a situation, what you observe, and how much of your observations you include are important in making your diary the kind you want to reread and remember.

BEGINNING YOUR DIARY

The best part of writing a diary is that you can start today. You don't need to check any of your records for dates or hunt for certificates. You are going to be writing about things you remember well. Yesterday is over now and you probably have forgotten what it was that excited you.

We tend to forget even important happenings. At the time of the event dates, details, people, and feelings are vivid in our minds. This is the time to record. As time goes by, we forget many of the details and dates. The event itself is put into perspective with that which went before and the events following. The emotions are re-evaluated into what you wanted to feel or what you think you should have felt. Or maybe you laugh indulgently at yourself for even having these feelings at all. For example, I had a boy friend, a possessive young man, who threatened anyone who might look my way. Finally, I told him I didn't want to see him again, but I was so upset, I cried all night. Looking back, I can say quite sensibly, that I didn't really like the boy that much; that he needed to realize he shouldn't bully others; that I was reacting sentimentally; or that I was simply experiencing an emotional release. Although I remember the incident generally, I cannot re-create the experience. The ironic part of it all is that I can't even remember the boy's name! This particular event was not that important to me as I grew older, but other events were, and I didn't write them down. If I had written a diary as a young person, I would have been able to go back and remember dates, facts, and people. But I didn't, and I am the loser.

"If I had written it down," a fatal statement. The past is behind us. There is no need to catch up on those twenty or thirty years you haven't kept a diary. Start today.

WRITE ABOUT ONE EVENT A DAY

How can you write then, and make your words interesting? First of all, don't let the idea of writing overwhelm you. At the end of each day, reassess what has happened to you and what you feel most strongly about. It may be an event, a relationship with another person, or it may be your reaction to a current event. Write clearly and in detail about one thing. Include your feelings or reactions to that event. Try to re-create exactly what happened and how you felt about it. Don't try to list your entire day's events, only the one that impressed you the most. Once you get into the habit of putting your thoughts down, the easier you will find it, and the more you will want to write. The stumbling block for most people is that they think they have to write about everything that happens to them, and the enormity of it stops them from writing anything at all.

If you know that at the end of the day you are going to want to record one discovery you have found that day, then your life is going to have more meaning to you. You will re-evaluate ideas, conversations, events and they will become more important to you.

Remember all those sections in the personal history about rewriting and readability? Those rules don't apply here. You can split your infinitives, fragment your sentences, and even abbrev. words. Your writing can have complete freedom. There are only three rules that will make your diary more meaningful:

- Write regularly, daily if possible.
- Write accurately. Keep your facts straight. You may want to check back.
- Tell your feelings.

Because you are writing about what is happening to you each day you may discover that you are observing what is going on around you and becoming more aware of the events in your life and your reactions to them.

MEDICAL DIARY/JOURNAL

I had a bad cut on my foot and went into the emergency room to have it checked and stitches taken.

"When was your last tetanus shot?" the nurse asked.

"Let me see. Four years ago. No, before that. I can't remember."

"We'd better give you another shot," the nurse answered.

Where do you keep your medical records? Do you rely entirely on your physician to keep records for you? Consider keeping a medical diary separate from your regular diary so important medical information can be accessed quickly and easily.

Document the following:

- Date of visit and reason for going
- Name of doctor
- Summary of the visit
- Shots or immunizations
- Diagnostic work done
- Prescription/prescriptions given
- Reactions to medicine
- Result of visit

Keep medical diaries for your children and aging relatives as well. You will find them invaluable in tracking medical progress and problems. *Genetic Connection: A Guide to Documenting Your Individual and Family History*[3] and *How Healthy Is Your Family Tree?*[4] are two helpful books in creating a medical family history.

Note: See Appendix B for a personal/family medical survey.

NOTES

[1]Frank, Otto H., *Anne Frank: The Diary of a Young Girl*, Doubleday & Co., Garden City, 1952, page 180.

[2]Simons, George F., *Keeping Your Personal Journal*, Paulest Press, New York, 1978, page 17.

[3]Nelson-Anderson, Danette L., and Cynthia V. Water, *Genetic Connections: A Guide to Documenting Your Individual and Family Health History*, Sonters Publishing, Washington Missouri, 1995.

[4]Krause, Carol, *How Healthy Is Your Family Tree?*, Fireside Books, New York, 1995.

Challenge

1. Start a diary.

2. Write about one event, idea or feeling.

CHAPTER TWENTY-ONE

Personal Letter Writing

$\mathscr{A}$mong my mother's many mementos was an envelope containing all the letters I had written to her starting when I was nine years old. It isn't earth shattering, but it was my first time away from home. I spent a week with a close friend, and it still brings back memories.

August 21, 1941

Dear Mother,

Shall I bring Jimmy a baby mouse. "Their" awfully cute. And they have no teeth. Shall I bring the mouse home? May I stay till next Monday? We have something planned for each day. Last night we slept outside. Today we were rather stiff. My ticket expires in 30 days. So I guess I'll stay awhile. PLEASE LET ME STAY.

Love Janice

The letters continued throughout the years including two summers when I was a teenager working in Yellowstone. After I married I kept a copy of all the personal letters I sent to friends and family. These letters, written regularly, constitute a history of my life and that of my family. I can go back and re-create events in my life. Informative letters to close friends or family can become an important record of the happenings in your life. They record the joys and sadnesses that have occurred. Weddings, births, deaths are all there.

I wrote to mother about the birth of my third son. I didn't write about all of my children, so I was quite excited when I found this one. I immediately made a copy and sent it to Dan to become a part of his scrapbook.

Sunday nite, July 20, 1958

It's finally over with and tonight I feel fine. Slept all day—am getting around. There were no stitches, so I don't have to go through with that discomfort. I'll probably go home on Wednesday. I think we'll name this boy Daniel James. He's another pugilistic looking, wise-eyed boy. He is so small, only 6 pounds 10 ounces and it's hard to imagine taking care of such a little one. Right now one side of his nose is flattened and it looks like he just finished a prize fight. He has lots of black hair all over his head and a little round face. I've quite fallen in love with the little fellow.

But even more important are the little annoyances, brief successes and minor decisions that you include in your letters because they will probably not be recorded anywhere else. In a desperate attempt to fill up the pages, you often include the day-to-day decisions that are really the substance of your life. What fun it is to read an off-hand comment in one of your letters and realize that this decision was one of the major turning points in your life, and you had no idea of its importance at the time.

Now I find that it is much too easy to pick up the telephone and talk to my sisters and brother, friends or to my children. This makes it more difficult to write many letters, and some of my history is being lost. And even though it is satisfying to hear their voices and have an immediate response to my familial needs, when the conversation is over, any record of personal history is lost. Personal letter writing, like beautiful penmanship, is becoming a lost art. In my case, the penmanship gave way to typing long ago.

PROTECT EXISTING LETTERS

As I went back over the years, I discovered that some of my old letters were already starting to disintegrate. The letters that I had folded were now tearing at the creases. In a few years portions of the letters would be lost.

I had written some of my letters on both sides of the paper with a ballpoint pen. The ink penetrated the paper and made it difficult to read either side of the paper.

I had typed some of my letters on light-weight, erasable paper. It was almost unreadable because the words had smudged. Words could disappear if I ran my finger across a printed page.

I was a person who did things the "easy" way. That meant that I wrote a family letter to siblings and close friends and did not want to retype or rewrite each letter separately. I devised many ways of making multiple copies of my letters. The first experiment in multiple copies was to type some of my pages on "ditto" paper and run a mimeographed letter. The mimeograph ink is now disappearing. Sometimes the paper had not been protected from water and the purple ink had run the words together. I lost some of those pages.

I then experimented in light sensitive copy paper. This was easier to type because I didn't have the awful purple ink on my fingers. However, in time the light sensitive paper went dark and with it the precious writing if exposed to any kind of light. Paper on the outside or anything left uncovered became almost black.

I now have the option of photocopying my letters or putting them on computer disc and making as many variations of one letter as I desire. E-Mail is becoming the popular mode of communication. Remember to make a hard copy of your correspondence.

Because these letters are important to me and to my history in a way that no other form of personal history could duplicate,

I was faced with saving or duplicating those letters which were quietly but steadily being lost.

Encase them in Polypropylene or Mylar Acid-Free Folders

First of all, I took the handwritten, but still folded letters and unfolded them. I placed each one separately in a polypropylene folder. This protects them from tears, oils in hands, and handling. It also keeps pages together. Unfolding them will keep them from tearing at the folds.

Retype or Recopy Damaged Pages

Some of the letters were damaged, but still readable so I photocopied them. Others needed to be retyped. This was a sorting and mending process. One by one I took each letter, evaluated its condition, retyped, recopied or merely placed in protective custody and went on to the next letter.

It was a process that took a while, because, of course, I had to read the contents first. What a memory jog that was! I had forgotten so many important things that had happened in my life.

Place in a Protective Binder

I purchased a three-ringed binder and placed the polypropylene folders each containing a single letter according to the date in sequence. Be careful that you don't use plastic with PVC (polyvinyl chloride) because they destroy paper and photographs. The vinyl pages of PVC have an oily residue. Photographs can wrinkle, shrink and even stick to the film emulsion. You can identify PVC by a strong plastic odor. This is a giveaway that it is PVC. Polypropylene or polyester (Mylar) envelopes or sleeves will save your paper or photographs and protect from the oils in your fingers. You can read your letters and look at your photographs without touching the surface of your letters.

Use Archival Supplies

With a lot of hindsight and new techniques being learned, I can recommend first of all that you write your letters on a good quality acid-free paper. If you have your letters duplicated by photocopy, request acid-free "archival" paper or bring it with you. A good carbon ribbon on the typewriter or printer will last longer and not produce acid fumes. Pens can be purchased that are archival quality. Do not use pencils as they will smudge. Archival binders using acid-free material can be purchased from companies that distribute archival materials.

Date your Letters

In reading old letters I learned that I hadn't always put in the date. Often, I found that I wrote, "November 3" or "April 27", and neglected to write in the year. Then I had to go back in my own memory and try to reconstruct from the contents of the letter exactly what year the letter had been written. If your letter contains more than one page you should date the other pages in case the pages are separated.

Make a Copy

Make a copy of personal letters you send. It contains a segment of you.

WHAT MAKES A LETTER INTERESTING?

I have talked about preserving the letters you have already written, but what makes a letter interesting and worth saving? I have found no book or article to even give suggestions. You are probably saying, "No one is going to tell **ME** how to write a letter or what to say."

But writing is writing. And if you could write better, wouldn't you try?

Begin to Write

First of all, write. Write a letter. Write to someone you trust and let them be a part of your life. Get in the habit of writing. Because if you don't write at all, you will get out of the habit. And then you forget how. Writing a letter is a bit like playing a piano. The more you practice, the better you become.

Include your Reader in your Actions

Write about what you are doing. Try to capture the enjoyment you had when you were doing it. What did you say to others? What did they answer? Tell about your enjoyment and the reactions of others. What were the consequences of what you were doing? What happened then? How did you feel about it? Capture the details and let others enjoy it with you. You don't have to write about everything you do. Choose the times that are most interesting to you.

Tell About Things that will Interest your Reader

Remember your audience. You know what your friend is most interested in. Write details. Write your feelings. Tell conversations. Tell about people.

I sent a post card to 3 year old Bryant. It was short. I told him things I thought he would like. I told how I went horse back riding on a horse named Chicago. I told him that my horse jumped in the air when I got on. And that he stopped and pooped on the ground. This was Bryant's kind of letter. He treasured that postcard, carrying it around with him all day, even when he went to the grocery store with his mother. Of course, what I would write to Bryant would be considered "silly" to my 18 year old grandson, or a close friend.

Choose a Theme or Single Event

Sometimes you may want to devote your letter to one subject or event. It's more interesting to know a lot about a little than a little about a lot. If you say, "This week on our vacation we went to Disneyland, Marineland and the beach" we get a vague impression of what you did. But if you talk about one part of Disneyland or Marineland or the beach, and what was the most fun, it will be more interesting.

When I went to French Guinea we went to see the great sea turtles coming in from the ocean to lay their eggs. This was such a fascinating part of my vacation that I spent nearly an entire letter to a friend telling about it.

Short Frequent Letters are Better than Long, Yearly Letters

Shorter fun letters are easier to read and remember than long involved letters. Don't save everything for a year and put it all in one letter. In these fast-paced times, people don't always have the time to read long letters. Yet they do want to hear from you. A quick, newsy letter written often is appreciated.

Let your Personality Show

Let your personality show. My style of writing is far different from that of my husband's. He would never have told about a horse pooping. He probably would have discussed the geological strata of the mountains, however, which is something I would never mention. We each have a distinctive way of expressing ourselves. I'm not right and he's not wrong because there is no right or wrong way to write a letter. Your personality will come out in your writing if you relax and write as you talk. Don't try to be someone else.

Use Portions of your Letters to Include in Scrapbooks

When I had a young family I would devote one paragraph to each of my children. I remembered fun things each one said or did. Then I made an extra copy of the letter and cut out each paragraph and pasted it in the child's photograph album. This way I had a photo and written account of each child as he grew up. This was written in 1976.

> July 20, 1976
>
> Danny is a very proud little eight-year old. He had a wonderful birthday party. One little boy couldn't come, but Danny said, "That's all right, you can send the present tomorrow." We had a nice long discussion on etiquette. He is playing football now. He isn't husky, but his nice long legs keep him out of the way of the hefty boys.

I copied this paragraph, cut it out and put it in Dan's photograph album next to pictures of his birthday party. The children look at the photos first, but they remember and quote things they did and said because I took the time to write about it.

Don't Apologize

"I'm sorry I haven't written sooner...." Some people ritually start a letter with these words. They can't get started without it. It's probably a letter-getting-started device, like doodling. Put it in and then once the words start flowing then cross out the apologies. Try to write often enough that you don't have to apologize.

WHAT CAN A LETTER DO FOR YOU?

When you are writing a letter the act of putting pen to paper, or fingers to keyboard can help you to sort your feelings and re-evaluate your thinking.

Letters are for Re-reading

You can re-read letters many times. This is the greatest value of a letter. I think my mother and father fell in love because of their letters. They were separated by many miles, but wrote regularly to each other. Dad spent two years in England while mother was in Mexico. Their courtship was carried on by letter a continent away. When they returned home, it only took one date before they knew they would marry.

Ask Questions, Re-evaluate and Explore Ideas

You can ask questions, even to yourself, answer them and then try again. Black and white words can be debated on paper and when you have finished, what was unclear before, now opens up to you.

You can re-evaluate your ideas, take an idea and explore it. Give pro and con thoughts about it and come to conclusions you hadn't even thought about before.

You can debate your feelings. Was it really that horrible, wonderful, catastrophic, exciting? Maybe what happened was for the best. What did you learn from the experience? Angry letters can be written down, but most of them should not be sent.

Writing Clarifies your Thinking

As you write your thoughts, you clarify your thinking. As you clarify what you write, you have a freedom you didn't have before. Decisions made now allow you to go on with your life.

Letters Give Immediate Responses

Letters are often written at a time of a happening. So the event is immediate, accurate (from the point of view of the writer) and emotional. Like a journal, you put it down as you see it. And that makes it vital.

SEND LETTERS OF KINDNESS

You can write things to people that you can't say to their faces. Sometimes you are embarrassed to tell someone how much you care for them. Maybe you are afraid of rejection or (even worse) reaction. It is easier to put your feelings on paper and mail it than to face them.

When someone does something thoughtful or nice for you, make a habit of sending a letter of thanks. During the many years I have taken in more than 20 people into our home. Sometimes I cared for them for short periods of time, and others have stayed up to four years of time. Of the 20 people, only two people have kept in touch with me. These two people have written, phoned and let me know that I have meant something to them. Too many times we forget to write thanks to others.

When a person dies, we don't always tell the family, "I really loved your Aunt Millie. She was there for me whenever I needed her. In fact, one time she....." But you can put these words in a letter and mail it to the family. They will treasure it. You will have written an incident in the life of someone which will be a memory of that person.

TEACH CHILDREN TO WRITE LETTERS

Children need to be taught early to write "thank you" letters for gifts received, services rendered, or just to say "I love you." This is a responsibility of the parent to make sure that appreciation is shown. This can be started even before the child can write. Have them "dictate" what to say or they can color a picture of thanks. Everyone understands a child's limits. Later on, when their writing skills become better, they can write a note of thanks or of love (with or without help). I received a letter from a seven year old grandchild this week. He said basically, "I miss you." On the back of the sheet was a stick picture of a child with tears running down his face and dropping onto the ground. This letter will go into an album I keep of his family. In twenty years he will enjoy the letter as much as I do now.

When that child is grown, he will know how to thank an aunt, friend, parent or grandparent for a graduation, wedding, baby or birthday gift. The tradition has already been established.

WRITING LETTERS
CAN ESTABLISH CLOSE TIES

Instead of giving material gifts to Grandparents, give them the gift of a monthly letter. They will appreciate hearing from you and maybe will write back. It could be the beginning of a closer relationship.

When you go on trips, send postcards to the grandchildren, letting them know what you are doing. Before you go, talk to them, tell them where you are going and ask what they would like you to look for. Then send a postcard telling them of your success. Maybe you could find a post card with a picture of the scenic view they were most interested in.

Write short messages to your children and slip them under their pillows, in lunchboxes, in their books. Let them know that you love them and that you care what they are doing. Young children like to have them written in code. But make the code simple and include the code where they will find it. Make secret code letters extra short. When the children get older, you can add more to the letters. Perhaps you could add a cartoon you like, a poem, a short thought, a memory that you want to share. Make your letters personal to that person. You could even add these thoughts to a husband's lunchbox, a wife's day-planner, in the car. Collect quotes, bumper stickers, t-shirt sayings your child, friend would like. Include them in a note.

Why not get a small notebook and write letters, thoughts, memories between husband and wife, each taking a turn. When you find a saying, a joke or poem, whatever, copy it into your notebook. It could be a quiet bond shared only by the two of you.

Try it. You'll like it!

You will find that as you write letters, you will become more proficient. Your letter writing will extend to other writings. Like any other talent, the more you do it, the better you will become. In this age of freedom in the world, we are becoming more isolated, more independent and more lonely. As we grow older, our families grow away from us, some more than others. Our friends develop other interests. Families and friends die. We are ultimately alone. We need an umbilical cord to connect us to others. The telephone is momentary. When you have finished, the warmth only lasts for a short time. Letter writing is one way to maintain connections to others.

Challenge

1. Write a letter to a friend.

    - Incorporate some new idea into the letter.
    - Keep a copy.

2. Write a thank you letter to someone for something they did nice for you.

3. Write a short note to a child.

    - Tell them something that will interest them.

CHAPTER TWENTY-TWO

Family Newsletters

One way for families to stay close to each other is to send newsletters to each member of the family. Now that our family has married and each one has moved away from the family home, it is easy for us to lose track of each other. In your family, you may find that some members of your family are getting lost. A family newsletter, sent at regular intervals, helps everyone to know what is going on in a family.

Talk to your family and find a way to correspond with each other. Written correspondence is more lasting than talking on the telephone because it provides a permanent record. Some of the more common family newsletters include the round-robin letters, having each member sending a letter to a central person who copies and sends on to other family members, or the printed newsletter with special features each month.

WHO WILL RECEIVE THE LETTER

What kind of a newsletter depends on how many people will be on your mailing list. In our family, we started out with five siblings. Then several cousins, aunts and uncles and finally our own children requested copies. At present, 40 families receive our packet of letters.

You need to decide how far your letter is going to extend. Are you going to choose your own generation and your children, or are you going to a previous generation or even a generation beyond that. Once you know how many newsletters you will be sending, then you can decide which is the best route to take. With our family we started small and the round robin letter was the best.

Round Robin Letter

The round robin letter is inexpensive. You write on your own stationery, put in an envelope and mail. The biggest cost is postage.

For the last ten years my family, which includes my brother and sisters and myself, have had a running newsletter. I can't even remember when it was started, but it has provided much happiness for us. This is the way it works. I write a letter and send on to the next sibling younger, who adds her letter and sends on both letters to the third sibling down. This continues until the first person receives all the letters, in our case five letters. She replaces her letter and sends the packet on again. Sometimes we add a cartoon, a funny article, or a photograph. In fact, we watch for new material to add to our letter packet.

At first we simply enjoyed our letters to each other, and then our married children and close cousins wanted copies. Three of our aunts and uncles asked for copies, and so it goes. This newsletter has worked well for us until now. But last week I received my packet of letters and it was one year old. Too long. Much too long. Each one of us took too long to respond and send the news on to the next sibling. All the news is old. We have seen each other during that year and have talked on the phone so none of the news was fresh. Although it has worked this long, and we have enjoyed receiving the news, it may be time for a change.

PRINTED NEWSLETTERS

If you decide to go with a printed newsletter there are many considerations:

- Number of copies to be made.
- Style of newsletter
- Cost of newsletter

Number of Copies

Because we started small, only brothers and sisters, we didn't worry about the number of copies. Now we know how many people are interested and how many copies we need to make.

If you are starting out with a family newsletter you need to send out a fun, interesting query letter to members of your family and see if they want to participate. Tell them some of the features you want to include, how often you want to publish, how many pages it will be, what you would like them to do, and that the newsletter cost will cover printing and postage. Then wait for a response.

Style of Newsletter

Don't try to start too big. Make it small and fun, and representative of your family. If you have members of your family who know desktop publishing or have a computer, let them help you. If you don't, you can always cut and paste your material. Use copy machines for final copy. In the newsletters I have printed for other organizations, I choose a size 11" x 17" good quality paper. This will make four sheets of standard size paper double-sided. If you want more pages you can add a second sheet the same size, which will make 8 pages, or you can insert a single 8" x 11" sheet. This keeps your newsletter flexible. Make sure your newsletter is divisible by two, so that you don't have an empty page. You can save a half page for the address, and then you don't have to put it into an envelope.

Another popular size is legal size paper. You can print this on both sides, but you don't have the flexibility of adding a single page in the middle. This means that you have to divide your pages by 4 to make sure you don't have the blank page extra.

Cost of Newsletter

Costs include postage, paper and copying. If you have it typeset, it will cost for the printer. You will probably not know how much the cost will be until after the first issue, but get some kind of estimate, to be adjusted. Add a little extra in case you want to include photographs which cost more to print. Leave one-half of one sheet on the outside for the address and it will save you the cost of an envelope. Be up-front with your family. Ask for a donation to help pay for these costs. Ask for a start-up fee and then when you have a better idea of costs, ask for a yearly fee.

HOW TO START

Choose a Masthead

Select a masthead with your family name in the title, if possible. The artwork can be selected in a variety of ways. Get a family member to draw one for you. Usually people are flattered to be asked. Have a competition for the masthead. Let everyone try his hand. Maybe you could use a different masthead each time until you find the right one. Create a masthead with a computer.

There are many art programs available on the computer now. Use borders and designs in the clip art books available at craft stores and office supply stores.

Typing or Typesetting

If you use a computer, try and find a good laser jet printer. Dot matrix is okay but doesn't print as well as a laser jet printer. If you want your newsletter to look more professional, you

The **ARMSTRONG** News

APRIL 1997   FROM THE ARMSTRONG HOME

EXERCISING GRANNY

Three times a week for an hour, I am now doing aerobics and/or step aerobics. This may not be an achievement for everyone, but to someone who hates loud music and physical exercise, this is a mighty step forward (or upward) as is the case. I am in a class with 30 young and beautiful girls who no more need to exercise than Jane Fonda. They sprightly jump up and down on their steps, roll on their exercise balls and lift their weights while I wearily move to every other one of the beats. When the cute young things roar with satisfaction at the end of the session, I roll over on the floor in exhaustion and pretend I am listening to my inner soul. I did find one girl who was at about my level, only to discover that she is 8 months pregnant.

WORDS FROM GREAT GRANDPA MARKHAM

Barbara give me Grandfather Markham's diary and notes. It came a s a surprise to learn that he worked, at least for awhile, as a Sheriff in Spanish Fork. I am enclosing a copy of them in the newsletter an do take time to read them. He talks about catching chicken thieves, (three young boys who steal 7 chickens) and the den of iniquity where men gamble in the wee hours of the night at the Boyack's house. He seldom goes home before dawn. We know so little about Great, Grandfather Markham, that this is delightful.

GRANDMA'S MAKEOVER

Lucy informed me that I have to have my picture taken for the book. She had a coupon for a session at The CoverLook, a photographer who does a complete makeover before taking glamour poses. "I have a picture of myself," I told her, but it was about 15 years old. She finally talked me into having this new one taken, but I insisted "no bare shoulders or sexy feathers." When I went in they took a "before" picture, and then proceeded to cover my face with gobs of makeup, eyeliner, eye shadow, mascara, several layers of lipstick, etc. Then the hair, teased and stiffened. I touched it and my hair cracked. When they finished, I did look great. Not me. But great. Willard wasn't excited about the "new me." He kept looking at me sidewards, like maybe I was some "hussy." But, of course, he wasn't critical. He said it would look good for my obituary. All he said after I washed away the goop, was that he liked me better without it. I saw the photos yesterday, and they are exactly the way I think I always look. Not the way the mirror reflects, but how I picture myself at my best. Look out Cindy Crawford.

may decide to choose a typeface other than courier. Most computers and printers have a variety of typefaces to choose from. Try not to use more than two different typefaces in your newsletter.

Typesetting is more expensive unless you have a large quantity of newsletters printed. Photographs can be included using halftones. Usually it is advisable to put most of your photos on one page to cut costs.

Before you copy your newsletter, be sure that you have proofread your copy more than once. Then give it to someone else to proof-read. Check for names, typographical errors, misspellings. Sometimes you say things and mean it one way, yet it can be misinterpreted. This is another reason to let a second person read it through.

FORMAT

Try using double or triple columns on your pages. It makes it easier to read and looks more professional. However, it is fun to vary the pages. Vary it with headings, clip art, photos, cartoons, illustrations, and white space. A newsletter is pretty boring without variety on each page. To give variety to your newsletter you can use light colored paper.

Headings

Use large headings to announce each article or special section. If you have a computer, then it is not difficult to adjust your headings whatever size you prefer, usually 16 to 20 points in a sans serif typeset. With a computer, it is fun to experiment with sizes and typefaces to get exactly the look you want.

Clip Art

You can also use clip art to give variety to your newsletter. There are many clip art books that you can buy. Your pages can be decorated around the edges, or the top and bottom of the page. Seasonal or representative line drawings liven up the articles. Computer programs now come with all kinds of clip art which can be enlarged or reduced according to your needs. Use the clip art to give variety and add interest.

If you have an artist in your group, let them have a chance to illustrate some of your features. Ask them to use a black pen so that it will reproduce better. Let a child illustrate some of your copy. The artwork can be reduced if the illustration is too big.

Photographs

Photographs are always good to use in a newsletter, but check the first copy to make sure you are getting the clarity you want. If you go to a copy shop, you may need to ask them to change the copier setting to "copyscreen" or "photo". Some regular copiers do a better job with photographs than others. Shop around for quality and price. Keep in mind that some copy centers can send your photo to a printer to shoot half-tones. This will give you even better quality. If you are having many newsletters copied you may consider having a printer do the whole job.

Be sure to put captions under your photos, so that family members will know who is in the photo and when it was taken. Do not use photos with a red cast to them, those out of focus, or those with a muddy look. If they don't look good before they are copied, they will look even worse after they've been copied.

You don't have to copy the entire photo, if you only want a part of it. You can ask your copy center to crop your pictures. Don't cut the photos though. This can be done without harming the photograph. Also, you can have your photos enlarged or reduced to fit your needs. Ask the copy center to adjust to size.

If you have a photograph taken by a photo studio in the last few years, they own the copyright to that photo, and you can't copy it without their permission. This is not true of old photos, or snapshots.

Cartoons

Draw your own, even if you have to use stick figures. Let members of your family try their hand at drawing.

Features

You may want to include some family photos, recipes, family history stories, update of what is happening to various family members, new births, marriages, birthdays, baptisms, family jokes, scouting news, new addresses, new jobs, anniversaries, deaths or retirement. You could also add poems written by family members, or short articles, artwork or stories if you have the space. Carol Ann Shepherd has an excellent book on family newsletters if you need more information. She gives examples and suggestions.[1]

Make sure that every branch of your family is represented. To do this, make assignments to family members well in advance. Give them deadlines to meet.

MAILING

You can fold your newsletters in half, staple them on both ends so that they don't get caught in the postal machines and send them out without an envelope. Check with your post office to make sure that your format can be legally sent and is in conformity for size.

You can get computer-generated self-adhesive labels so that you don't have to type up addresses each mailing. Once you have the master list on the computer, it is no problem to update addresses and generate the labels for a disk.

If you don't know how to do this, you can buy the self-adhesive labels and make a master on a sheet of paper. Then you can run these labels on a copy machine from a master. Ask a business supply house for these labels. Specific instructions are included with the labels.

If you have left a space on the newsletter for the address of the family member and your return address in the upper left hand corner, then it is not difficult to put on a label and send it. If you have over 200 newsletters, you can send it bulk rate, but you have to be a legal non-profit organization in order to do that. Otherwise, you will have to send it first class.

FAMILY SUPPORT

The strength of a family depends on the active support of each family member. We all need the feeling of being included in a strong support system and the closest support is that of a family. We can all attend the funerals and the weddings, but between these events is the everyday living that needs to be shared. Grief can be endured if you know that a group of loving family is there to hold your hand and give you a hug. Joys and success are even sweeter when there is family to send you a card or make a phone call. With family we can brave the most difficult times, and enjoy the day to day challenges. Even if there have been rifts (we all have them), a family newsletter is one way to let each family member know that he is loved and needed.

INTERNET CONNECTIONS

Everton Genealogical Helper has an interactive Website that can provide technical support and set up. Phone 1-800-443-6325 for more information. http://www.familyletter.com/

NOTES

[1]Shepherd, Carol Ann, *How to Create a Family Newsletter, An A to Z Guide to Make a Living History, Strengthen Family Ties, and Keep in Touch with Each Other*, 1984, 431 Mobley Drive, Boise, Idaho 83702

Challenge

1. Evaluate your need for a family newsletter.

2. Write a letter to a family member.

Section Five

Polishing and Publishing
Personal and Family History

CHAPTER TWENTY-THREE

Polishing Your Writing

Write your autobiography and family history first including all of your stories, memories, tributes and humorous anecdotes. Finish everything you want to include before you start to
polish your material. Read it through from the first page to the
last page without making corrections. Try to do it in a day or
two so that you will get the feel of your book. What have you
left out? What part of your life have you slipped over?

If you are working on your family history, be sure you have
included everyone. If you have ancestors in your family who
do not measure up, be sure to include them anyway. Make sure
of your facts.

Check for Corrections

Now, go back over it for corrections. Don't worry if everything is not perfect in your first draft. The first draft is supposed
to be the putting down of words, feelings, emotions, etc. I have
several friends who say they want to write, but they have yet to
write down any words. This is because they want it to be perfect the first time and get frustrated when it isn't. Don't be so
critical of your writing that you don't try a second time. I hope
you don't have a tiny editor perched on your shoulder whisper-

ing all the things that were wrong about your writing. There is nothing worse for any writer than to be stopped by his own self-editing.

After the first draft is finished, then you can go over it again and take out all of the rough edges. Add and correct material as necessary. Cut out unnecessary phrases and words. Adjectives can often be deleted. Substitute better words for inadequate words. Check for accuracy, clarifying all of your meanings and taking out the unnecessary material that slipped in. Simplify. Keep your sentences simple and your words short. You don't need to impress people with flowery words. Now you can start making it better. But you can't correct your material until you have written it down on paper the first time. All of those published autobiographies you may have read have been polished and edited many times before they get to the readers.

At this time, make sure you have at least two copies of your work. If you are writing on a computer, make sure you have a back-up disk, and a hard copy. If you have only made one copy of your writing, hurry fast to the closest copy center and have another copy made. You are going to be working with one copy, perhaps letting a trusted friend or family member read another copy, and you don't want to risk losing what you have already written.

Check for Inaccuracies

Dates, places, people. These are facts that you will want to have as correct as possible. Can you document your sources? If you have any question about your facts, say so. You can call it "family folklore" if you can't prove your source.

You may want to let another person read your work for accuracy, but don't let both copies go at the same time. Another person's perception of an event may be different from yours, but the basic facts should be the same. If you have family records, you should consult them. Make sure that birth dates, marriage dates and death dates are correct. Often we don't keep track of everyday happenings, but we will know the approximate year. Another common mistake is the spelling of names. Who else would know that person's name or the date that you are searching for? Make phone calls, write letters, make sure of your facts. Go back to diaries, letters, scrapbooks, yearbooks, certificates in search of facts.

Correct your Mistakes

I have a friend who still writes everything by hand, then has it typed for him. He writes many autobiographical papers, sometimes amounting to over a hundred pages. At this writing he is revising it about the eighth time. By the time he has finished, I know it will have at least ten revisions. I keep telling him that the easiest way to work is by using a computer, but he does it the way that works best for him.

If you are using a computer, you will find it a simple matter to go into your copy and add words or sentences, move a paragraph from one spot to another, do any revisions that you think necessary and all this at a minimum of physical labor. The only work is the decision-making process that comes with any change you decide is necessary.

However, if you are not comfortable with a computer and want to revise from the handwritten or typewritten copy, here are some suggestions:

- Do not start retyping or handwriting until you have made all the necessary changes.

- If you use an underliner felt tip pen, you can cross out any words you wish and still see the original. It is not as painful to eliminate words if you know it is not irreversible.

- Add words or phrases right on the copy.

- If you want to add a paragraph, don't retype the entire page. Use a pair of scissors and tape and splice in the paragraph where you need it.

- If you need to add an extra page, add letters to the page numbers, that is 5, 5a, 5b, 6. This will keep your pages in order without having to redo the page numbers every time you make an addition.

If you are brave enough, read your manuscript to someone. Don't listen while they say, "That's great! You're the most talented person!" or else the opposite with, "Who said you could write? It isn't worth finishing!" There will always be both kinds of critics. Usually they are people who have never written and are either jealous or in awe. Occasionally you can find someone who says, "It's good because..." or "I don't understand that part..." Maybe they are right and maybe not, but at least they are thinking constructively. After the immediate comments, listen for the questions, "How come you did...?" or "Why did you..." Don't defend your piece of work. Listen. Make notes. Then look back and see if you have really put into writing what you intended. Maybe you thought you did, but didn't.

MECHANICS OF TYPING

When you are all finished with your corrections, you need to start typing the finished copy. You should finish your work on a good grade of 8 1/2" x 11" white acid-free bond paper, at least 20 pound. Archival paper will last the longest of any paper.

If you are using a computer you can choose two typefaces, but no more than that. Try to choose typefaces that are different in appearance. If you use the typeface such as Times Roman, New Century Schoolbook, Bookman, Palatino or Helvetica it will look more professional than if you use the usual typeface of Courier.

An Alkaline Pen is available at some office supply stores. Or you can write to Printers Pacific, Inc., Sutter Creek, CA 95685 and ask for a paper test pen. You can test your paper to see if it is acid-free by making a mark on the paper. The pen I have will designate acid with a yellow mark, neutral with a green mark and alkaline with a blue color. Testing pens will vary so check directions on the pen. pH testing strips are also available for the testing of colored papers.

If paper, adhesives or protectors contain acid, the paper will become brittle or turn brown with age. It is estimated that within 15 years, paper containing acid will start to deteriorate. The more inexpensive the paper, the better chance it will contain acid. If you have important papers you want to save, you can spray it with *Wei T'o* which will neutralize the acid.

Double space on one side of the paper with at least one inch margins on three sides. Leave 1 1/2" on the left margin for binding. Make sure you have clean ribbons on the printer or typewriter. You can use dot matrix printers or electric typewriters with carbon ribbons, but the laser, ink jet or letter quality printers are preferred. After you decide how you are going to include your illustrations, then you can put on the page numbers.

Before you start typing the final copy, make a decision how you are going to print or copy your book. If you are going to publish your book through a publisher, they have their own requirements on page size, margins, double columns, etc. The typing is a lot of work and there is no reason to do it twice if you can avoid it.

MECHANICS OF HANDWRITING

There are some who prefer to handwrite their personal histories because they feel it gives it a more personal touch. This is definitely a choice you have.

Restoration Source has a "journal paper" which is lined on one side of good quality. Never write on both sides of a paper as the ink may bleed through. If your handwriting tends to slant upward, place a guide underneath. Many office supplies will carry a preprinted guide.

Use a permanent carbon ink pen. Many ballpoint pens will fade or wash off if any moisture touches it. There are pens that are better for permanent storage. A uniball pen can be used. These have a roller type device inside and most of them can be purchased at office supply stores. A mono-pen such as Tomko can also be used. These come in fine point and extra-fine. You can check at office supply houses or at archival supply houses. You can also find carbon ink pens used in accounting or legal writing.

ILLUSTRATIONS

If you are going to use illustrations, such as photographs, newspaper clippings, or certificates, etc. you need to decide how you are going to include them. Are you going to place your illustration in context with the writing, or are you going to put them in a section in the middle or at the end of your book? If you decide to publish your book there is a "screening" charge for each page. This may make a difference in how you format your book. You may decide to place photographs together to save costs.

Use clear photos with good contrast. Do not include blurred or out of focus photos. If they have a red cast to them, they are not going to copy well. You may also decide that you need to crop your photos. The printer or copy center can crop your photographs for you. Don't destroy your photographs.

You need to clearly caption each photograph or illustration to include dates and the names of people and places. Mount with photograph film tape, 3M double sided tape, or mounting corners. Type the captions and glue/tape them underneath the illustration or you can write under the illustrations with an archival pen as suggested. Place photographs in protective sleeves or envelopes which can also be bound with the rest of your writing. Black and white photographs last longer than color photos. Use good quality film and take film to a quality photo shop, not one that gives 1-hour service.

Copy machines are now copying photographs with far better clarity than ever before. You may want to photocopy a few of your photographs as an experiment. If you are making many copies, this may be a less expensive way to go. You can always have extra copies made of your most precious photographs. I have seen photos that have been photocopied that would be difficult to tell if they are copies or photos. At this present time, I can find copy centers that will copy color photos for a dollar a page. If you have more than one photo on a page, it is still only a dollar. When you copy black and white photos, ask for the color copier with the color over-write. It gives the photo an extra dimension and clarity. You may decide to scan your pictures into your history. Reread the photography section on scanning.

Newspaper clippings yellow easily. Make a photo copy of them. Copy certificates, except those that prohibit it. Birth, marriage, death certificates could be included in your book. Your original certificates should be placed in a file for safe-keeping. Do not use rubber cement or white glue. Do not dry-mount, as the heat causes the acid to destroy your photographs. Don't staple or use paperclips, rubber bands or pressure sensitive tapes. They can harm your prints.

If you have a coat-of-arms, the original or copy can also be included. An ancestral chart using names or a picture ancestral chart will present a good overview of the family in a comprehensive manner. A family group chart also shows family relationships. Maps, pictures of gravestones or photos of homesteads add to the quality of the book.

At this point, you are ready to copy or publish your manuscript. Turn to chapter 24, *Publishing or Reproducing Your Book,* on how to proceed.

Challenge

1. Check for omissions.

    *   Be as objective as you can.
    *   Be aware of what you have, and what you don't have.

2. Check for corrections.

    *   Substitute favorite phrases and words for more variety.
    *   Clarify your meanings.

3. Check for inaccuracies.

4. Correct your mistakes.

5. Make copies of your writing.

6. Type your manuscript.

7. Choose illustrations.

CHAPTER TWENTY-FOUR

Publishing
or
Reproducing Your Book

If you have written a family history, you may want to go to your family organization and let them know what you have written. They may be willing to help subsidize the book. They can also let others know that you are ready to publish about Great-Grandpa and you can get publishing orders. You can also write to various family members asking if they are interested in receiving a copy which will cost $... This gives you an idea of how many copies to have printed and the type of bindings you can afford.

If you take an order, be sure to follow through. Keep good records, so that you don't lose names and addresses.

You may decide to publish your own Personal History. If you have children or grandchildren, they are going to want a copy. Whether you photocopy, typeset or self-publish, there are some guidelines to follow.

Assembling your Book

A title page with your name and date is the simplest beginning for your book or you can use some or all of the following pages. These are included in published books, and yours is beginning to look professional.

- Half-title page. This is only the title of your book, nothing more.

- Title page. This contains title, subtitle (if any) your name and date. (Published books also include the name of the Publisher)

- Copyright page. You can copyright your own work for a minimal fee. This protects you from having someone take your writing and use it without your permission. The copyright lasts for fifty years. In case of your death, it extends to your heirs. All you need to do is write the words:

    Note: Copyright, your name and the date
    ie. Copyright, Janice Dixon, 1997

You could also include the copyright symbol, or the abbreviation copr.

You don't need to register a copyright with the Copyright Office for it to be valid. Some people have mailed a copy of the work to themselves in a sealed envelope (which is not to be opened). This proves that you wrote it on a certain date.

However, if there is a problem, and someone does take some of your writing and claims it as theirs, you cannot take anyone to court with an infringement suit unless it is registered with the Copyright Office. It is very easy to register your autobiography. Write to the Register of Copyrights, Library of Congress, Washington, D.C. 20559 for an application form.

Fill out the application form and send the required fee along with one copy of your writing. This ensures the fact that you indeed did write this and it is registered in your name. If you publish it, then you would need to send two copies of your writing. If you register your work with the Copyright Office they will send you a Library of Congress cataloging date, ISBN (International Standard Book number, and date.) You should include this information underneath the copyright notice.

If you are quoting from other sources, you need to reference your quote. If the quote is only a line or two, then it is considered "fair use." If it is no longer copyrighted and has not been renewed, then you can use the material without getting permission. The rule of thumb for copyright is 56 years if it is not renewed and 25 years beyond that if it has been renewed. For books published since 1980, the copyright term is the life of the author plus 50 years.

- Foreword. This is an introduction to your book and is written by someone else. This is an optional section.

- Preface. This is another optional section and is your statement about your book. You may want to say why you wrote it, who you wrote it for and what is your purpose in writing it. You may also want to include anyone who helped you write it, and your thanks.

- Table of Contents. If you have written in chapters, then it is easy to include a Table of Contents.

- Illustrations. If you placed your illustrations throughout the book, you may decide to give them a page number, and this list should be included in the front of your book.

- Prologue or Introduction. If you want an introduction you are free to add to it here. Sometimes the first chapter serves as that introduction.

PHOTOCOPY

The easiest way is to photocopy it and have it bound at a copy shop. Ask the copy shop to use good quality paper with acid-free 20 pound bond. A good bond paper will last about forty years without turning yellow. However, if you choose a paper with 50% rag content or rag bond Permalife document bond it will last about 500 years. You can supply the copy shop with the paper you prefer using to make sure you get the quality you want. You can send for a catalog of available materials to archival quality suppliers:

University Products, Inc.
P.O. Box 101
South Canal Street
Holyoke, MA 01041

Light Impressions
439 Monroe Avenue
Rochester, New York 14607-3717

Restoration Source
P.O. Box 9384
Salt Lake City, Utah 84109
(801)278-7880 or (801)278-3638

Conservation Materials Ltd.
340 Freeport Blvd.
Sparks, NV 89341
(702)331-0582

If you photocopy, each page will cost about the same no matter how many copies you make. For example, the copy center may charge you three cents to five cents a page. However, if you are making many copies you may be able to negotiate a better price per page.

If you are going to include photographs and illustrations, place them before you bind it. Make a minimum of three copies, but it would probably be better to make more than that. For family histories, you are going to want many copies, depending on the number of family members interested in your book.

It is also possible to change the size of your book by reducing or enlarging it on the copy machine. Once your manuscript has been typed, it can now be adjusted to your needs.

Docutech printing is another option for those who want only a few copies. This has a double sided printer which is toner based. Some copy shops and some small printers have them.

DESKTOP PUBLISHING

Computers have become so advanced that you can achieve a printed look without the need to have it typeset. Desktop publishing combines words and images to create an attractive presentation of your book.

If you are comfortable with computers, there are programs available so that you can do the work yourself. You can change type set, use double columns and include graphic designs. Most people who know how to use a computer can manipulate a page so that it looks exactly the way you want it. Ask a computer software salesman which program would be best for your particular project. Aldus Pagemaker or Quark XPress are two programs which can make your work look more professional.

If you don't want to format the pages yourself, but have typed the material on a computer, you can take your disk to a Service Bureau. They can convert it to other programs, such as Quark XPress or Aldus Pagemaker and make it look professional. You have already done the keyboarding which is the time-consuming part. It will be less expensive if you do the typing. They can format it according to your directions to give it a more professional appearance.

If you are going to self publish your manuscript then it needs to be "camera" ready. The larger sized books which can be the size of a typewritten size 8 1/2" x 11" fall into this category. You can also use 7" x 11". When you photocopy, it can be reduced to the desired size. Or you may decide to choose a smaller format.

Popular sized formats are 5 1/2" x 8 1/2" or 6" x 9". Ask the publisher which formats work best for printing. Each company has its own format and if you can work within that format it will be less expensive for you to have it printed.

You can also change the print so that you can use a bolder, bigger print for headings or a smaller, italic print for footnotes.

An image processing or scanning software will allow you to put in special effects such as artwork. Photographs can also be added by using a scanner. I have worked with a program which will allow you to scan a photograph onto a computer screen and then let you re-touch the photo. I found a photo I wanted to use, but it had a second person in the photo. I was able to crop the photo and then blend the background. There was a bright light above the person's head which was distracting for my purposes. Again, this was re-touched. Imagesetters are expensive, however, and you may decide to send pages which include photographs to a professional for this type of work.

Some of these companies are called "pre-press businesses." Kinko's and AlphaGraphics often have this capability. A Service Bureau can do the image processing or scanning for you. Perhaps you may want to use a color copier for your photographs (even for black and white photographs). This is the least expensive. Try it on a few of your photographs and see if that is acceptable to you. Try more than one copier to get the best resolution for your needs.

If you are not comfortable with computers, you can contact a desktop publisher or service bureau and talk to them. They will charge for their time and know-how, and it could be an expense you will not want to get into. The price will depend on the number of pages, amount of artwork or photographs you want to include and how many copies you want. The initial cost is higher, but will go down in price with the number of copies you need. Do not get involved with a desktop publisher without getting a quote first. Find out what they will do for you, how they will proceed, how the photographs will look, and who will own the original copy. If you decide you are going to publish and sell your book, you don't want a desktop publisher to come back in for a cut in your profits.

SELF-PUBLISHING

Unless you are going to be printing 500 or more copies of your book, it will not be advisable to self-publish. You can cut your expenses if you are willing to sub-contract each phase of the publishing. That is, you could have it printed by one company, photos copied by another, and bound by a third company. Get quotes from more than one company on each phase. Make sure you get the quality you want. Remember that, if you decide to print photos in color or choose a high quality paper or binding, your costs are going to increase substantially.

You will be having running costs no matter which way you decide to go. Running costs include the cost of the paper and the binding.

When you self-publish, then the initial setup costs are expensive, but the cost of the book will go down with increased number of copies. A setup cost will include the typesetting, photo resizing, photo screening, etc. The more copies you make, the less it will cost per copy. But you will still have the running costs (paper, binding) and the setup costs (typesetting, photo plates, etc.) It will be less expensive to photocopy, if you are making less than 500 copies.

There are many offset presses in every city. You can check them out and find out costs. The quality of the work will depend on how much you are willing to pay. The more work a press will do such as cleaning up the negatives and taking out any defects, the more it will cost you. Again, the price will come down as the number of copies you want made goes up. You can write to The Printing Industries of America, Inc., 1930

North Lynn St., Arlington VA 22209 and ask for a list of commercial printers who do small press runs in your area. You
might also phone your local Chamber of Commerce or Better
Business Bureau for references for a reliable printer. Get more
than one bid, and be sure to know exactly what you are going
to be getting for the price. Does it include photographs or binding, quality of paper? Get it in writing that, if you want to print
more copies, you can do so without penalties.

Write to the Genealogy Club of America and ask about their
publishing service. They may include editing and printing. Be
sure to ask for a written estimate.

VANITY OR SUBSIDY PUBLISHERS

There are publishers who are willing to take all the problems of publishing off your shoulders. They are called "vanity," "subsidy," "co-publishers," or "cooperative publishers."
They are usually excited and enthusiastic about your book
because you are footing the bill. Before you sign anything with
these publishers, be sure to have a good contract, one you
understand. Be sure you have in writing how much it is going
to cost and what the quality of the work will be before you sign
anything. Usually the vanity publisher will not do any market-
ing for you, which means that if you contract for 1000 books,
you know that you will be the person selling them. Usually a
bookstore will not sell vanity press books in the bookstore.
Also be sure that you are not giving any of your rights to the
publisher and that he is not going to be making a profit from
your book if you are subsidizing it. You will probably do better by publishing it yourself than by accepting the services of a
vanity press publisher.

Gateway Press, Inc. does a lot of family and genealogy publishing. They seem to publish a quality book with a professional appearance and durable books. They will give you an
estimate of cost.[1]

ROYALTY PUBLISHING

If you feel that you have written a book that will appeal to a wide market outside your own family, you can send your manuscript to a publisher. A current list of publishers is listed annually in the *Writers Market* published by Writers Digest Books. This book gives editor, address, and information about most of the major book publishers. It will tell you if it publishes non-fiction, specifically autobiographies and family histories. It will tell you if you can send unagented manuscripts to them, and the procedure for doing so. Some publishers only publish specialty books, such as books on dogs, guns, art, photography, etc. Make sure that your book would fit into their interests, otherwise you will be wasting your time and money.

If you find a publisher that includes your type of book, send a letter with an outline and perhaps a sample chapter and a self addressed stamped envelope. These royalty publishers will pay you for publishing your book. They will list their terms. Read the contract carefully before signing.

BINDINGS

There are many kinds of bindings including ring binder, velobind, wire roll, plastic comb, perfect bind or hard bind. A copy center can bind your copies with velo-bind, wire roll or plastic comb. If you are only going to have a few copies made, these are convenient ways to go.

Plastic Comb

A plastic comb can open flat. Holes are punched in the paper and the plastic teeth go through the holes. There are different sizes of combs depending on the size of your book. These books aren't too sturdy and sometimes the pages tear out. You can even buy your own plastic comb binder at most office supply stores and bind your own.

Velo Bind

A velo bind punches holes in the side and uses a plastic strip with plastic rivets to hold it together. These books will not open flat.

Spiral Wire

Spiral wire binding are often found in books that need to lie flat, such as how-to books, cook books, computer books. It is easy to tear pages out. They aren't too professional looking, but they are probably more sturdy than comb binding.

3-Ring Binder

You may decide that you want to place your personal or family history in a 3-ring binder and continue adding to it as you desire. There are binders that are also acid-free, but they are difficult to find. Don't use vinyl binders. Cloth binder or buckram are preferable. Light Impressions has a Journal Binder and Mylar sheet protectors which are archival quality. The binder measures 10 3/4" x 11 3/4" x 1 3/4". They have other sizes, so write for a catalog. Restoration Source also has a good journal binder with a dust cover as well as other archival materials. I've also noticed that some bigger photograph retailers are starting to carry acid-free journal binders. You can also spray old binders with *Wei T'o* to de-acidify. Genealogy supply stores may also have archival binders.

Hard Bound

Family history books should be more permanent and, where possible, should be hard bound. Some families work together in family organizations and produce lengthy books for many family members. A hard bound book will protect the information the best way. If you are having a number of copies bound the price per book will go down in price.

Hand Binding

Hand binding is an option most people do not have. We had one family member who wanted to have an old family journal published and he wanted to have it leather-bound and hand-finished. He brought a sample of the book the way it would look when finished to a family reunion. Those who were interested placed an order and paid him upfront. When it was finished it was a work of art and highly treasured. Those that ordered were thrilled with the copy and those that hesitated were out.

Perfect Binding

You can also choose a perfect binding, which is the same as most soft cover books. These are glued on the back and placed in a cover. Otabind is a variation of the perfect binding. The book needs to be at least 50 pages before a perfect binding will work.

NOTES

[1]Poynter, Dan, *The Self-Publishing* Manual, Para Publishing, P. O. Box 8206, Santa Barbara, CA 93118-8206, (805)968-7277, 1996.

[2]Gateway Press, Inc., 1001 N. Calvert Street, Baltimore, Maryland, 21202, (410)837-8271.

Challenge

1. Gather your writings together.

   - Bind them in an appropriate manner so that they don't get lost.

2. Finish your history.

3. Present it in its finest form.

Appendix A

Memory Joggers

CHILDHOOD TIMES

- What is your first memory? How old were you then?
- What is your favorite childhood story, or nursery rhyme?
- What is the earliest dream you remember?
- What were some of the early home remedies you had?
- How were you disciplined as a child?
- What is the first Christmas (or special holiday)
  you remember?
- Can you remember your first home?
- What was your favorite toy as a child?

ELEMENTARY SCHOOL YEARS

- What activities did you do with brothers and sisters?
    Did you ever fight with them?
    What fun things did you do together?
- Can you remember any of your teachers?
    Which was your favorite teacher? Why?
- What was your school like?
    Which subjects did you enjoy?
- What were your favorite holidays?
- Did you have any sicknesses or accidents?
    How were they treated?
- Did you have any vacations?
- Where did you live?
- What family responsibilities did you have?
- What activity out of school did you enjoy?
- Is there any event in this period that changed your life?
- Who were your friends?
    What games did you play?
- Did you have religious training?
- What were you like as a child?
    Describe yourself.
- What did you want to be when you grew up?
- What did you do on holidays as a child?
    4th of July

> Birthday
> Christmas
> Easter
> New Years

- What were some of your family traditions?
- What was the first book you read (outside of school)?
- Was music a part of your growing up?
    Art?
    Dance?
- What year was the happiest for you?
- What year was the worst?

JUNIOR HIGH YEARS and HIGH SCHOOL YEARS

Many of the questions asked in the earlier section may apply here, but the answers may be different. As you go into your junior high school years and then into your high school years, you can ask the same questions.

- Did anything happen in this period of time that changed your life?
- Did any important deaths occur?
- What was your first date?
- Who were your friends?
    Do you know what happened to them?
- What Junior High or Middle school did you attend?
    Who were your teachers?
    What subject did you enjoy the most?
    What teacher was the most influential in your life?
    What teacher had a negative influence on you?
    What was the craziest thing you did in school?
    Who were your heroes in school?
    Movie stars? Sports stars?
    Did you go to dances? What kind of dances were they?
    What was the "in" fashion in clothes? Hairstyle?
    What were the fads of the time?

What classes, hobbies and activities became interesting to you?

What honors and awards did you receive?

- When did you set your lifetime goals, and what were they?
- What sports were you interested in?
- Did you ever get into trouble?
- What work experience did you have?
- What services did you perform for others?
- Did you attend church?

What were your religious beliefs?

- Were you a Boy Scout or Girl Scout? 4-H?
- What President was in office in your youth?
- What responsibilities did you have as a youth?

POST HIGH SCHOOL YEARS

Military Service

- What branch of the service were you in?
- What years did you serve?
- What was your serial number?
- Why did you decide on a military experience or profession?
- Were you drafted or did you enlist?
- What was the political climate at that time?
- Where did you receive basic training?
- Where were you stationed?
- How did you feel about basic training?
- How did your family feel about your going into the military?
- What special training did you receive?
- What rank did you achieve?
- Where did you go after basic training?
- Did you see any combat?
- Were you wounded?
- What experiences did you have?

- How did you feel about war?
- What was your closest experience with death?
- Did you make special friends in the military service?
- Have you kept in touch with them?
- Do you have any stories about your military service that you would like to tell?
- What is your best military experience?
- What is your worst military experience?

COLLEGE or VOCATIONAL SCHOOL

- Why did you choose the particular school that you did?
- Were you the only one in your family to attend college?
- What classes did you enjoy the most?
- What classes did you enjoy the least?
- Did you have favorite teachers?
- How did you finance your schooling?
- Did you work part-time (or full time) while you were attending school?
- Did you leave home to go to school?
- Where did you live while you were at school?
- Did you join a fraternity or sorority or other school social club? What other organizations did you join?
- Were you involved in any theater art, music or dance organizations?
- What kind of a student were you?
- Have you used your education in the field you studied?
- Who was your favorite friend in college?
- Do you keep in touch with him (her)?
- What were some of the funny things you did in college?
- Were drugs or alcohol a problem in your college?
    What were your feelings about drugs?
    Was it ever an issue?
- What kind of sports did you enjoy?
    Did you participate in any sports?
    Were you on a school team?

- Did you have any crisis times during your college years?
- Did you date anyone special during this time?
- Did you graduate from college?
  What year?
- Did you attend graduate school?
    Was undergraduate different than graduate school?
    Did you write a graduate paper?
    Dissertation?

SERVICE

Mission, Peace Corps, Red Cross, etc.

- Why did you choose to serve others?
- Where did you go? To what people?
- How were you financially supported?
- What training did you take with you?
- Did you receive special training in this service?
- What friends did you make?
- What did you do?
- How did you help others?
    How do you feel about it?
- Did you have any experiences you would like to tell?
    How did you affect others?
- How has this experience affected your life?

COURTSHIP and MARRIAGE

- When was the first time you met your future spouse?
- What was the occasion?
- Was it love at first sight?
- What attracted you to your spouse?
- Tell about your courtship.
- Did your courtship go smoothly?
- What type of dates did you enjoy most?
- When was the first time you met your future in-laws?
- How did you ask her to marry you?

How did he ask you to marry him?
- Did you ask her father for her hand in marriage?
  Did he ask your father?
- Did you get along with her/his family?
- Did anything funny happen during your courtship?
- Tell about the wedding day.
  Where and when were you married?
  Who attended? Who officiated?
- What was your spouse like at the time of your marriage?
  Physical attributes, personality, financial
- Where did you go on your honeymoon?
- Where was your first home?
- What was the best thing he/she knew how to do?
  What was the worst?
- What happened the first time you went
  shopping together?

BUILDING A BUSINESS or CAREER

- What was the first job that started you toward your present business or career?
- How did you decide to choose this particular work?
- What training did you have to prepare for this work?
- What promotions or honors did you have?
- What was the biggest problem you had in adjusting to your work?
- What successes/failures did you have?
- How did your work affect your family?
- Did you have any experiences on the job that are particularly important to you?
- What was it like to turn 40?
- Did your career change (grow, turn-around)?
- Did you ever wish you had pursued a
  different occupation?
- What was your most important achievement?

RAISING A FAMILY

- Give names and birth dates of your children?
- What were the circumstances of giving birth then as opposed to now?
    Where did the births occur?
    Who assisted you?
    Did you have natural childbirth?
    Did you have any trouble getting to the hospital?
    Were there any funny/interesting stories about
    their births?
- What are the characteristics, talents, hobbies, personalities of each child.
- What has each meant to you in your life?
- Have these children given any challenges to you?
- What did you do as a family?
    Vacations?
    Daily routines?
- As they have grown, how have you adjusted in your personal life?
- What philosophy did you use in raising them?
    How did you discipline/praise them?
    Did they present any challenges to you as a parent?
    Did you raise your children the same way you
    were raised?
- What were some of the family rules in your home?
- Did your children receive a college education?
- Would you raise your children the same way if you had a second chance?
- Are any or all of your children married?
- Whom did they marry?
    When? Where?

SETTLING IN

- In what community service are you involved?
- How have you expanded or changed in your business

or work?
- Are you involved in politics?
  In what way?
- How is your health?
- What friends do you have?
  Are they the same ones with whom you grew up?
  What new friends have you made?
- How are they important to you?
- Have you had special trips or vacations?
- What honors have you had?
- Are you living in the same home, or have you moved?
- How have you planned for your retirement years?
- What is your social life?
  What activities do you prefer?
- Do you have any grandchildren?
  How many?
  What are their names?
  Tell about each one.

RETIREMENT YEARS

- What activities interest you most?
- Tell about your friends.
- Which of your goals have you achieved?
- How is your financial situation now?
- Do you have any hobbies?
- What are your future plans?
- What changes do you see in your lifetime that are most significant?
- What is your philosophy?
- How is your health?
  Do you have a physical fitness plan?
- What is the most healthful diet for you?
- Do you need more or less sleep than when you were younger?
- What positions do you now hold?

- What organizations do you belong to?
- What contributions have you made in your life to making the world a better place?
- What is the most important thing a person can strive for?
- What is the most unusual thing about you?
- What are your biggest problems now?
- What do you most fear?
- How is the world different now from the world you grew up in?
- What is the best thing about your current age?
  The worst thing?
- What has made you the happiest in this life?

There is a book[1] that contains just about every question you could possibly ever ask. If these kinds of questions are of a help to you, you might find this book helpful.

NOTES

[1]Fletcher, William, *Recording Your Family History*, Ten Speed Press, Berkely, CA.

Appendix B

Family History Survey

Family History Survey

*Y*ou will save yourself time if you will prepare a list of dates and places in your home where vital information is kept. If one spouse has all the information and doesn't communicate it to the other, it can be devastating to try to find needed information, especially in a time of stress, such as a death.

If you are doing research on a family member, this is a quick way to get all the information in front of you and let you assess exactly what information you have about this family member. This way you can refer back to this list easily without having to stop and look up the needed information. It will also save you time if the work has already been gathered or printed.

Birth Information

Name of person _____

Birth _____
        Day   Month   Year

Place   City   State   Country

                          Yes   No

Do you know the circumstances of your birth? ☐ ☐

Where can this information be obtained? _____

What certificates are available: Where are they kept?

☐ Birth Certificate _____

☐ Christening Certificate _____

☐ Blessing Certificate _____

☐ Baptism _____

Letters or newspaper accounts of birth? _____

Baby books or scrapbooks? _____

Baby pictures or photo albums? _____

Genealogy records? _____

Additional records? _____

ℳother's Background

Mother's name —————————————————————————

Birth ——————————————————————————————
                         Day   Month   Year

Place   City   State   Country

Where are they kept?

Do you have any records of your mother? —————————

Do you have any histories of your mother?—————————

Do you have any biographies
   or written stories of your mother?—————————

Was your mother married more than once?—————————

Give name of any other husband. —————————————

Is your mother still living?—————————————————

    If yes, give the address. —————————————

If she has passed away, what is the date of her death?
                      Day   Month   Year

Where is she buried?—————————————————————

Certificates Available?
   ☐ Birth Certificate—————————————————
   ☐ Marriage Certificate —————————————————
   ☐ Death Certificate —————————————————

Additional Records?—————————————————————

Father's Background

Father's name _____

Birth _____
                                 Day   Month   Year

_____
Place   City   State   Country

Where are they kept?

Do you have any records of your father? _____

Do you have any histories of your father? _____

Do you have any biographies
    or written stories of your father? _____

Was your father married more than once? _____

Give name of any other wife. _____

Is your father still living? _____

    If yes, give the address. _____

If he has passed away, what is the date of his death?

                             Day   Month   Year

Where is he buried? _____

Certificates Available?

   ☐ Birth Certificate _____

   ☐ Marriage Certificate _____

   ☐ Death Certificate _____

Additional Records? _____

Homes

Childhood home			
	Address	City	State

Other home			
	Address	City	State

First home after Marriage			
	Address	City	State

Other home			
	Address	City	State

Current Home:

Do you have any of the following: Where are these documents kept?

- ☐ Deeds
- ☐ Loans
- ☐ Mortgages
- ☐ Leases
- ☐ Contracts
- ☐ Land grants
- ☐ Water rights
- ☐ Abstracts of title
- ☐ Tax notices

Additional documents?

ℐiblings

Names of brothers and sisters

Full name: _____

Birth date: _____
                      Day   Month   Year

Name of spouse: _____

Current address   _____
                      Address   City   State

Full name   _____

Birth date: _____
                      Day   Month   Year

Name of spouse: _____

Current address   _____
                      Address   City   State

Full name   _____

Birth date: _____
                      Day   Month   Year

Name of spouse: _____

Current address   _____
                      Address   City   State

Make additional copies of this survey as needed

Marriage Information

Name of spouse: _____

Birth date: _____
                Day   Month   Year

Spouse's parents: _____

Marriage date: _____
                Day   Month   Year

Name of place married: _____

Location: _____
         Address   City   State

Marriage performed by: _____

Witness: _____

Witness: _____

	Yes	No
Do you have a copy of your marriage certificate?	☐	☐

Where is it kept?

	Yes	No
Were you married more than once?	☐	☐

Provide name and data.

	Yes	No
Were you divorced?	☐	☐

If yes, when and where

	Yes	No
Was your marriage annulled?	☐	☐

If yes, provide name and data

Where do you keep these papers?_____

Health Records

Which of the following do you have: Where are these papers kept?

☐ Living will _____

☐ Hospital records _____

☐ Doctors records _____

☐ Immunization records_____

☐ Xrays _____

☐ Blood donor records _____

☐ Insurance papers _____

☐ Health insurance _____

☐ Funeral insurance _____

Personal Records

Have you kept any of the following: Where are they kept?

☐ Journal _____

☐ Diary _____

☐ Letters _____

☐ Photograph albums _____

☐ Scrapbooks _____

☐ Autograph book _____

☐ Wedding book _____

☐ Patriarchal Blessing _____

Family Records

Do you have any of the following: Where are they kept?

- ☐ Family bible   _____
- ☐ Family group sheet   _____
- ☐ Pedigree charts   _____
- ☐ Family histories   _____
- ☐ Family newsletters   _____
- ☐ Local histories   _____

Do you have any announcements or   Where are they kept?
newspaper clippings of the following:

- ☐ Wedding   _____
- ☐ Divorce   _____
- ☐ Obituaries   _____
- ☐ Birth announcements   _____
- ☐ Honors   _____
- ☐ Graduation   _____
- ☐ Birthday   _____
- ☐ Golden anniversary   _____
- ☐ News announcements   _____
- ☐ Professional news   _____
- ☐ New home   _____
- ☐ Travel   _____

School Information

Place and Dates

Elementary school _____

_____

Middle school _____

_____

High school _____

_____

College _____

_____

Specialty school _____

_____

Do you have any of the following: Where are they kept?

☐ Diplomas _____

☐ Transcripts _____

☐ Honor rolls _____

☐ Yearbooks _____

☐ School publications _____

☐ Report cards _____

☐ Awards _____

☐ Scholarships _____

Employment Records

Social Security #   _____

Union Name and #   _____

Employed by   _____

Address   _____

Date of employment _____

Manager's name   _____

Employed by   _____

Address   _____

Date of employment _____

Manager's name   _____

Do you have any of the following: Where are they kept?

   ☐ Pension plans   _____

   ☐ Retirement papers   _____

   ☐ Honors   _____

   ☐ Union Records   _____

Make additional copies of this survey as needed

Financial Records

Do you have any of the following: Where are they kept?

☐ Account books   _____

☐ Checkbook stubs   _____

☐ Bills   _____

☐ Estate records   _____

☐ Wills   _____

☐ Stocks or bonds   _____

☐ Safety deposits   _____

Licenses

Do you have any of the following: Where are they kept?

☐ Drivers license   _____

☐ Vehicle registration   _____

☐ Business license   _____

☐ Hunting license   _____

☐ Occupation license   _____

☐ Professional license   _____

Military Records

Do you have any of the following: Where are they kept?
- [ ] Service records _____
- [ ] Awards _____
- [ ] Discharge papers _____
- [ ] Pension _____
- [ ] Separation papers _____
- [ ] National Guard _____
- [ ] Disability _____
- [ ] Citations _____

Citizenship Records

Do you have any of the following: Where are they kept?
- [ ] Passport _____
- [ ] Visa _____
- [ ] Naturalization _____
- [ ] Green Card _____
- [ ] Deportment _____
- [ ] Directories _____

Family Medical History

Because the health of your family can affect you and your posterity, it is important to find out as much about your ancestors as you can. Build a family medical pedigree. Start with yourself, parents, your brothers and sisters, grandparents, great grandparents, aunts and uncles.

Search death certificates, obituaries, cemetery, funeral, insurance, service, pension, and medical records. Be sure to record what you already know. See page257 for medical diary information and references.

Take a portrait pedigree chart, fill in the names of your ancestors, and instead of a photograph, include cause of death and any known medical problems. Use the numbers listed below to indicate those that might apply to each person.

1. Heart Condition
2. Mental Problems
3. Hearing Loss
4. Multiple Sclerosis
5. Strokes
6. Liver Disorder
7. Hysterectomy
8. High Blood Pressure
9. Asthma
10. Cancer/Leukemia
11. Kidney Disease
12. Deformities
13. Paralysis
14. Ulcers
15. Arthritis
16. Substance Abuse
17. Smoker
18. Blindness
19. Osteoporosis
20. Thyroid Problems
21. Eating Disorder
22. Intestinal Problems
23. Colitis
24. Diabetes
25. Convulsions/Seizures
26. Other (Explain)

Personal Medical History

Who is your present primary physician? _____

List previous physicians/specialists. _____

_____

Where are your medical records? _____

List the medications/vitamins you take regularly.

_____

_____

_____

What major operations have you had?   Include name of surgeon.

_____

_____

Where are the records/xrays from these operations located?

What is your average height? _____ weight? _____

Describe your general health?_____

_____

List immunizations and date of last inoculation.

Tetanas toxoid _____   Mumps _____

Diphtheria _____   Rubella _____

Pertussis _____   Polio _____

Measles _____   Other _____

Note: Please refer to the Family Medical History survey for additional medical questions.

Appendix C

Vital Satistics Information
State Archives & Records
Historical Societies
Archival Supplies

Vital Statistics Information

ST	OFFICES	ADDRESS	TELEPHONE	PRICE
AL	Center for Health Statistics	PO Box 5625, Montgomery, AL 36103-5625	(205) 242-5033	$12.00
AK	Bureau of Vital Statistics	PO Box 110675, Juneau, AK 99811-0675	(907) 465-3391	$10.00
AZ	Vital Records	PO Box 3887, Phoenix, AZ 85030	(602)255-3260	$9.00
AR	Division of Vital Records	4815 W Markham, Slot 44, Little Rock, AR 72205	((501)661-2336	$5.00
CA	Vital Statistics Section	304 S. Street, Sacramento, CA 95814	(916)322-1356	$19.00
CO	Colorado Dept of Health, HSVRD-VR-A1	4300 Cherry Creek Drive. South Denver, CO 80222-1530	(303)692-2200	$15.00
CT	Vital Records Section	150 Washington St., Hartford, CT 06106	(203)566-1124	$5.00
DE	Office of Vital Statistics	PO Box 637, Dover, DE 19901	(302)736-4721	$5.00
DC	Vital Records Branch	613 G Street, NW 9th Floor, Washington, DC 20001	(202)727-9281	$12.00
FL	Office of Vital Statistics	PO Box 210, Jacksonville, FL 32231	(904)359-6920	$9.00
GA	Vital Records Unit	47 Trinity Ave., Atlanta, GA 30334	(404)656-7456	$10.00
HI	Vital Records Section	PO Box 3378, Honolulu, HI 96801	(808)548-5819	$2.00
ID	Bureau of Vital Statistics	450 W. State St., 1st Floor, Boise, ID 83720-0036	(208)334-5980	$8.00
IL	Division of Vital Records	605 W. Jefferson St., Springfield, IL 62702-5097	(217)782-6555	$15.00

IN	Division of Vital Records	POI Box 1964, Indianapolis, IN 46206	(317)633-0276	$6.00
IA	Vital Records Section	321 East 12th St., Des Moines, IA 50319	(515)281-4944	$10.00
KS	Vital Statistics,	Rm. 151, Landon St. Off. Bldg.		
		900 SW Jackson, Topeka KS 66612-2221	(913)296-1415	$10.00
KY	Vital Statistics	275 E. Main St., Frankfort, KY 40621-0001	(502)564-4212	$7.00
LA	Office of Vital Records	PO Box 60630, New Orleans, LA 70160	(504)568-5152	$13.00
ME	Vital Records	State House Station II, Augusta, ME 04333	(207)289-3184	$10.00
MD	Division of Vital Records	PO Box 68760, Baltimore,MD 21215	(410)225-5988	$4.00
MA	Registrar of Vital Statistics	150 Tremont St. Rm. B-3, Boston, MA 02111	(617)727-0110	$11.00
MI	Office of State Registrar	PO Box 30195, Lansing, MI 48909	(517)335-8656	$13.00
MN	Minnesota Dept.of Health	717 SE Delaware, Minneapolis, MN 55440	(612)653-5121	$11.00
MS	Office of Vital Records,	PO Box 1700, Jackson, MS 39205	(601)960-7981	$12.00
MO	Bureau of Records -Statistics	PO Box 570, Jefferson City, MO 65102-0570	(314)751-6387	$10.00
MT	Bureau of Records -Statistics	1400 Broadway, Helena, MT 59620	(406)444-4228	$10.00
NE	Bureau of Vital Statistics	PO Box 95007, Lincoln, NE 65509-5007	(402)471-2871	$8.00
NV	Dept of Vital Statistics	505 E. King St., Rm 102, Carson City, NV 89710	(702)885-4480	$11.00
NH	Vital Records	6 Hazen Dr., Concord, NH 03301-6527	(603)271-4654	$10.00
NJ	Bureau of Vital Records	CN 370 Trenton, NJ 08625	(609)292-4087	$4.00
NM	Vital Statistics Bureau	1190 St. Francis Dr., Santa Fe, NM 87503	(505)827-0121	$10.00
NY	Vital Records Section	Empire State Plaza, Tower Bldg, Albany, NY 12237	(518)474-3077	$15.00
NY	New York City Dept of Health	125 Worth St., New York, NY 10013	(212)285-9503	$15.00
NC	Office of Vital Statistics	PO Box 27687, Raleigh, NC 27611	(919)733-3526	$10.00
ND	Division of Vital Records	State Capital, 600 E. Blvd., Bismarck, ND 58505-0200	(701)224-2360	$7.00

OH	Division of Vital Statistics	65 S. Front St., Rm. G-20, Columbus, OH 43266-0333	(614)466-2531	$7.00
OK	Vital Records Section	PO Box 53551, Oklahoma City, OK 73152	(405)271-4040	$5.00
OR	Vital Records	PO Box 14050, Portland, OR 97214-0050	(503)731-4095	$15.00
PA	Vital Records	555 Walnut St., 6th FL, Harrisburg, PA 17101-1900	(412)656-3126	$4.00
RI	Division of Vital Statistics	3 Capitol Hill, Rm 101, Providence, RI 02908-5097	(401)277-2811	$12.00
SC	Office of Vital Records	2600 Buff St., Columbia, SC 29201	(803)734-4830	$8.00
SD	Vital Records	445 E. Capital, Pierre, SD 57501-3185	(605)773-4961	$5.00
TN	Tennessee Vital Records	312 8th Ave., N. 3rd Floor, Nashville, TN 37247-0350	(615)741-1763	$10.00
TX	Bureau of Vital Statistics	1100 W. 49th St., Austin, TX 78756-3191	(512)458-7380	$11.00
UT	Vital Records	PO Box 16700, Salt Lake City, UT 84116-0700	(801)538-6105(6368)	$12.00
VT	Vital Records	PO Box 70, Burlington, VT 05402-9962	(802)863-7275	$5.00
VA	Division of Vital Records	PO Box 1000, Richmond, VA 23208-1000	(804)786-6228	$5.00
WA	Vital Records	PO Box 9709, Olympia, WA 98504-9709	(206)753-5936	$11.00
WV	Vital Records Office	State Capital Complex, Bldg 3, Rm. 516, Charleston WV 25305	((304)348-2931	$5.00
WI	Vital Records	PO Box 309, Madison, WI 53701	(608)266-1371	$10.00
WY	Vital Records Service	Hathaway Bldg., Cheyenne, WY 82002	(307)777-7591	$11.00

Also write for a more complete list,
"Where to Write for Vital Records
Births, Deaths, Marriages and Divorces
DHHS Publication No. (PHS)93-1142

US Department of Health and Human Services,
Public Health Service
Centers for Disease Control and Prevention
National Center for Health Statistics
Hyattsville, Maryland 20780

State Archives & Records

Alabama Dept. of Archives
624 Washington Ave.
Montgomery, AL 36130
205-242-4441
Fax: 205-240-3433

Alaska State Archives & Records
Management Services
141 Willoughby Ave.
Juneau, AK 99802-1720
907-465-2275
Fax: 907-465-2465

Arizona State Archives
Dept. of Library, Archives & Public Records
1700 W. Washington Street
Phoenix, AZ 85007
602-542-4159
Fax: 602-542-4402

Arkansas History Commission
One Capitol Mall
Little Rock, AR 72201
501-682-6900

California State Archives
201 N. Sunrise Ave.
Sacramento, CA 95561
916-773-3000
Fax: 916-773-8249

Colorado Dept of Administration
Division of State Archives & Public Records
1313 Sherman St., I-B20
Denver, CO 80203
303-866-2055
Fax: 303-866-2257

Connecticut State Archives
Connecticut State Library
231 Capitol Ave.
Hartford, CT 06106
203-566-5650
Fax: 203-566-2133

Delaware Bureau of Archives & Records
Management
Hall of Records
Dover, DE 19901
302-739-5318
Fax: 302-739-6711

Florida State Archives
R.A. Gray Bldg (M.S. 9A)
Tallahassee, FL 32399-0250
904-487-2073
Fax: 904-488-4894

Georgia Dept of Archives & History
Box RPM
330 Capitol Ave., S.E.
Atlanta, GA 30334
404-656-5486
Fax: 404-656-2940

Hawaii State Archives
Iolani Palace Grounds
Honolulu, Hawaii 96813
808-586-0310
Fax: 808-586-0330

Idaho Library & Archives
210 Main St.
Boise, ID 83702
208-334-3890
Fax: 208-334-3198

Illinois State Archives
Archives Bldg.
Springfield, IL 62756
217-782-4682
Fax: 217-524-3930

Indiana State Archives
Commission on Public Records
State Office Bldg., Rm. W472
Indianapolis, IN 46204-2215
317-232-3373
Fax: 317-232-3154

State Archives of Iowa
State Historical Society of Iowa
Capitol Complex
600 E. Locust
Des Moines, IA 50319
515-281-8837
Fax: 515-282-0502

Kansas State Historical Society
120 W. Tenth St.
Topeka, KS 66612-1291
913-296-3251
Fax: 913-296-1005

Kentucky Dept for Lib/Arch.
Public Records Division
Archives Research Room
P.O. Box 537
Frankfort, KY 40602-0537
502-875-7000, ext 173
Fax: 502-564-5773

State of Louisiana
Secretary of State
Division of Archives, Records
Management, and History
P.O. Box 94125
Baton Rouge, LA 70804-9125
504-922-1206
Fax: 504-925-4726

Maine State Archives
Capitol - Station House 84
Augusta, ME 04333-0084
207-289-5790
Fax: 207-289-8598

Maryland State Archives
350 Rowe Blvd.
Annapolis, MD 21401
301-974-3915

Massachusetts Archive
Office of Secretary of State
Boston, MA 02125
617-727-2816
Fax: 617-727-2826

Michigan State History Bureau
State Archives
Lansing, MI 48906
517-373-1401
Fax: 517-373-0851

Minnesota Historical Society
345 Kellogg Blvd. W.
St. Paul, MN 55102-1906
612-297-4502
Fax: 612-296-9961

Mississippi Dept of Archives & History
100 S. State St.
Jackson, MS 39205-0571
601-359-6850
Fax: 601-359-6905

Missouri State Archives
600 W. Main St.
Jefferson City, MO 65102
314-751-4717

Montana Historical Society
Division of Library & Archives
225 N. Roberts St.
Helena, MT 59620
406-444-4775
Fax: 406-444-2696

Nebraska State Historical Society
1500 R St.
Box 82554
Lincoln, NE 68501
402-471-4785
Fax: 402-471-3100

Nevada State Library & Archives
100 Stewart Street
Carson City, NV 89710
702-687-5210

New Hampshire State Archives
71 S. Fruit St.
Concord, N.H 03301-2410
603-271-2236
Fax: 603-271-2272

New Jersey State Archives
CN 307, 2300 Stuyvesant Ave.
Trenton, NJ 08625
609-530-3203
Fax: 609-530-6121

New Mexico Commission of Public Records
New Mexico Records & Archives
404 Montezuma Ave.
Santa Fe, NM 87503
505-827-7332
Fax: 505-827-7331

New York State Archives
State Education Department
Albany, NY 12230
518-474-1195

North Carolina State Archives
Department of Cultural Resource
109 E. Jones St
Raleigh, NC 27601-2807
919-733-7305
Fax: 919-733-5679

North Dakota State Archives & Historical
Research Library
612 E. Blvd. Ave.
Bismarck, ND 58505-0830
701-224-2668
Fax: 701-224-3000

Ohio Historical Society
Archives/Library Division
1982 Velma Ave.
Columbus, OH 43211-2497
614-297-2510
Fax: 614-297-2411

Oklahoma Department of Libraries
200 North East Eighteenth St.
Oklahoma City, OK 73105-3298
405-521-2502
Fax: 405-525-7804

Oregon Secretary of State
Archives Division
800 Summer N.E.
Salem, OR 97310
503-373-0701
Fax: 503-373-0659

Pennsylvania State Archives
P.O. Box 1026
Harrisburg, PA 17108-1026
717-787-2891

Rhode Island State Archives
337 Westminister St.
Providence, RI 02903-3302
401-277-2353
Fax: 401-277-3199

South Carolina Department of Archives
and History
1430 Senate St.
Columbia, SC 29211
803-734-8577
Fax: 803-734-8820

South Dakota Historical Society/State
Archives
900 Governors Drive
Pierre, SD 57501-2217
605-773-3458
Fax: 605-773-6041

Tennessee State Library & Archives
403 Seventh Ave. N.
Nashville, TN 37219-1411
615-741-7996
Fax: 615-741-6471

Texas State Archives Division
Lorenzo de Zavala State Archives and
Library Building
P.O. Box 12927
Austin, Texas 78711-2927
512-463-5480
Fax: 512-463-5436

Utah State Archives & Records Service
Archives Building, State Capitol
Salt Lake City, UT 84114
801-538-3012
Fax: 801-538-3354

State of Vermont Archives
Secretary of State's Office
26 Terrace Street
Montpelier, VT 05633-1103
802-828-2369
Fax: 802-828-2496

Commonwealth of Virginia
Virginia State Library and Archives
11th St at Capitol Square
Richmond, VA 23219-3491
804-786-2332
Fax: 804-786-5855

Washington Secretary of State Office
Div. of Archives & Records Management
1120 Wash St., S.E.
P.O. Box 40238
Olympia, WA 98504-0238
206-753-5485
Fax: 206-586-5629

West Virginia Archives
Division on Culture and History
1900 Kanawha Blvd. E.
Charleston, WV 25305-0300
304-558-0230
Fax: 304-558-2779

The State Historical Society of Wisconsin
816 State St.
Madison, WI 53706-1488
608-264-6480
Fax: 608-264-6472

Wyoming Archives
Parks & Cultural Resources Division
Barrett Building
Cheyenne, WY 82002
307-777-7013
Fax: 307-777-6289

Historical Societies

Alabama Historical Association
P.O. Box 2877
Tuscaloosa, AL 35486

Alaska Historical Library & Museum
P.O. Box G
Eighth Floor, State Office Building
Juneau, AK 99811
Phone: 907-465-2925

Alaska Historical Society
524 W. Fourth Ave., Suite 208
Anchorage, AK 99501

Arizona Historical Society
Century House Museum
240 Madison Ave.
Yuma, AZ 85364
602-782-1841

Arkansas Historical Association
History Department
Ozark Hall, 12, University of Arkansas
Fayetteville, AR 72701
501-575-5884

Arkansas Historical Society
422 S. Sixth St.
Van Buren, AR 72956

Arkansas History Commission
1 Capitol Mall
Little Rock, AR 72201
501-682-6900

California Historical Society
2090 Jackson St.
San Francisco, CA 94109

Colorado Historical Society
Stephen H. Hart Librqary
1300 Broadway
Denver, CO 80203
303-866-2305

Connecticut Historical Commission
59 S. Prospect St.
Hartford, CT 06106

Connecticut Historical Society
1 Elizabeth St. at Asylum Ave.
Hartford, CT 06105
203-236-5621

Connecticut League of Historical Societies
P.O. Box 906
Darien, CT 06820

Historical Society of Delaware
Town Hall
505 Market St.
Wilmington, DE 19801
302-655-7161

Florida Historical Society
P.O. Box 3645, University Station
Gainesville, FL 32601

Georgia Historical Society
501 Whittaker St.
Savannah, GA 31499
912-651-2128

Hawaiian Historical Society
560 Kawaiahao St.
Honolulu, HI 96813

Idaho Historical Society
610 N. Julia Davis Dr.
Boise, ID 83706
208-384-2120
208-334-3356

Illinois State Historical Library
Old State Capitol
Springfield, IL 62701
217-782-4836

Indiana Historical Society
State Library & Historical Bldg.
Family History Sectiohn
315 W. Ohio St.
P.O. Box 88255
Indianapoolis, IN 46202
317-232-1879

State Historical Society of Iowa
Library/Archives Bureau
State of Iowa Historical Building
600 E. Locust
Des Moines, IA 50319
515-281-5111

State Historical Society of Iowa
Library/Archives Bureau
Centennial Building
402 Iowa Avenue
Iowa City, IA 52240
319-335-3916

Kansas State Historical Society
Archives Division
Memorial Building
120 W. Tenth St.
Topeka, KS 66612
913-296-4776
913-296-3251

Kentucky Historical Society
300 Broadway
Old Capitol Annex
P.O. Box H
Frankfort, KY 40602
502-564-3016

Louisiana Genealogical & Historical Society
P.O. Box 3454
Baton Rouge, LA 70821
504-343-2608

Maine Historical Society
485 Congress St.
Portland, ME 04111
207-774-1822

Maryland Historical Society
201 W. Monument St.
Baltimore, MD 21201
301-685-3750, ext. 359

Massachusetts Historical Society
1154 Boylston St.
Boston, MA 02215
617-536-1608

Historical Society of Michigan
2117 Washtenaw Ave.
Ann Arbor, MI 48104

Michican Historical Commission
505 State Office Building
Lansing, MI 48913

Minnesota Historical Society
690 Cedar St.
Saint Paul, MN 55101
612-296-2143

Historical & Genealogical
Association of Mississippi
618 Avalon Rd.
Jackson, MS 39206

Missouri Historical Society
Research Library & Archives
Jefferson Memorial Building
Forest Park
Saint Louis, MO 63112-1099

State Historical Society of Missouri
1020 Lowry St.
Columbia, MO 65201
314-882-7083

Nebraska State Historical Society
State Archives Division
1500 R St.
P.O. Box 82554
Lincoln, NE 68501
402-471-4771
402-471-4751

Nebraska State Historical Society Room
Chadron State College
Chadron State Library
Chadron, NE 69337

Nevada State Historical Society
1650 N. Virginia St.
Reno, NV 89503
702-789-0190

Nevada State Museum & Historical Society
700 Twin Lakes Dr.
Las Vegas, NV 89107
702-486-5205

Association of Historical Societies
of New Hampshire
Maple St.
Plaistow, NH 03865

New Hampshire Historical Society
30 Park St.
Concord, NH 03301
603-225-3381

New Jersey Historical Society
230 Broadway
Newark, NJ 07104
201-483-3939

Historical Society of New Mexico
P.O. Box 4638
Santa Fe, NM 87501

History Library Museum of New Mexico
Palace of the Governors
Santa Fe, NM 87501

The New York Historical Society
170 Central Park W.
New York, NY 10024-5194
212-873-3400

North Carolina Society of County &
Local Historians
1209 Hill St.
Greensboro, NC 27408

State Historical Society of North Dakota
State Archives & Historical Research
Library Heritage Center
612 E. Blvd. Ave.
Bismarck, ND 58505
701-224-2668, Division Office
701-224-2091, Reference Desk

Ohio Historical Society
Archives- Library Division
Interstate Route 71 and 17th Ave.
1985 Velma Ave.

Columbus, Ohio 43211
614-466-1500   614-297-2510
614-297-2300

Oklahoma Historical Society
Library Resources Division
Wiley Post Historical Building
2100 N. Lincoln Blvd.
Oklahoma City, OK 73105
405-521-2491

Oregon Historical Society
1230 S.W. Park Ave.
Portland, OR 97268
503-222-1741

Heritage Society of Pennsylvania
P.O. Box 146
Laughlintown, PA 15655

Historical Society of Pennsylvania
1300 Locust St.
Philadelphia, PA 19107
215-545-0391

Rhode Island State Historical Society
121 Hope St.
Providence, RI 02909
401-331-8575

South Carolina Historical Society
100 Meeting St.
Charleston, SC 29401
803-723-3225

South Dakota State Historical Society
South Dakota Archives
Cultural Heritage Center
900 Governors Drive
Pierre, SD 57501
605-773-3804

Tennessee Historical Society
Ground Floor
War Memorial Building
300 Capital Blvd.
Nashville, TN 37243-0084
615-242-1796

Tennessee Historical Commission
Conservation department
701 Broadway
Nashville, TN 37203
615-742-6717

Texas State Historical Association
2306 SRH, University Station
Austin, TX 78712

Utah State Historical Society
300 Rio Grande
Salt Lake City, UT 84101
801-533-3500

Virginia Historical Society
428 N. Blvd.
P.O. Box 7311\Richmond, VA 23211
804-342-9677

Washington State Historical Society
Hewitt Library
State Historical Building
315 N. Stadium Way
Tacoma, WA 98403
206-593-2830

West Virginia Historical Society
Division of Archives & History
Department of Culture & History
Science and Cultural Center
Capitol Complex
Charleston, WV 25305
304-348-2277
304-348-0230

The State Historical Society of Wisconsin
816 State St.
Madison, WI 53706
608-262-9590, Reference Librarian
608-262-3338, Reference Archivist
608-262-9580   608-262-2781

Wyoming State Archives
Barrett Building
2301 Central Ave.
Cheyenne, WY 82002
307-777-7826

Archival Supplies

Archival Products, Inc.
2134 East Grand
P.O. Box 1413
Des Moines, IA 50305
Phone: 800-526-5640

Conservation Materials Ltd.
240 Freeport Boulevard
P.O. Box 2884
Sparks, NV 89432
Phone: 702-331-0582

Conversation Resources
International, Inc.
8000-H Forbes Place
Springfield, VA 22151
Phone: 800-634-6932
Fax: 703-321-0629

G. M. Wylie Company
P.O. Box AA
Washington, PA 15301-0660
Phone: 800-747-1249
Fax: 412-262-5254

The Preservation Emporium
2707 N. Stemmons Fwy./Ste. 140
Dallas, TX 75207

Solar Screen
53-105th Street
Corona, NY 11368
Phone: 718-592-8222

TALAS
213 West 35th Street
New York, NY 1001
Phone: 212-736-7744

Light Impressions,
439 Monroe Avenue
P.O. Box 940
Rochester, NY 14603-0940
Phone:1-800-828-6216,
FAX 1-800-828-5539,
Catalogue available

University Products, Inc.
517 Main Street,
PO Box 101
Holyoke, MA 01041-0101
(800)762-1165 or (413)532-9431
Catalogue available

If you would like to know the name of a conservator in your area you can write to:

American Institute for Conservation of
Historic and Artistic Works
1717 "K" Street
Suite 301
Washington, DC 20006
202-452-9545

For information on paper and photograph preservation, write to:

Society of American Archivists
600 S. Federal, Suite 504
Chicago, IL 60605

or

National Archives
Washington, DC 20408

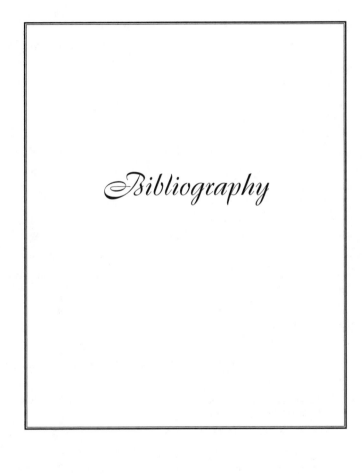

Bibliography

Personal History Section

Alessi, Jean and Miller, Jan, *Once Upon a Memory*, Your family tales and treasures, Betterway Publication, Inc., White Hall Virginia, 1987.

Bruening, Sylvia, *The Story of Your Life*, A workbook for preparing and writing your personal history, published by the author, Salt Lake City, Utah, 1974.

Cannon, Elaine, *Putting Life in your Life Story*, Deseret Book Company, SLC, Utah, 1977.

Daniel, Lois, *How to Write Your Own Life Story*, A step by step guide for the non-professional writer, Chicago Review.

Dixon, Janice and Flack, Dora, *Preserving Your Past*, A painless guide to writing your autobiography and family history, Doubleday & Company, New York, 1977.

Duncon, Lois, *How to Write and Sell Your Personal Experiences*, Turning everything that happens to you into salable writing, Writer's Digest Books, Cincinnati, Ohio, 1979.

Edwards, Charlotte, *Writing from the Inside Out*, Learn how to make full use of your emotions and experiences to make a more powerful impression on your readers—whether you're writing fiction or nonfiction, Writers Digest Books, Cincinnati, Ohio, 1984.

Fletcher, William, *Recording Your Family History*, A guide to preserving oral history using audio and video tape, Ten-Speed Press, Berkeley, CA, 1983.

Hartley, William G., *Preparing a Personal History*, Primer Publications, Salt Lake City, 1976.

Heslop, J. Malan, and Orden, Dell Van, *How to Write Your Personal History*, Bookcraft, Inc., Salt Lake City, Utah, 1976.

Holmes, Marjorie, *How to Write and Sell Your Life Experiences*, Writing Articles from the Heart, Writer's Digest Books, Cincinnati, Ohio, 1993.

Knott, William C., *The Craft of Fiction*, Reston Publishing Company, Reston, Virginia, 1973.

Metzger, Deena, *Writing for Your Life*, A guide and companion to the inner worlds, Harper, San Francisco, CA, 1992.

Norton, Don, *Composing Your Life Story*, Ten practical guides to creating a personal history, 599 East Center Street, Orem, Utah, 19

Perret, Gene, *How to Write and Sell Humor*, Learn how to write comedy and make your punchlines pay off, Writers Digest Books, Cincinnati, Ohio, 1982.

Provost, Gary, *Make Your Words Work*, Proven techniques for effective writing--for fiction and nonfiction, Writers Digest Books, Cincinnati, Ohio, 1990.

Schwarz, Ted, *The Complete Guide to Writing Biographies*, How to research, interview for, and write marketable biographies, including as-told-to autobiographies and authorized, unauthorized historical, literary, academic and young reader biographies, Writer's Digest Books, Cincinnati, Ohio, 1990.

Stillman, Peter R., *Families Writing*, Writers Digest Books, Cincinnati, Ohio, 1989.

Thomas, Frank P., *How to Write the Story of Your Life*, Writer's Digest Books, Cincinnati, Ohio, 1984

ℱamily ℋistory Section

Billington, Ray Allen, and Martin Ridge, *Westward Expansion*, Macmillan, New York, 5th ed., 1982.

Block Mark, *The Historian's Craft*, Reflections on the nature and uses of history and the techniques and methods of the men who write it, A Vintage Book, Division of Random House, New York, 1953

Bowen, Catherine Drinker, *Biography, the Craft and the Calling*, Little, Brown and Company, Boston, 1970.

Dixon, James D., *History of Charles Dixon*, Forest City Publishing Company, 1891.

Eastman, Richard, *Your Roots, Total Genealogy Planning on Your Computer*, Ziff-Davis Press, Emeryville, California, 1995.

Family History Monthly, Diamond Publishing Group Ltd., 45 St. Mary's Road, Ealing, London W5 5RQ.

Felt, Thomas E., *Researching, Writing and Publishing Local History*, Nashville: American Association for State and Local History, 1976.

Fletcher, William, *Recording Your Family History*, A guide to preserving oral history with video tape, audio tape, suggested topics and questions, interview techniques, Dodd, Mead & Company, New York, 1983.

Galeener-Moore, Laverne, *Collecting Dead Relatives*, Genealogical Publishing, Co., Inc., Baltimore, Maryland, 1987.

Haley, Alex, *Roots*, The saga of an American family, Doubleday & Company, New York, 1976 Howard, Jane, *Families*, Simon and Schuster, New York, 1978.

Jones, Vincent L., and Eakle, Arlene H. and Christensen, Mildred H. *Family History for Fun and Profit*, Genealogical Copy Service 1972, Publishers Press, Salt Lake City, Utah, for The Genealogical Institute, 1978.

Lichtman, Allan J., *Your Family History*, How to use oral history, personal family archives and public documents to discover your heritage, Vintage Books, a Division of Random House, New York, 1978.

Rawlyk, George A., *Nova Scotia's Massachusetts*, McGill-Queens University Press, Montreal, 1973.

Smith, Frank, *The Lives and Times of our English Ancestors*, Everton Publishers, P.O. Box 368, Logan, Utah, 1969.

Schumacher, Michael, *Creative Conversations*, The Writer's complete guide to conducting interviews, Writer's Digest Books, Cincinnati, Ohio, 1990.

Shumway, Gary L. and Hartley, William G., *An Oral History Primer*, Salt Lake City, Utah, by the authors, 1976.

Watts, J. F. and Davis, Allen E., *Generations,* your family in modern American history, Alfred A. Knopf, New York, 1983.

Willard, Jim and Terry, *Ancestors*, A beginning guide to family history and genealogy, Houghton Mifflin Company, Boston, New York, 1997.

Wright, Norman E. *Preserving Your American Heritage*, A guide to family and local history, Brigham Young University Press, Provo, Utah, 1974.

Photography Section

Bannister, Shala Mills, *Family Treasures:* Videotaping your family history, A guide for preserving your family's living history as an heirloom for future generalions, Clearfield Co., Baltimore, 1994.

Bishop, John Melville and Bishop, Naomi Hawes, *Making Home Video*, How to get the most from your videocassette recording equipment, Wideview Books, 1980.

Conservation of Photographs, Eastman Kodak Company, 1985.

Eastman, Richard, *Your Roots,* Total genealogy planning on your computer, Ziff-Davis Press, Emeryville, California, 1995.

Frisch-Ripley, Karen, *Unlocking the Secrets in Old Photographs, Ancestry*, Salt Lake City, 1992.

Greenberg, Seth and Adele Droblas, *Digital Images,* A practical guide, What everyone needs to know about computer graphics, Osborne McGraw-Hill, Berkeley, CA, 1995.

Miller, Ilene Chandler, *Preserving Family Keepsakes*, Do's and Don'ts, Shumway Family History Services, 5041 Stone Canyon Avenue, Yorba Linda, CA 92686 (714)693-8703.

Noren, Catherine Hanf, *The Camera of My Family*, The 100-Year album of a German Jewish family, photographs and mementos of five generations, from their lives in Germany before the turn of the century to the American present, Alfred A. Knopf, New York, 1976.

Rempel, Siegfried, *The Care of Photographs*, Lyons & Burford Publishers, New York, 1976.

Shull, Wilma Sadler, *Photographing Your Heritage, Ancestry*, Salt Lake City, 1989.

Smith, Kenneth L. *Focus on the Past*, A genealogist's guide to photography, AGLL Press, P.O. Box 329, Bountiful, Utah 84011-0329, (801)298-5446.

Sturm, Duane, and Pat Sturm, *Video Family History, Ancestry*, Salt Lake City, 1989.

Tuttle, Craig A., *An Ounce of Preservation,* A guide to the care of papers and photographs, Rainbow Books, Inc., 1955.

Weinstein, Robert A., and Larry Booth, *Collection, Use, and Care of Historical Photographs*, American Association for State and Local History, Nashville, 1989.

Genealogy

Bentley, Elizabeth Petty, *The Genealogist's Address Book*, Genealogical Publishing Co., Baltimore, 1994.

Cerni, Johni, and Arlene H. Eakle, *Ancestry's Guide to Research, Ancestry*, Salt Lake City, 1984.

Cerny, Johni, and Wendy Elliot, *The Library: A Guide to the LDS Family History Library,* *Ancestry*, Salt Lake City, 1988.

Clifford, Karen, *Genealogy and Computers for the Complete Beginner*, Genealogical Publishing Company, Baltimore, 1992.

Clifford, Karen, *Genealogy and Computers for the Determined Researcher*, Genealogical Publishing Co., Baltimore, 1993.

Everton, George B., Sr., *The Handy Book for Genealogists*, The Everton Publishers, Logan, Utah, 1988.

Guide to Genealogical Research in the National Archives, National Archives Trust Fund, Washington, D.C., 1982.

Harland, Derek, *Genealogical Research Standards*, Bookcraft, Salt Lake City, 1970.

Jaussi, Laureen R., *Genealogy Fundamentals*, Jaussi Publications, 284 E. 400 South, Orem, Utah 84058, 1994.

Przecha, Donna and Joan Lowrey, *A Guide to Genealogy Software*, Genealogical Publishing Company, Baltimore, 1994.

Szucs, Loretto Dennis and Sandra Hargreaves Luebking, *The Source,* A guidebook of American genealogy, Ancestry, P.O. Box 476, Salt Lake City, 84110-0476, 1997. (This book is one of the best on the market for source material.)

Wright, Raymond S., *Genealogists Handbook,* modern methods of researching family history, American Library Association, Chicago and London, 1995.

Diaries, Letters & Newsletters Section

American Diaries: An annotated bibliography of published American diaries and journals, Gale Research Co., Detroit, 1983.

Baldwin, Christina, *One to One*, Self-Understand through journal writing, M. Evans and Company, New York, N.Y., 1977.

Bender, Sheila, *Writing Personal Essays:* How to shape your life experiences for the page, Writer's Digest Books, Cincinnati, Ohio, 1955.

Krause, Carol, *How Healthy Is Your Family Tree?*, Fireside Books, New York, 1995.

Nelson-Anderson, Danette L., *Genectic Connection: A guide to documenting your individual and family health history*, Sonters Publishing, Washington, Missouri, 1995.

Shepherd, Carol Ann, *How to Create a Family Newsletter*, 1984.

Simons, George F., *Keeping Your Personal Journal*, Paulist Press, New York, 1978.

Polishing & Publishing Section

Bell, Herbert W., *How to Get Your Book Published,* An insider's guide, practical advice, based on the author's 33 years in publishing--on the entire publishing process, with an emphasis on issues vital to your book's success, Writer's Digest Books, Cincinnati, Ohio, 1981.

Chickering, Robert B., and Hartman, Susan, *How to Register a Copyright and Protect Your Creative Work*, A basic guide to the new copyright law and how it affects anyone who wants to protect creative work, Charles Scribner's Sons, New York, 1980.

Hatcher, Patricia Law, *Producing a Quality Family History*, Ancestry, Salt Lake City, 1996.

Kiefer, Marie, *Book Publishing Resource Guide*, Includes a bibliography of over 500 books, Ad-Lib Publications, Fairfield, IA, 1993.

Miller, Ilene Chandler, *Publishing a Family History from P.A.F.*, A five step guide, Shumway Family History Services, 5041 Stone Canyon Avenue, Yorba Linda, CA 92686 (714)693-9803.

Shushan, Ronnie and Wright, Don, *Desktop Publishing by Design*, Everyone's guide to page-maker 5, Microsoft Press, Redmond, Washington, 1994.

Poynter, Dan, *Publishing Short-Run Books*, How to paste up and reproduce books instantly using your Quick Print Shop, Para Publishing, Santa Barbara, CA, 1988.

Poynter, Dan, *The Self-Publishing Manual*, How to write, print and sell your own book, Para Publishing, Santa Barbara, CA, 1995.

Mathieu, Aron, *The Book Market*, How to write, publish and market your book, Andover Press, Inc., New York, 1981.

General

Brown, Barbara and Tom Ninkovich, *Family Reunion Handbook*, A guide for reunion planners, reunion research, 3145 Geary Blvd. #143, San Francisco, CA 94118, 1992.

Brown, Vandella, *Celebrating the Family*, Steps to planning a family reunion, ancestry, Salt Lake City, P.O. Box 476, 1990.

Fisk, Margaret, *Encyclopedia of Associations*, Gale Research Book Tower, Detroit, MI 48226. Lists all fraternal and foreign interest and ethnic groups.

Internet Yellow Pages, The Fun, Fast, and Easy Way to Get Productive Online, New Riders Publishing, 201 West 103rd Street, Indianapolis, IN 46290, 1997.

Kirkham, E. Kay, *A Genealogical and Historical Atlas of the United States of America*, N.P., 1976.

Miller, Olka K. Miller, *Migration, Emigration and Immigration*, The Everton Publishers, Inc., Logan, Ut, 1974.

National Geographic Society, Historical Atlas of the United States, National Geographic Society, 1988.

Sagaves, Barbara, *A Preservation Guide*: Saving the past and the present for the future, ancestry, Salt Lake City, 1995.

World Conference on Records,*Personal, Family and Local History*, Volume 2, (39 talks given at the World Conference of Records in Salt Lake City, Utah in 1980).

World Conference on Records, *Historical Change in Population, Family and Community*, Volume 12, 1980, (11 talks given at the World Conference of Records in Salt Lake City, Utah in 1980.)

Index

Order Form

- **Fax orders**: (801) 486-0849
- **Telephone orders**: (801) 486-0800
- **On-line orders**: mtoly@wasatch.com
- **Postal orders**: Mt. Olympus Publishing, P.O. Box 3700, Wendover, Nevada 89883, USA

Please send me the book *Family Focused*.
I understand that I may return the book for a full refund–for any reason, no questions asked.

Name: _____

Address: _____

City: _____ State: _____ Zip: _____ - _____

Telephone: (___)_____

Sales tax:
Please add 6.50% for books shipped to Utah and Nevada addresses.

Shipping:
$4.00 for the first book and $2.00 for each additional book.

Payment:
Check or Money Order